Leading High Performance

Murray Eldridge

Dear Robin,

Written by an
Associate of Gemini Methods.

Happy "hammock" reading

With you a healthy recovery

crimson

~Shaun~

Leading High Performance

This edition first published in Great Britain in 2014 by Crimson Publishing Ltd, The Tramshed, Walcot Street, Bath BA1 5BB.

© Murray Eldridge, 2014

British Library Cataloguing in Publication Data.
A catalogue record for this book is available from the British Library.

ISBN 978 1 78059 213 8

Typeset by IDSUK (DataConnection) Ltd
Printed and bound in the UK by Bell & Bain, Glasgow

CONTENTS

LIST OF FIGURES

LIST OF TABLES

INTRODUCTION

Most people never run far enough on their first wind to find out they've got a second.

William James (1842–1910), professor in psychology, philosophy and physiology

This book is first and foremost about people.

It is about leaders and leadership but more importantly it is about 'followers' and what it is that they want from their leaders.

This book explores the relationship between leaders and followers and the responsibilities followers have. It provides insights into how this relationship is managed in high-performance sports teams and how these concepts can be transferred to companies and organisations.

By combining current ideas of leadership in business with coaching in sport and modern sports science I aim to show that high performance is not a holy grail. It is not some remote aspiration achievable only by an elite, brilliant few. It seeks to explain how high performance in business can readily be achieved and how leaders can create a high-performance environment through good leadership, good coaching and, of course, through their people.

By way of explaining why you should make the effort to create a high-performing organisation, this book sets out the case that the majority of modern organisations are, at best, average. It describes how most incentive regimes predominantly reward mediocre performance. It shows how average leaders are able to obscure poor results and that stakeholders are either unaware of the situation, powerless to influence it or even collude in rewarding mediocrity.

Part 1 of this book draws out the differences and the similarities between business and sport in terms of leadership and coaching. It shows that good coaching is not about great leadership. The very best coaches are deliberately not leaders because they know that leadership must come from within the team. Conversely, it shows that good leaders must be exceedingly competent coaches. While great coaches do not (and, I would argue, should not) aspire to be great leaders, the reverse is not the case. If they desire to be great leaders and create an environment that enables their people to excel and deliver sustained high performances then they will have to be great coaches. Many of today's top leaders cite the ability to coach and mentor talent as a key requisite of good leadership.

This poses one of the key questions this book seeks to answer: 'Are leaders getting the same performance out of their "followers" at work as coaches get out of their athletes in sport?' If not, why not?

Just as it is the responsibility of the coach to create a high-performance environment in their squad so it is the leader's responsibility to do the same in a company. In almost all cases, creating the right environment and culture that secures raised performance makes for a much more enjoyable working life. Where it is achieved a virtuous circle is created – a more enjoyable working life leading to increased performance creating increased rewards (and not just extrinsic ones), thereby leading to a more enjoyable working life, and so on.

Unfortunately, business leaders, especially poor ones, are able to disguise and conceal weak performance behind any number of excuses. As we see almost every day in the global media, company leadership not only gets away with low performance but secures ever-increasing rewards for it. The same is not true for those lower down the corporate hierarchy where the ramifications of poor leadership are often much more painful. Coaches in sport, however, have nowhere to hide when it comes to average performance. The performance of their athletes is a lens that focuses attention on the coach's performance. It is visible, immediate and on display at the end of every exercise, every development test and every competitive encounter. Good coaches cannot and do not make excuses.

If, as a leader, you are reading this and mentally looking around your organisation thinking 'How on earth can we beat the competition with this lot?', then the organisation's limitations may just be you! Look at high-performing sport clubs and think again. Within every successful club there are multiple layers of squads and teams competing at various levels of competition. At the top are the fully committed – perhaps even professional – players, but as you move down through the layers there are many athletes of varying abilities playing for the love of the sport, the excitement of competition and that feeling of exhilaration when they win. If you delve deeper into the workings of these clubs you will discover that not only are there excellent coaches at work with each squad and team but there is good leadership as well. It is the blend of both that makes not just individual teams great but the club as a whole successful.

I must stress that sport is not always about money or material gain. Not one of the athletes in the rowing club where I coach is a professional sportsperson – they all have full-time day jobs. Not one of the coaches in my club is a paid professional – they too have full-time day jobs. However, over the years the club has produced rowing crews that have won gold medals at the highest levels of the sport both nationally and internationally. It also produces its share of Great Britain trialists. Only in professional sports or at the highest level of amateur sport do coaches and athletes see material or monetary rewards. There are tens of thousands of athletes and thousands of coaches out there devoting huge energy and hours to their sport for no reward whatsoever, other than the joy of competing and creating winning performances by athletes and teams. It is this innate desire to be the best they can be that drives these individuals.

If you think they are unusual, take a look around your own organisation – you will find many of them already working for you. In any company you will have runners, rowers, footballers, rugby players, racquet-sports players and any other number of highly competitive individuals. A medium or large company will have lots of employees who are highly committed in terms of the hours, dedication and desire to learning and improving themselves in their activities outside of work. You will find in the majority of people a natural desire to fulfil themselves. This desire may take many forms, of which sport is just one. Nonetheless, the psychological drivers to do well, to be recognised and to belong to something exciting and worthwhile are all things that the best coaches recognise and positively and actively develop to achieve high performances out of their individuals, squads and teams.

Part 2 of this book focuses exclusively on organisations and how they can use the principles discussed in Part 1 to build a high-performance environment. It emphasises good goal setting and analyses processes that will deliver the target outcome of high performance.

Some years ago I developed a framework I call the 'performance triangle' to guide my approach, planning and philosophy in developing successful squads and teams of athletes. Over time I have adapted this for use in business. The resulting model is a mix of my development and learning as a sports coach combined with 40 years of experience running medium-sized and international companies and has become a model that I use all the time, both in sports coaching and in my business and consultancy work. The elegance of this model is that it provides a performance-enhancing framework that can be used at all levels of an organisation. It can be applied to individuals, to teams, to business units or at the organisational level. It can be used 'statically' to help frame, shape and resolve issues at a particular point in time. Its real value, however, comes when it is applied dynamically. It can be used over the full timeline assumed by the top-level strategies, help deliver goal-congruent performance and management of people, and guide strategic alignment of all staff across the organisation.

It is important to understand that a number of the ideas, developments, regimes and techniques employed at the top levels of sport can be successfully adapted to suit mere mortals. In looking at the ideas taken from sports coaching and their suitability for adaptation in business, it is also important to note that ordinary people can and do achieve extraordinary things when they are well-led, well-supported, and excited and engaged in their endeavour.

The coaching principles contained in this book are used at the elite levels of sports as well as at club level. Holding true to the desire to make the ideas in this book relevant and accessible to small and medium-sized entities as well as large corporations, many of the examples focus on club level. This proves that high performance is not just the preserve of the large, the highly resourced or the wealthy. It must be remembered that many national and international record-setting athletes and teams are first developed and come to prominence at club level.

This raises a very important aspect that I must clarify early on. You may already be thinking about the rarefied levels of Olympic, international or premiership-level sports and the phenomenal, supra-normal athletic specimens they often produce. If you are, you may also be wondering about the ideas in this book and their application to the average people that work in average organisations. What chance does Albert in accounts have of clearing the finance equivalent of the six-metre pole vault when he can't seem to clear his desk? What this book shows is that ordinary people are not actually that ordinary if they can be 'turned on'. I have been in business for 40 years and have led companies internationally in four different industries. I am also a qualified rowing coach. I have employed the many relevant elements of coaching principles and techniques (including elements of sport psychology) in my businesses to excellent effect. I have also seen good coaches (and occasionally good leaders) in action and observed the galvanising impact they have on the performance of people in their teams and organisations.

This book is not just about the people in a company or organisation who are committed sports athletes. It is about achieving high performance from the majority, if not all, of the staff. It is about enabling them to enjoy the feelings and rewards that such high performance creates. Anyone with a normal degree of self-esteem wants to feel they are good at what they do, whether in sport, hobbies, home or work. People want and need only a few (albeit critical) elements to be in place. If these are in place people will respond with raised levels of commitment, enthusiasm and, not unsurprisingly, higher performance. Just as in sport, everyone in a business organisation has within them the scope for significantly raised performance.

I have deliberately grounded this book in the real world, not the theoretical or the politically adjusted one we often see. In drawing on real life experiences I hope you will find it stimulating, interesting and enjoyable. Delivering winning performance is generally great fun for both leaders and followers – and winning certainly is. I hope you find the ideas, examples and experiences offered interesting. More importantly, I very much hope you find them useful in helping you develop your own ideas on how to achieve higher performance though people at whatever stage you find yourself in your career.

Notes:
1. Throughout this book I use the term 'follower'. This is not used in any disparaging or pejorative way. It is used broadly in three ways. The first is as a convenient way of identifying and expressing the difference between those who are not employed in any formal leadership role. The second is to ensure that we are clear that there is a properly identified 'group' apart from leaders who have distinguishable needs that good leaders must recognise and address. Lastly, it is to ensure that followers understand that they are not 'passive actors' in their organisation and that they have just as much responsibility to engage themselves in achieving high performance as their leaders.
2. Having defined follower, it may also be helpful to define 'leadership'. The danger here is that, rather like economics, there are as many different theories and schools of thought on leadership as there are leadership experts. Thus a definition will depend on what theories of leadership you ascribe to. For the purposes of clarity the definition I use is as follows: leadership is the ability to envisage a future, set a direction towards that future and enable people to follow that direction of their own free will.

3. I use the word 'average' throughout the book and in many cases apply it to people. This again is not meant in any disparaging or pejorative way. It is used in order to differentiate between those who deliver average performance and those who deliver high performance in order to show how one moves from the lower to the higher state.

Murray Eldridge
April 2013

PART 1

COACHING IN SPORT AND ITS USEFUL APPLICATION IN ORGANISATIONS

An exploration of concepts, models and techniques from the world of coaching relevant to organisations

CHAPTER 1
WHY COMPANIES ARE AVERAGE
AND LEADERS GET REWARDED

They [leaders of corporations] come from an order of men, whose interest is never exactly the same with that of the public, who have generally an interest to deceive and even oppress the public, and who accordingly have, upon many occasions, both deceived and oppressed it.

Adam Smith, ***An Inquiry into the Nature and***
Causes of the Wealth of Nations, **1776**

No doubt you have found yourself at some time or other sitting in yet another meeting room in front of yet another corporate leader who flashes through a slick slide presentation exhorting you to do more to be 'part of the team', to 'get on board with the programme' and to 'work hard to deliver results'. Also, no doubt, this message was sugar-coated in all the usual ways: the 'you people are our greatest asset' speech, the 'we are all one team' lecture, the 'these are tough times but together we will win' call to arms and no doubt many more such phrases. These 'leaders' deliver their rather superficial messages, answer a few questions and are whisked away by their executive clique. In the case of average and poor leaders, rarely do their actions match their rhetoric. Rarely does the senior team around them seem to exhibit the leadership required to match their grandiloquent exhortations. Consequently, rarely do these 'leaders' see the performance they so badly desire and need. This chapter examines how and why leaders of averagely, even poorly, performing organisations are able to continue leading them.

FOLLOWERS PAY FOR THE MISTAKES OF
THEIR LEADERS

Why is it that so many leaders get away with being, at best, only average at what they do? Why is it that the frequently reported failure by leaders to achieve performance in business not only goes unpunished but more usually secures handsome rewards? Why is it that, more often than not, the ramifications of failing to achieve good performance are visited upon the followers, not the leaders? And why is it that some companies do achieve the holy grail: superior performance derived through people who seem to have fun whilst doing it?

The undeniable fact is that even poor leaders intrinsically grasp the fact that within all the rhetoric the underlying message is absolutely true. People really are the greatest asset. Good people, if they are led well, really can make great teams. Great teams really do win and outperform – and can keep on doing so for long periods of time. The problem is that so few leaders are real 'leaders' in the true sense of what that really means. Often they will have been good managers who have been promoted over time. Sometimes they have been around so long that it is just deemed to be 'their turn'. There are some who have progressed by being a 'safe pair of hands' – certainly not the strongest endorsement for future stellar performance! More frequently, people succeed by being very good at corporate politics. In the world of large companies, they may often be part of an 'old boy' network who take it in turns to move the deckchairs around all the Titanics they captain until one of them hits an iceberg! At such times a metaphorical helicopter usually clatters over the horizon as their mates whisk them off the bridge and onto another ship.

There are a number of cases of individual companies where poor leadership and its lack of ability, strategic incompetence, venality, criminality or just plain stupidity have bankrupted otherwise good businesses. In extreme cases the failures of leaders on an industry-wide scale have taken whole sectors down. Arguably the financial crisis of 2007 and subsequent full-blown global recession is indicative of this average level of competence. The technology crash of 2002 certainly was.

It is usually the case in business that the incompetence of the few is visited on the many. These failures rarely impact materially on the leaders, who generally receive handsome 'abandon ship' payments. They do, however, often punish tens of thousands of otherwise competent 'followers' who not only lose their jobs but often their houses and even their pension funds. The failure of leaders is not much fun for creditors and shareholders either.

POOR PERFORMANCE! WHAT POOR PERFORMANCE?

The lack of penalty for failure at the most senior levels of corporations is easy to understand. Elements have been outlined above but the real reason corporate failure goes unpunished, even below the level of the ultimate leaders, is that the causes of poor performance in the business world can be easily concealed or obscured. Leaders at all levels in an organisation are almost always able to mask their own direct failures by blaming factors outside their control. The market collapsed. A competitor launched a new product. The government changed the rules. A war broke out. Or any other of the myriad reasons you have probably heard many times before.

This masking of performance can only occur if there is a conscious, or even unconscious, collusion between two parties – those who wish to portray it (the leaders) and those who wish to believe it (the owners and/or investors). It also requires an absence of will to implement regimes that:

■ *properly* determine what is good and bad performance, and
■ *properly* measure that performance.

Note: the word 'properly' is used here deliberately to make the distinction between what usually happens in organisations, namely almost exclusive use of internal measures of performance, rather than taking comparative and relative measures against external industry, sector and competitor performance.

For this to occur as consistently as it does in modern business means a number of things are happening:

- average (even poor) performance is tacitly planned for by the senior leadership team
- average (even poor) performance is accepted by the business's owners and investors – or they are powerless to do anything about it
- average (even poor) performance at the top of an organisation is well rewarded
- employees of the business (who are neither stupid nor blind) will know that average (even poor) performance is not just acceptable but attracts rewards.

We have all seen how the performance and rewards game is played, especially in large corporations. No doubt most of us have even participated in it. Typically it goes something like this:

> Here at Gamble & Hope Limited we operate an employee performance reward scheme with a bonus system linked to both corporate and personal performance. Personal performance is determined by our comprehensive employee appraisal system and corporate performance goals are set each year by the board. Any performance related awards are at the discretion of the management.

In most organisations this means that corporate performance targets get plucked from the business plan, e.g. revenue, profit, earnings before interest and tax, or some mixture of these or other elements. Since, more often than not, the business plan is little more than a glorified financial budget it is quite likely that all the players in the game, from the bottom up, have tacitly conspired to 'minimise' the performance levels wherever they can get away with it. There follows a bit of negotiating by the chief financial officer and his managers with the respective heads of business units. Eventually a consensus set of company 'performance' figures are agreed and an annual business plan derived.

The above process generally ensures that, provided an employee's personal performance appraisal is at least average and provided the company meets its corporate (massaged) targets, some level of performance-related rewards get paid. Chapter 12 outlines why average appraisal results nearly always mean below-average performances.

It is interesting to note that invariably the leaders of the business will be on significantly different, and always more lucratively rewarded, schemes. They are less likely to be linked to personal ability appraisal schemes than their followers. In listed companies they are more usually tightly linked to share performance. This opens up a completely different set of problems that include short-termism, decision-making based on self-interest, inordinate risk-taking and even unethical and illegal behaviours. These problems are not the subject of this book, but Roger Martin in *Fixing the Game* addresses superbly all of these elements and more.

THE REWARDS OF MEDIOCRITY

Actions, symbols and signals are far more effective than words. The actions, symbols and signals from almost everyone at the top of the corporate world is that average performance is not just acceptable but extremely well remunerated, and that even poor performance has little impact on personal gains.

Gary Winnick, who in 1997 was the founder and chairman of start-up telecommunications company Global Crossing, sold over $700m worth of shares in advance of his company going into Chapter 11 bankruptcy protection in 2002 where it subsequently lost over 95% of its value. He was later given an honorary doctorate by his alma mater and still plays a large part in US corporate life as chairman of Pacific Capital Group.

In 2008 Fred Goodwin, Chief Executive Officer (CEO) of the Royal Bank of Scotland (RBS) and one-time close ally of the then UK Prime Minister, struck a rather cosy deal with the UK government that saw him depart the bankrupted institution he presided over with a pension deal worth £693,000 per year for life, starting at the age of 50 – an age he had conveniently already reached. This deal was reputedly valued at £16.9m and considerably more than his contractual pay and bonus severance package would have been. The resulting furore around the scandal later saw this severance package reduced to a mere £2.7m tax-free lump sum and a £342,000 per annum pension. A year later he was back in employment as an adviser to a prestigious engineering and architect firm. Meanwhile, RBS has made 36,000 people redundant since the UK government bailout in 2008.

Similar to Goodwin, Tony Hayward, CEO of BP, walked away with enhanced and early pension rights in a deal said to be worth over £10m. Anyone who will recall his handling of the BP oil spill in the Gulf of Mexico must wonder how much you get for mediocre performance in such large, listed organisations if this is what appalling performance can achieve. Within 12 months of his ignominious exit from BP he had been installed on the board of TNK-BP and became a director of a Rothschild-backed energy acquisition vehicle looking to spend up to £8bn. This could see him on the board of another quoted company in short order.

Other examples are easy to find. Robert Nardelli, CEO of Home Depot between 2000 and 2007, departed with a severance package reportedly in excess of $200m. Share price performance during his tenure was a negative 4%. Henry McKinnell, CEO of Pfizer between 2001 and 2006, managed to reduce the share price of Pfizer by almost 40%. For this stellar performance he exited with just under $200m. From the sub-prime debacle, Richard Syron, CEO of Freddie Mac between 2003 and 2008, allegedly ignored internal warnings on the credit risk Freddie Mac was exposed to. Together with Fannie Mae almost $150bn was required from the US government as a bailout, on top of the $78bn they lost of their own money. Syron exited with a reputed $3.8m.

Performance failure does not come much bigger than these examples from the worlds of telecoms, banking, energy, retail and pharmaceuticals and neither, it appears, do the rewards for failure. If this is what is happening in the glare of the media spotlight imagine how much poor, let alone average, performance is being rewarded every single day in companies all over the world that operate away from media attention.

By comparison, Johnson & Johnson, founded in 1886 and consistently recorded as one of the world's most admired companies, saw its share price rise from an average $42 in 2000 to $64 in 2006. Despite the financial crash and global recession, Johnson & Johnson's shares were at $70 by the end of 2012. Interestingly its leader, Chairman and CEO Bill Weldon, had been at the helm for 10 years and had been in the company for 41 years – almost his entire career. During a time of global financial crisis and double dip recession, when many of Johnson & Johnson's competitors (and most companies in other sectors) were going backwards, the company's positive results go to show that poor or even average performance is not the result of external forces. High-performance people find ways to harness every situation to their advantage. I have even worked with a few, rare people who positively relish industry downturns because they see them as times of massive opportunity for the well prepared.

SUMMARY

This chapter highlights the fact that poor, even grossly incompetent, performance is in many circumstances able to secure handsome rewards, albeit just for the leaders. Of much greater concern, however, is that if this can happen with outright poor performance, what is happening in entities where performance is hovering around average? It is the case that the majority of organisations I have been involved with are rewarding mediocre performance.

The good news in all of this is that if you are a leader seeking to create above-average outcomes you do not have to do too much to start driving performance beyond sector norms. Even better news is that the basic, psychological needs of followers are aligned to what is required to drive high performance, if only the leader can tap into these needs.

Further good news is that winning teams in sport not only survive changes in coaches but often go on to bigger and better results. If the right performance ethos, frameworks, measures and other factors are in place winning teams can survive and even relish change. What sporting teams cannot do is survive poor coaching. The same is true for business: high performance cannot survive poor leaders. Poor leaders predominantly rely on rules, constraints, procedures and financial measures. As we shall see, in the hands of poor leaders, these create a climate that minimises rather than maximises performance.

CHAPTER 2
COACHING AND LEADERSHIP:
DIFFERENCES AND SIMILARITIES

A leader is best when people barely know he exists, not so good when people obey and acclaim him, worse when they despise him. But of a good leader who talks little when his work is done, his aim fulfilled, they will say 'we did it ourselves'.

Lao Tzu

I start this chapter by reiterating:

Great coaches should not be great leaders – but those who wish to be great leaders must also be great coaches.

Since leadership is critical to driving performance we need to establish an early reference point for the ideas put forward in this book. In this chapter we look at the differences and similarities between leading and coaching and set out the key elements for each.

In most team sports, once the team takes to the field or arena, it moves beyond the coach's immediate control. At this point the team needs a highly competent leader who is part of that team. If an overly strong and forceful coach deliberately sets himself up as both coach and leader then often the team is left leaderless on the field of play. The effect of this may be temporarily masked if the team is successful. However, if performance comes under pressure from a better side the speed at which a highly coached but leaderless team disintegrates can be spectacular. The best coaches not only have the ability to create strong teams but also have the ability to identify team leaders. They quietly and almost unobtrusively build up those leaders at the same time as developing the teams.

Corporate leaders who do not have great coaching skills will find it difficult to achieve the highest levels of performance that are the essence of this book. This chapter introduces key aspects of leadership and coaching and explores the differences and similarities between them. It also looks at each role from the perspective of the follower in business and the athlete in sport. By examining those aspects of coaching in sport that are relevant and applicable to business, this chapter begins to provide ideas, models and techniques that business leaders and their followers can adopt to secure high performance.

LEADERSHIP: A DIFFERENT VIEW

When we talk about high performance, whether in sport or in business, there are many variables to be taken into account, planned for and managed on a continual basis. We will come to all of these later but before we do we must to address the crucial matter of leadership.

I have had the good fortune to lead a number of companies. I have also run numerous leadership programmes and workshops with senior people from well-known blue chip companies as well as smaller entities. Typically, when running a leadership programme I will start with a simple question: 'What do leaders need?'. This exercise, without fail, elicits 10 minutes of filling flip charts with characteristics that include:

- interpersonal skills
- charisma
- competence
- vision
- communication skills
- empathy
- strategic ability
- technical skills
- experience.

This exercise can run to 30 or more attributes, skills and abilities.

I have to own up here and say I am being deliberately misleading when asking the question. I want participants to go down the blind alley of thinking of the leader as a 'superhero' in order to show how unrealistic it is to list all these amazing characteristics and expect to be able to 'check box' them against a leader and say 'this is a good one' or 'look at these scores, our leader must be awful'.

There are myriad papers, books and seminars on leadership that have investigated a plethora of aspects of leaders and leadership styles, behaviours, attributes, habits and actions. All good stuff, often very interesting reading and without doubt some fascinating insights. But they nearly all miss the point from a high-performance view. Since performance, especially high performance, can only be delivered through people, the primary question relevant to leaders is: 'What do followers need or want?'

If you agree that outstanding performance can only be achieved through your followers, then if as a leader you can work out what it is that they really need and what turns them on, then the whole leadership question in many respects becomes simplified. This is because, in broad terms, the needs of followers are not inordinately complex, especially if you address them at the level of our most basic human drivers.

With respect to our basic human needs most business people will be aware of the 'hierarchies of needs' addressed by a variety of researchers and authors. The theory

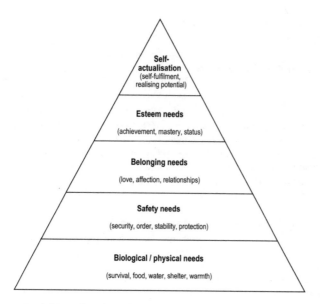

Figure 1: Maslow's hierarchy of needs.

and hierarchy probably best known in business is that of Abraham Maslow who developed a hierarchy of five basic needs in 1943 (see Figure 1).

In terms of leaders and followers, and specifically with respect to organisations and the work environment, we can simplify even these five basic needs. If we accept that in most developed and developing countries the state and/or societal frameworks provide for the first two basic needs, physical and safety, we are left with Maslow's belonging, esteem, and self-actualisation. Understanding how these might translate into the needs of followers within organisations is critical for leaders to understand.

WHAT FOLLOWERS NEED
Returning to the basic question 'What do followers need?' and interpreting from the above, we are looking at some rather important human 'needs'.

A need to belong
In corporate or workplace terms this often looks and feels like being part of a 'tribe' that has some meaning for the individual. We see tribes every day in work and they can be very small, right down to the department level. While they can be a powerful driver for good they can also be highly destructive and cause organisations to tear themselves apart. This tribalistic need to belong poses both huge opportunities and significant challenges for leaders. Good leaders maintain a high awareness of the tribes in their organisation and are able to use their power positively to increase feelings of belonging. However, the best leaders are also aware that this can be a

double-edged sword and are acutely tuned to managing the negative aspects of tribalism.

A need to be stimulated

This is the desire for excitement. Most people would like to wake up on a workday morning and be able to feel a sense of excitement and a positive buzz of anticipation for what the day ahead may bring. It may not necessarily come from the task or role. It may come from the people they work with but it is more likely to come from the environment created. Good leaders have an ability to understand the levels of stimulus that will excite their people and create structures, practices and organisational environments that provide that stimulus. It is important to note that one person's excitement may be another person's terror. Leaders have to be attuned to and dynamically manage this continuum.

A need to feel valued and recognised

This can come from two sources. It may come from the job itself in that the work being undertaken has a clearly visible, meaningful purpose and is deemed important and valued by others outside the organisation, e.g. by society itself. Examples are surgeons, teachers, police officers, etc. The second source is where the job or tasks have little or no external recognition. In this case the status and self-esteem must come from how it has been structured and framed within the company itself. This means that the work has been positioned to have meaning and purpose internally to those in the company that the followers value. An example might be a company's receptionist. There is little external status or external recognition for the role but if the company leadership takes the view that this first point of contact for the outside world is critically important and visibly does things that shows the role is crucial then the person performing that role will feel highly valued and perform well. The less natural recognition, purpose or external status a job has, the harder leaders have to work at creating that recognition internally. If a role or job is valued neither externally by society nor internally by leaders, the chances of securing anything more in performance terms than a vertical human being with a pulse are limited.

A need to believe in and trust the leader

Regardless of the degree to which someone wants to be led it is important that leaders do not set themselves up as some form of 'idealised construct', trying to act out a role of some archetypal leader they may have read about or studied and want to try to model themselves on. Followers are not stupid and will flush out actors even if their mistakes have not given them away already. People buy into genuineness in whatever form it comes. Leaders can lead in almost any way that suits their character as long as it is real and they are being themselves.

SITUATIONAL CONSIDERATIONS FOR LEADERS

While it is crucial to understand what followers need and want the other critical question that is often not asked is, 'What is the situation?'. Situational in this context means that what followers want depends not just on the mindset and needs the followers themselves bring to the organisation but on the circumstances in which that organisation, its leaders and followers find themselves at any given time.

There are many publications that talk about leadership and even a few that now recognise followership as being perhaps more important in terms of truly understanding leadership. In some cases they focus on the leaders and in others the followers – even to the extent of saying followers don't want to feel they are being led. The belief, in these more enlightened and egalitarian times, is that followers, even though they may not be part of the leadership, want to feel they are at least engaged and involved in direction setting. This all sounds very desirable but in reality it is highly situational. Take the following example. A previously strong, growing, egalitarian and highly empathetic company suddenly comes under heavy attack from competitors. It rapidly begins to lose market share with revenue and profits plummeting. The previously democratic followers are not going to be too impressed with a leader in such a situation who is highly consensual and inclusive and who uses problem solving encounter groups, egalitarian voting systems and feedback mechanisms that result in fatally slow decision making and ultimately the company going under.

Conversely, take the follower who is blissfully happy working in a slow, stable, bureaucratic entity with a dominant market position in a benign environment. The leader who comes along trying to generate a gung-ho, sharp, lean, mean and aggressive organisation will be a terrifying prospect and will alienate such followers. That leader may well find difficulties not just in making things happen; he might not even be speaking a language the followers understand.

It is therefore evident that, despite what the 'normal' needs and desires may be for followers and what they look to their leaders to provide, these will undoubtedly change depending on the situation. In an emergency situation even followers in a typical bureaucracy will suddenly want to see high competence, incisiveness, speed of decision making and the ability to execute from their leaders.

These situational aspects of leadership become clearer when set out in Figure 2 below. Without doubt there have been undeniably great leaders in war or emergency situations who have been hopeless in more benign and less threatening conditions, and vice versa. We have often seen leaders, especially the more Machiavellian ones, creating and even fabricating threatening and fearful situations to enable them to embark on a particular course of action or simply to try to deflect attention away from some issue or event that might damage them.

WHAT MAKES A GREAT COACH?

To understand why good leaders need to be good coaches we need to examine what makes a great sports coach. There are two aspects that are critical. First, the best coaches have very high technical domain knowledge. This is not just about the sport itself but about what it requires of the athletes in terms of physiology, biomechanics, conditioning and even psychology and mental skills development. Coaches may not have expert knowledge in all these fields but they will secure it from those that do. Second, the best coaches have exceptional empathy and people skills, the key elements of which are listed below.

- Strong focus on people and their needs (physical and psychological) in everything they do.

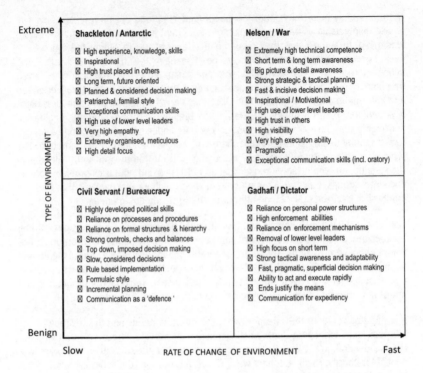

Figure 2: Situational leadership styles.

- Putting the athlete first: placing the individual and their needs at the forefront of everything they do.
- Commitment and adherence to the highest of standards.
- The ability to identify weaknesses and areas for improvement in positive ways so that individuals feel empowered, even desperate, to turn them into strengths.
- The ability to devise and implement 'improvement' regimes, tailored to suit each athlete based on the their intimate and broad understanding of each individual in their squad.
- Highly developed ability to communicate complexity and change requirements positively such that the athletes work hard to implement them. Even the type of language used will change from athlete to athlete.
- Strong empathy with and psychological awareness of both their squad and each individual.
- Ability to get their athletes to believe in them, their approach, training regimes, etc.
- Creation of an environment that feels like a powerful 'can do/try anything' one to the athlete, but in which the coach is aware of and in control of the risks as much as they can be without making it so safe nothing worthwhile can happen.

- Non-hierarchical: does not rely on position and creates a powerful, positive team spirit.
- Being a 'real' and authentic person who is genuinely interested in their athletes.

We can complete this exploration into the differences and similarities between coaches and coaching and leaders and leading by finally looking at the coach roles through the lens of their athletes. In the same way that we earlier asked, 'What do followers need?', we can similarly ask 'What do athletes want or need?'.

It is important to note that athletes are a little different from people in organisations in that they already have a mentality that has moved them very firmly into the esteem and self-actualisation areas of Maslow's hierarchy (see Figure 1, p.17) The 'need' below this, that of belonging, is generally subordinate to the two higher drives. For those who seek out team sports, belonging is clearly important but the need to be the best they can be as an individual takes priority. On this basis we can get an appreciation of what the needs of top performing athletes might be. While true athletes exhibit a much higher and more visible order of these drives to be the best they can be, they also exist to a greater or lesser degree in the majority of followers in business (especially if a strong degree of selectivity at the recruitment stage is practised – see Chapter 9). By gaining an appreciation of what drives athletes to high performance in sport, business leaders will gain insight into how these may be adapted for use with followers to obtain increased performance in organisations.

WHAT ATHLETES NEED

A need to be challenged
In order to achieve continuous development and improvement athletes want to be challenged, tested and measured. They want demanding goals to be set and they want those targets raised as often as sensibly possible. They are seeking to find and challenge limits. A term used in training in sport is 'progressive overload'. This means training that overloads the athlete (for whatever period is appropriate for the particular sport being coached) and then dropping below that limit for a predetermined recovery period. During this recovery period adaptation takes place in the body and brain. Repeating this cycle results in a progressive increase in whatever performance levels are being targeted.

A need to trust and believe in their coach
At the heart of this trust is the need for the athletes to believe that their coach can help them achieve the high-performance levels that will place them in a position to be able to win. A strong element in this deeply trusting relationship is the further belief in their coach's absolute competence in all aspects of their sport. This competence must be wide ranging. Obviously technical competence is critical. But athletes also have to trust that their coach can identify problems and fix them in ways that enhance performance in both the individual and the team. In this respect athletes generally are very open to having weaknesses exposed. Either they recognise, or good coaches help them recognise, that turning a weakness into a strength has a far greater impact on performance than simply building an existing strength a tiny

percentage higher. Identifying and exposing weaknesses needs to be handled well and good coaches must also be highly aware of the psychological needs in training and in competition. Athletes look to their coach to address these mental skills as well. As a squad becomes a team there is also a great need for the athletes to trust and believe in each other. This is also within the coach's sphere of control.

A need for performance and achievement to be recognised

In seeking to master themselves and their chosen discipline athletes require recognition. They need frequent reference points that help them gauge their progress and that help define and measure their development. Acknowledgement and respect are critical in this regard. While one of the greatest recognition factors is winning it is not necessarily the top one. Much depends on whether an athlete is extrinsically or intrinsically motivated. These crucial aspects of motivation in individuals are covered more fully in Chapter 6.

In many respects, because top athletes drive themselves so hard and recognition is so critical, they can often become quite fragile mentally if they fail to meet whatever goals or targets they set. Coaches have to be capable of handling difficult psychological situations, especially where an individual's fragility issues impacts on a team.

Not only individuals have such crises of confidence: teams do too. Good coaches have the ability to work through these difficult patches but great coaches seem to recognise them before they become visible. Coaches recognise that in most cases overcoming bad patches successfully together often builds a much stronger team as a result.

A need for the right environment to be created

Athletes need to be able to concentrate, focus and dedicate themselves to driving performance ever upwards. In order for athletes to achieve this focus coaches must be able to provide an environment and regimes that enable the athlete to single-mindedly work on their all-round development. This will cover everything from fitness programmes and technical competence development right through to travel and accommodation arrangements. This is not about mollycoddling. It is about recognising exactly what it is that the athletes need in order to bring all their training and skills to bear with the minimum of distractions.

Hopefully it can be seen from the above that if a leader already has the 'technical' business skills and some degree of leadership ability, then having great coaching skills along the lines outlined above will without doubt enable that leader to build strong, high-performing teams across the wider organisation. The good news is that coaching skills and abilities are probably easier to develop than those required for leadership. This book provides a number of models, concepts and techniques adapted from sport coaching and sport science that will help leaders understand and employ good coaching practices.

OVERCOMING THE 'COMFORT ZONE'

The model shown in Figure 3 (developed by sports psychologist Willi Sten Railo in 2002) encapsulates very clearly what it is that great coaches and leaders have to

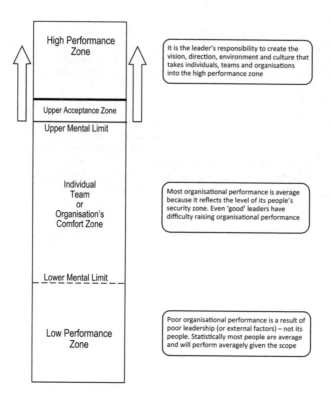

Figure 3: Railo security model.

overcome to achieve high performance. Even potentially high-performing people in either sport or business have a tendency to gravitate towards their 'comfort zone'. With high performers this tends to be towards the upper mental limit and with low performers it will be well towards the lower mental limit and even into the poor performance zone.

To achieve high performance coaches and leaders have to create an environment and encourage a culture that actively moves people out of their comfort zone. In sport this is easier because competitive athletes are usually already working continuously at the upper limits of their security zone. Good coaches can relatively easily construct 'stories', goals and targets to move them higher. With athletes the stories tend to focus less on the 'why' and more on the 'how' because top athletes are already committed to and understand why they are seeking these goals and have these desires.

Except for the best organisations, the picture is a little different. Most people are working only within their security zone and prove very difficult to move out of it. This is generally for the following three reasons.

1. The innate human propensity for caution.
2. The extra effort and personal stress is not seen to be worth it.
3. Most organisations, whether they realise it or not, primarily seek compliance not performance from their people. Control is at best through hierarchy, rules, processes and contracts. At worst it is achieved through cultures of fear, fault and blame.

SUMMARY

While there are some similarities between leaders and leading and coaches and coaching, there are also some very interesting differences. It is in these differences that the opportunity lies for leaders of companies to achieve enhanced performance. The chapters that follow explore key aspects more fully and provide models and methods by which they may be adapted and implemented in companies or other organisational environments.

CHAPTER 3
SUCCESS AND FAILURE: THE ACID TEST OF COMPETITION

Only one who devotes himself to a cause with his whole strength and soul can be a true master. For this reason mastery demands all of a person.
Albert Einstein

How many times have you heard a corporate leader in a media interview saying, 'Our company welcomes competition'? How many times have you believed that they really mean what they say? I have heard leaders in my own companies and industries say exactly this. Yet, what they privately want is a dominant market position, so they can make easy profits, reap substantial personal rewards for little risk or effort and have a comfortable journey into wealthy retirement. I am also sure that shareholders, whose general experience is of average corporate leadership with its attendant average performance, shudder in horror when they hear CEOs of companies they are invested in say 'We welcome competition'.

How different in sport. For the athlete and especially the coach, the mantra 'We welcome competition' is not simply a media sound bite. It is an absolute truth. Competition is the inescapable arena in which athletes and coaches test themselves time and again. It is the single, black-and-white measure that defines them – publicly, visibly and with no hiding place from the result or the consequences of it. Coaches and the athletes they work with really do mean 'we welcome competition'. Not only do they welcome it, they seek it out. It is their *raison d'être*. Competition is where they learn and where they improve. They positively thrive on it. It provides the buzz and the rush they need to commit to the gruelling training regimes, the physical pain, the mental discipline and often the loss of any normal social life. This chapter explores the difference between coaches and leaders in relation to success and failure.

THE SPOTLIGHT AND SHADOWS OF FAILURE
Even a modest amateur athlete commits many hours a week on the road or in the gym for their sport, building fitness, improving technique and developing their ability in addition to competing. For top professional athletes who get paid for their sport this is all they do. It is how they earn their living and they commit to their sport and their team mates every day. This commitment stems from the fact that they are predominantly intrinsically motivated to be the best they can possibly be. They are self-driven to improve their performance. As we saw in the previous chapter, they are seeking to realise the top two needs (esteem and self-actualisation) in the psychological hierarchy and to do so at the highest possible

levels of personal achievement. This requires dedication, focus and commitment over long periods.

How do they know if all the work and pain they devote themselves to is successful in achieving their fundamental drive to be the best? They find out by testing themselves in competition and by doing so as often as they sensibly can. And if they fail? Good coaches and athletes (and certainly the top ones) drive even harder to eradicate those causes of failure.

It is in these failure situations that the coach has absolutely nowhere to hide. It is a fact that the best coaches tend to draw back when there is success and let their team and athletes bask in the glory of winning. When there is failure the opposite is true. The spotlight falls well and truly on the coach. It is the coach who first comes under pressure from those above them. Franchise owners, club management and billionaire shareholders can and often do make almost instant firing decisions. In high-profile sports the coach will also come under pressure from the media and probably fans and supporters as well. Because failure is so visible there truly is no hiding place for the coach. The ramifications of failure can very quickly end up in the coach losing his job – almost regardless of the circumstances or how good he really is. This may be to appease a capricious owner, an athlete revolt, a media feeding frenzy or even supporter-based pressure.

Coaches also come under substantial pressure from those 'below' them, namely their athletes and their coaching team. Where there is performance failure they can often be more difficult and judgemental than those above. Good athletes have incredibly high expectations of themselves and similarly expect their coach to be a key element in delivering their personal performance goals and aspirations. When these are not met and confidence wanes athletes are often as ruthless as owners.

It can be seen quite clearly that both coaches and athletes are not only prepared to place their personal performance and that of their team on the line, they are prepared to do it frequently, highly visibly and with no possible chance of hiding poor performance either from themselves or others.

In business, things are a little different! As we often see in sport it is the athlete and/or the team that takes centre stage and who receive the accolades when they win, not the coach. I have often seen great success in companies achieved by employees who have received no recognition whatsoever for that success. When a business is doing well it is the leaders who usually take all the glory and most of the rewards that go with what is often only modest success. This is because, unlike sport, what predominantly triggers business rewards is more often than not based solely on internal measures of success rather than on relative or comparative performance. We need to remember that 'doing well' is predominantly a measure set by the business leaders themselves.

COMPARATIVE AND RELATIVE PERFORMANCE

It is important to note that we are not talking just about absolute failure with respect to performance. Absolute failure in performance is easily visible – at least for those who truly want to see it. However, since this book is about achieving high performance, a worse situation is that of the poor leader failing to maximise the potential of the business. This means a failure to achieve the best or highest performance that the market, environment and the resources available could allow if properly led and managed.

I have been in situations where a market is booming and the company is seemingly doing well, securing year-on-year growth of 10% or more and everyone getting great bonuses. Everything looks fine until you realise that the underlying market sector was growing at 15% and the main competitor was squeezing almost 20% of it. The reality was the company going backwards, losing market share and not performing as well as the competition, but its leaders were still getting handsomely rewarded for it.

Not only is very average performance being well rewarded in businesses but relative and comparative performance rarely gets a mention in bonus schemes or short and long-term incentive plans. By relative performance I mean the level of performance that could be achieved with the people and resources available to the leader if they were properly marshalled and effectively employed, i.e. relative to what the company has achieved against what the company could have achieved. Comparative performance is the performance achieved compared with that of competitors.

An example would be an around-the-world sailing race. A team wins four out of the seven stages and thus compared with its competitors it is the winner. However, if you then look at the boat and team's performance more closely you discover that the boat could have completed the race 15 days faster and established a new world record for which there was an additional prize. In this example the team has succeeded on a comparative basis but failed on a relative basis. Businesses do this all the time, especially when they are comparing themselves against other businesses that are similarly achieving poor relative performance. Few owners or shareholders even seem interested in these aspects of performance. For coaches, athletes and teams in the sporting arena performance is always relative and comparative. It is not just about beating your rivals, it is about winning well and setting records.

As a simple business example, when Shell reported in their 2010 Annual Report that 'oil and gas production volumes increased by 5%' their performance on the face of it looked good and their annual report was very upbeat. As an investor you might be impressed – that is until you see Exxon Mobil's report for the same period 'oil equivalent production grew to 4.4 million barrels of oil per day, a 13% increase year on year'.

THE RAMIFICATIONS OF FAILURE IN SPORT

While we often see that success is treated very differently in the business environment from that in the sporting world, the more interesting question may be 'How is failure treated?'. If business leaders are the first on the podium to take the medals and plaudits when things are going well, what about when they are going badly? You are no doubt well ahead of me in the prediction game! If we take a sample of poorly performing companies in the FTSE 100 and Fortune 100 companies we can see an impressive degree of dissembling by their business leaders in the face of poor performance even in such high-profile, index-leading firms.

Given the Shell and Exxon examples above it is interesting to start with BP's reporting of its production performance in the same 2010 period:

> Reported production in 2010 was 4% lower than in 2009 due to the effect of entitlement changes in our production sharing agreements, the effects of acquisitions and disposals and the impact of events in the Gulf of Mexico.

Despite poor comparative and relative performance executive directors in BP still received substantial cash bonuses and stock awards.

It would be easy to continue with examples but I think the point is clear. Unlike coaches in sport, business leaders are able to hide poor performance behind any number of 'business environment' rationales and frequently do. Predictably, in all these cases there is little or no recognition that the leadership may be to blame for average or even poor performance. It is even more worrying that, if this is what high-profile leaders can get away with in market-leading and highly scrutinised firms, what must be happening in companies outside the leading stock exchanges where less attention is being paid? This goes back to one of the opening premises of this book regarding poor performance in firms.

- Average (even poor) performance is planned for by the senior leadership team.
- Average (even poor) performance is accepted by the owners and/or shareholders of the business, or they are powerless to do anything about it.
- Average (even poor) performance at the top of an organisation is handsomely rewarded.
- Employees of the business (who are neither stupid nor blind) can see that poor/ average performance is not just acceptable but is rewarded.

The central argument of this chapter is that in sport coaches cannot hide from their poor performance whereas business leaders can and often do. Given these facts the ability to hide, or not hide, poor performance must have some ramifications for how both leaders and coaches behave with respect to future performance. There is plenty of evidence showing that it is the responses to failure that set apart consistent winners from habitual losers. On this basis, if business leaders can and do conceal or deflect poor performance and do not take responsibility for it, then it is clear they are unlikely to learn anything that will make them improve. If this ability to hide their shortcomings similarly has little impact on their rewards there is also no incentive to improve. It is my experience and that of thousands of shareholders that this is often proven in reality. Fortunately there are sufficient examples in business of good leaders who do manage to achieve high performance and even more clear examples in sport.

What happens in sport when things are going wrong? In sport, if you are in the firing line, poor performance will be as visible as great performance. When things are going wrong there is another crucial difference between sport and business: because the effort required by both the coach and athletes is high (extreme at the top levels) the psychological impact of failure is often much more severe on the individual athletes.

When you are committing to high levels of training, when your diet is strictly controlled and when your entire life is regimented and directed towards winning, then failure can have a greatly increased impact. While athletes have to be extremely mentally tough to endure the training regimes they commit to, they can also perversely be quite fragile when it comes to failure. This is when coaches become critically important – in the management of failure and turning it around. While athletes always look to their coaches to identify areas of improvement, they look even harder when there has been a failure. Good coaches will be able to say what, how, why, where and when things went wrong. They will be able to identify weakness at both individual and team level. They will have the competence, knowledge and experience to adjust current programmes and regimes or even develop completely new ideas to overcome those performance weaknesses. These changes will be made at both individual athlete level and at team level.

Rate of improvement

With a good coach the athletes themselves are generally spurred on by failure to train better – which does not necessarily mean harder! Along with the coach they study those who beat them; they learn from every competition and every setback and use them as platforms from which to launch the next level of performance development. Not only is there a master plan, there is a master attitude: to train better, to improve faster, to test more, to measure, to compare and thus maintain the required rate of improvement. From a business leader's perspective this approach to individual, squad, team and even organisational development can readily be transferred into the business environment. Later chapters in this book address the key elements, concepts and techniques (including frameworks) for doing exactly this.

The rate of improvement is a concept that businesses would do well to embrace and embed in their corporate thinking. Coaches and athletes live and breathe rates of improvement, so much so that it almost does not need to be mentioned. Not only are athletes aware of their competitors, they measure them as much, if not more, than themselves. They know that there is no point carrying out their training and development programmes if they are not helping them to improve faster than the competition. In a 2,000 metre rowing race the winning margin can be down to centimetres – the difference between an Olympic gold and an Olympic silver can come down to a margin as little as the length of a mobile phone.

Response to failure situations

Coaching a team that is not performing well or, even worse, one that used to perform well and is now failing requires the highest levels of skill, experience and 'leadership' qualities from the coach. I have placed leadership in quotes because you will no doubt remember what I said in the opening to this book about coaches and leading: 'Great coaches should not aspire to be great leaders but great leaders should be great coaches'. The failure situation, especially repeated failure after repeated success, is where a coach does have to 'lead' to a degree, although prefer- ably very cleverly and without appearing to do so.

It is in these situations where all the coach's technical knowledge, experience, skills and abilities are required. He has to have the background and technical competence to be able to analyse what is going wrong at the technical and mechanical level. He must also understand the environment of his sport: how it works, even how it is adminis- tered and how he has to manage his squad within the rules and norms of that sport. He has to have expert knowledge of the physical and physiological demands of the sport and the capability of his athletes to meet them. He must be a good psychologist, able to understand and work with the mental strengths and weaknesses of his ath- letes and be able to harness them to advantage. He has to understand what is going on with each of the athletes in his squad. He has to understand the make-up and driv- ers of each individual and how these impact on the team dynamic. Lastly, he has to be able to take all these hard and soft elements and come up with an all-encompassing strategic, tactical, physiological, even psychological solution that returns the team to winning ways. It is his knowledge of both the external and the internal elements of his sport, the competition, his individuals and his squad and how he uses his skills and abilities to harness them that will enable the coach to turn around a failing situation.

Competitor and environment analysis

The resulting, all-encompassing solution will include the aspects you would expect of a competitive situation where what you were doing in the past (that used to be successful) is beginning to fail in the present and likely to get worse in the future. It is a total review that starts not with what you were doing before but with what you need to do now and in the future. Therefore it starts with the competition: what it is that they are doing that is making them successful. This does not mean slavishly copying them but understanding exactly how and why they are successful.

Among others, you need to ask questions such as:

- Have they changed equipment?
- Has their squad been refreshed?
- Have they changed coaches?
- Have they engaged new sports scientists or employed new training regimes?
- How big are the improvements and have the changes been fast or slow?
- What have been the environmental conditions in the recent competitions?
- What have we been doing that is different?

This questioning process is the critical part in assessing what has changed. All assumptions must be examined and challenged. This process must involve everyone – the coaching team, the athletes, even some 'off the wall' observations by 'outsiders' can be useful triggers for new thinking.

It also requires putting the competition and your own athletes and teams into con- text. This means understanding the environment in which competition is taking place, the current requirements, the trends and the future likely needs. It may mean the creation of a new strategy rather than a retuning of the existing one. Creation of this new strategy must be based on new knowledge. This means that the coach will have assessed the causes of failure and will have found either some clear visible causes (the easy route) or will not have found a simple explanation and will be relying solely on their experience to make changes (the more difficult route).

Sometimes the changes come down quite simply to new equipment and latest technology; but this is rarely the cause for a once successful team to start failing. It may come down to new techniques, advances in the sport, or greater understanding of how the body and/or equipment can work better. Developments in physiological understanding and measurement may lead to changed and better training regimes or diet. But, as you may already have guessed, more often than not it comes down quite simply to the 'human factor'. Either the coach or the athletes, or sometimes both, were just not performing at the levels required. It is also quite likely the levels were raised by the competition and there was a failure to notice or respond in time. And sometimes a great coach comes along who just has a eureka moment and tries something so different that it changes the very nature of the competition. More usually it is an amalgam of all of these complexities.

Actions after analysis

This is where what appear to be difficult decisions need to be made, for example dropping athletes out of the team. I say 'appear to be difficult' because two things are nearly always true in high-intensity, competitive teams.

- The first is the athlete or athletes who are underperforming already know they are doing so.
- Second, the athletes in the team who are not underperforming usually know who is.

Therefore the coach who does not deal with this situation effectively is doing far more to damage the team attitude and dynamic than any competitor could.

As we will see later in this book, exactly the same is true in business. If, as a business leader, you believe your employees do not know who is and who is not performing you had better think again. Everyone in an organisation or department or team knows who is performing and who isn't, who is brilliant and who is average, who is competent in their role and who is failing and who is just a slick talker and not an effective 'doer'. If your performance management system merely ratifies the status quo then there should be no surprises if the status quo is exactly what you get going forwards. Except, just as in sport, there is no such thing as the status quo in business. If you are not developing, improving, changing and leading your sport or business then you will be falling behind. If you are not failing now you are likely to fail in the future because the best of your competitors are definitely seeking to improve faster than you.

Absolutely critical to a coach in turning around a failing situation is the fact that their athletes, their team, have to believe that not only can they themselves turn failure into success but that the coach is the one who can help them make it happen. It is this last aspect that is crucial. Unless the team absolutely, 100% believes that their coach can deliver everything that is required for them to achieve success then that coach, and therefore his squad, are doomed. This aspect touches upon the emotional and psychological contract between coach and athletes as well as the very obvious one of technical competence.

There is recognition in sport that sometimes failure is not due to a lack of fitness, ability or attitude of the athletes or incompetence of the coach but solely due to the fact that the vital and indefinable 'spark' you need in the coach/athlete/team relationship is missing. This aspect of a psychological contract between a leader and his followers in business is often missed. Regardless of the written, formal contract of employment and/or the processes and procedures by which the organisation is managed, there still exists a 'psychological contract' between a leader and his followers. This is not something that a leader fully controls; in fact average leaders rarely know that it exists and even if they do it is rare for them to acknowledge the fact. It is something that the followers, both individually and as a collective, attribute to their leader and is borne out of the actions, signals and symbols the leader employs and the cultural context of the organisation itself.

Poor and average leaders rely on their position of power, the rules and procedures of the organisation and the employment contract to manage their organisation and followers. Under these circumstances what is normally seen is leadership and management by control (often even fear). Great leaders intimately understand the psychological contract and are adept at employing this to energise and motivate the organisation rather than seeking compliance and control through rules and regulation. What poor leaders achieve is follower compliance rather than free, willing, enthused and engaged followership. What great leaders achieve is engagement, empowerment and a belief that anything is possible.

It may be seen from the above, especially with an understanding of the psychological contract between leaders and followers or coaches and athletes, that by far the most critical (and most difficult) part of the failure analysis is the requirement for the coach to take a very close look at himself. The hard truth in sport is that if coaches are not honest enough to look at themselves and their role in any failure, it is without doubt the case that the athletes and the employing body will do it for them. Competition ensures poor coaches get found out very quickly.

THE RAMIFICATIONS OF FAILURE IN BUSINESS
How different for poor leaders in business! Apart from being able to blame external factors 'beyond their control', poor business leaders do not come under pressure from their followers in the way coaches do from their athletes. Poor leaders are protected by their position. This protection often comes from the group think of their clique of immediate subordinates. It always comes from the rules, procedures and processes companies put in place to ensure compliance. And of course there is almost always employee fear: the fear they have for their careers if they make adverse comments.

Unlike in sport the ramifications of performance failure in business are rather more difficult to investigate. This is because, as we have seen, the first problem is in trying to ascertain just when a failure has occurred. The reality is that the primary external measurements for a business tend only to be once a year and are generally against 'targets' set internally by the company's leaders in the first place. An analogy might be that you are a 400 metre hurdler. You only have to run one race a year, you have your own stadium and you are allowed to set the height of your own hurdles. While you know that other hurdlers in other stadia are running this same 400 metre race your prize money will be secured not by beating the times and heights of all those other competitors but only for clearing most (not even all) of the hurdles on your own track. The outcome for the height setting of the hurdles is entirely predictable!

It is therefore almost impossible under normal trading conditions to determine not just that outright failure in relative performance has occurred but that any significant performance has occurred at all. Any assessments of comparative performance will generally only be made by external agents, e.g. market analysts and stock markets, if the company is quoted. Unquoted companies rarely see this comparative analysis done and thus most business leaders avoid the discomfort of having their performance failures compared with the successes of others in any meaningful way. Even where there are catastrophic and unavoidably visible failures in performance, we often see the existing leaders managing to survive and continue leading their organisations.

In situations where there is a highly visible failure in performance in companies we often see the organisation's leaders making a variety of excuses or seeking to confuse and disguise the real causes of that failure. Some examples of these from the banking, telecoms and energy sectors have been shown earlier in Chapter 1. However, the ramifications of such failures are quite different in business compared to sport. Whereas in sport all eyes turn to the coach and their performance, quite often in business the focus swings onto the organisation or the environment rather than the leader. Because excuses get made (and generally accepted) that extraneous factors are to blame for a company performing badly, often the last element that comes under scrutiny is the quality and competence of the leader and leadership. The owner who might normally be expected to undertake such scrutiny is often an amorphous mass of shareholders whose powers are diluted and diffused and therefore limited at best.

Unless it is a quoted company, analysts also do not bring any pressure to bear. Even if it is quoted and the market and/or media do take an interest it has little immediate effect. Thus a poor leader in business can retain his position for a long time while still failing to perform and doing damage. Obviously, in time, if there is continued poor performance, the leadership eventually comes under fire; but eventually can be many years away. In that time the business 'athletes', the team and indeed the whole 'club' can be terminally damaged.

The worst outcome from this inability to recognise early enough when business performance is sub-optimal or failing is the delay in taking actions to correct performance failure. Late recognition more often than not results in a knee-jerk reaction just to stop the financial haemorrhaging. Invariably this results in the first response of business leaders in a failing situation being cost cutting and restructuring – otherwise known as getting rid of people. This is followed by asset sales, structural retrenchment, etc. Eventually, once the accountants are happy that the bleeding has stopped the leadership may be allowed to look at the real problem that caused the performance failure in the first place. However, even this becomes a suspect and probably flawed action. On the basis that the leader is still in situ then his excuses for the failures will have been believed and accepted by the owners. As a result the still incumbent leader will look to fix what was publicly stated as the problem and not the more fundamental issues, such as their own leadership and competence.

SUMMARY

We know that many great coaches have been at the top of their sport for many years. Coaches such as Alex Ferguson with 26 years at Manchester United alone, or Jurgen Grobler who has been the men's coach of the GB rowing team since 1991 and won gold medals in every one of the six Olympic Games since his appointment. They are the very best at what they do. These are not dilettante journeymen flitting from football to tennis to swimming like some chief executives flit from energy to construction to electronics. These are people who have become experts in their particular sport. They have honed their knowledge and skills in that sport, its requirements of their athletes, the intensity of its competition and the environment (physical, legal, financial, organisational) in which their team is required to perform and win. They have what is known as domain knowledge and in the case of the very best coaches and leaders it is absolute.

Coaches in sport accept and relish the responsibility that goes with taking on the role of coach. They understand the performance visibility the role places upon them and they relish the challenge it entails. It energises them and galvanises them to always improve. This is because they, like their athletes, are primarily intrinsically motivated. Few (if any) go into the sport for material rewards. Conversely, most business leaders are extrinsically motivated and thus almost diametrically opposite to sports coaches in terms of what makes them seek the role. It is often desire for its power, status, rewards and ability to feed the ego.

Generally the last thing that business leaders seek is to place themselves in the centre of an arena of highly visible competition and performance. However, often when talking to followers you find they would enjoy competing more visibly: they would relish seeing how good they are and how they stack up against the competition. You only have to see the excitement and celebration that goes on in good departments in companies when a contract is won or a project well delivered to know people can and do enjoy winning at work. Average performance is almost always the result of average leadership. Good leaders, like good coaches, understand that people like succeeding. They tap into intrinsic motivations and create an environment where motivated people can flourish, as we will see in subsequent chapters.

CHAPTER 4
THE PERFORMANCE TRIANGLE
(STATIC MODE)

Don't measure yourself by what you have accomplished, but by what you should have accomplished with your ability.
John Wooden, basketball coach, winner of 10 NCAA championships in 12 years

If we accept that, in most cases, company performance is generally average and that company leadership has more to gain in performance-related rewards by setting lower rather than higher targets, then what do we do about it? Coaching and sport can provide some interesting ideas, models and even some lessons. It can be argued that the critical factors that go into developing high performance in sport have advanced significantly faster than in almost any business sector. Focusing on a few key factors from high-performance development in sport that can be adapted to business can help organisations achieve equivalent performance improvements.

This chapter introduces a key model called the performance triangle. Through a detailed examination of the constituent elements of the model, namely attributes, fitness, ability and attitude as they are applied in sport, this chapter goes on to show how the model can be adapted for and used in organisations.

THE RISE OF RIGOUR, DETAIL AND SCIENCE IN THE HUNT FOR HIGH PERFORMANCE

The 1968 Mexico Olympics are frequently held as being a watershed in modern coaching. Regardless of exactly when such a watershed occurred, there is no doubt that the change in modern sports coaching around 40 years ago was driven by two key elements. The first was the increase in the importance of international sporting success, both politically and because of the increasing wealth sport was beginning to generate. The second was the rise of sports science and its ability to empirically examine, test, validate and change established coaching techniques and training methods. With increasing scientific understanding of physiology, biomechanics, nutrition and latterly neurology and psychology in sport it became possible to derive brand new approaches to athlete and team development.

As with any revolutionary change of this nature, the battle between the traditionalist coaching world, with its experiential and intuitive approach, versus the new scientific one was predictable and in many cases still goes on. Also, predictably, neither side could hold itself up as being the absolute and definitive best solution for either athlete or team development. There are examples of each being applied exclusively and achieving occasional success. However, without doubt sustained high performance comes from the artful blending of the rigour of the scientific approach together with the practical experience, creative flair and intuition of the great coach.

This blend of the rigour of the sports scientist with the creativity and intuition of the skilful coach shows that the thoroughness and painstakingly detailed approach of modern sports coaching on a broad front of specialisms is often well in advance of the haphazard approaches frequently seen in modern business. How many business leaders undertake the business equivalent of $VO2_{max}$ (maximal oxygen capacity) tests, blood sampling athletes during stress tests and pushing aerobic/anaerobic (lactic acid) thresholds? How many undertake the equivalent of designing programmes to alter the physiology of a body, build muscle mass, work on fast twitch or slow twitch muscle fibres and know why they are doing all these things and the effects they will have on performance? How many business leaders immerse themselves in what their competitors are doing? How many spend large amounts of their time doing the business equivalent of watching videos of their competitors' performance, minutely examining every element of their strategic and tactical approach in previous events or encounters for areas to exploit? How often do they assess each individual in a competitor's team for points of weakness then test counter strategies and tactics?

Targets and stretch

I hope it is obvious that obtaining high performance is not achieved as a result of just setting high goals and targets. Setting goals that are not inextricably aligned with corporate direction, that are not harnessed to performance targets and that are not grounded in the reality of the talents and resources at your disposal will have the opposite effect to that which you wish to achieve. No matter what level of current performance you are starting from it is critical that the targets and goals are achievable. Regardless of whether it is athletes in sport or employees in business, goals and targets must require a significant degree of high performance and personal 'stretch'. From a self-esteem perspective people want to feel they have achieved something worthwhile.

Easy targets devalue how people feel about having achieved them and end up minimising performance. It is more difficult, arguably impossible, to see the effects of easy targets in business but their impact in sport is obvious and becomes readily apparent. If as a coach you fail to stretch athletes or fail to achieve their continuous and effective development they very quickly become aware they are falling behind their competitors (both inside and outside their own squad). They will very swiftly let the coach know they are not happy.

In business it is more difficult as followers will still take the easy target bonuses and any other rewards, but they will lose the satisfaction and excitement that comes with knowing they have genuinely done well. Over time their performance will degrade since they will know high individual performance and the associated higher levels of effort make little difference. Low targets lead to a low performance culture. Often employment contracts and appraisal systems reinforce this performance-minimising culture. This aspect of both individual (and team) stretch is worth dwelling on as it is one of those virtuous circles so crucial for improving performance. In business this aspect of stretching individuals is exclusively associated with psychological aspects. However in sport, in addition to the psychological elements, stretch also fits in neatly with the significant physiological improvements brought about by the principle of 'progressive overload' in training regimes.

In terms of the virtuous circle the fitter athletes become the more they can train. The more they can train the more their ability can be developed. The more their ability develops the more they can be stretched. As they recognise that they are getting fitter and better the more they engage and want to be stretched. This leads to a positive feedback 'loop' for continuous performance improvement being inculcated that feeds into the psyche of the athlete's development. They feel the burn, enjoy the buzz, see the results and thus seek ever more improvement. One of the crucial skills when coaching athletes is knowing just how far progressive overload can be taken in each cycle without breaking the athletes or imploding the team. It can be seen that achieving the highest possible performance from that athlete or squad is a constant balance between overload and recovery. It is more about the minute and detailed planning of a pathway to high performance over time than about instantaneous change especially where you are starting from an initially low fitness and ability base.

Coach-athlete symbiosis and the ways leaders seek to avoid it

As with anything in life, expecting people to follow your ideas and plans cannot be achieved unless they fully understand what it is you want them to do. They also need to know how you and they together are going to do it. Where they are required to invest a significant amount of themselves and their time into the endeavour it is also critical they understand what they might gain from their efforts and why. Consequently there is a requirement for high order communication skills in good coaches and no less so for those who aspire to be great business leaders.

With athletes the 'why' and the gains to be achieved are pretty much a given. They know why they are giving up any semblance of normal life and dedicating it to years of pain, trials and tribulations! However, because they know the high personal cost of their commitment, athletes are much more difficult to manage than people and teams in organisations. When an individual athlete's performance is suboptimal he will expect the coach to have the answers. If those answers do not produce visible results the athlete will let the coach know in no uncertain terms. If it is the team's performance that is suffering life can become very tough for the coach.

As mentioned in the opening chapters, coaches are not leaders in the sense that a CEO or managing director would understand the word. There is no corporate hierarchy, no position of power or cosy company procedures to protect or shield the coach from his athletes. If the coach's ideas, plans and regimes are not delivering the performance the athletes require it very rapidly becomes apparent. Because of the high physical and emotional commitment required of the athletes they will challenge the coach often and vigorously. The symbiosis between coach and athlete in sport is much greater than that between leader and follower in business. With an unremitting focus on performance, measurement and frequent testing in the heat of competition, the attainment of high performance, or the lack of it, is much more visible and immediate in sport than in business. Because coach and athletes are so tightly bound together around these aspects of high performance and winning it is often easy for emotions to run high. This is why managing high-performance athletes requires a high order of interpersonal skills, especially in situations when you are not winning.

In the business environment, leaders are able to get away with a great deal more than coaches in sport with respect to poor performance. Earlier chapters have shown how poor leaders can use external factors as excuses for dismal performance. Even worse is the fact that they are able to protect themselves from the sort of internal pressures coaches come under. First, there is not the same symbiosis in the relationship between leaders and followers in business as there is between coach and athletes. As a result, the followers' commitment is not so intense in business, nor does it need to be to achieve high performance. However, without some intensity and immediacy there is no spark to fire up a follower to question his leader's performance even if they feel brave enough to do so. Second, all leaders are protected from internal criticism and pressure as a result of their position. It is achieved by hierarchy, rules, procedures, employment contracts, appraisal systems and just plain old fear and possibly even bullying. Quite often this protection exists from the simple fact that the leader is the company owner and does not wish to be questioned. Poor leaders use these mechanisms to both reinforce their power and also secure immunity from blame. In the worst cases they will abuse their position power and blame others – even firing them from their jobs – to avoid their own culpability.

COMMUNICATION AND ALIGNMENT

The ability to communicate the what, why, how and when of often complex development ideas and rationales and securing the athlete's belief in them is what sets good coaches apart. It is no less essential in good leaders. An inability to derive relevant visions, formulate strategies, translate them into meaningful targets and goals and communicate plans, or indeed any complex set of ideas, is one reason why organisations fail in their strategic ambitions. However, a more common reason by far is the failure of leaders to achieve the alignment of everyone in the organisation to its vision, direction and goals. Without alignment there is unlikely to be commitment. This is a failure of leadership not just communication. It is an inability to create a vision and a story of a desired future that grabs the imagination and attention of the people you need to bring it to life. This is one of the key reasons why businesses fail to achieve the higher performance they think their strategy is designed to secure. Research shows that around 70% of all business strategies fail to achieve what they set out to do.

This issue of 'organisational alignment' and its impact on strategy implementation and success is both critical and complex. It is something sports coaches do all the time, as do the very best business leaders. The alignment of training regimes and plans with targets and goals is easier and more visible in sport but no matter how difficult or complex alignment may be for a business the failure to achieve it is at the leader's peril.

GOALS AND GOAL SETTING

Before moving on to the core model it is important to clarify a few aspects of goals and goal setting since they are a key part of any performance management system.

In general the core principles of goal setting are common in both sport and business. Goals are used to closely focus attention and effort on securing those elements of the 'vision' or long-term direction that are crucial for ensuring it is achieved. While many people in business are aware of the three different goal types, they generally tend not to think too deeply about them or even them use them. Organisations usually just refer to goals as goals and make no distinction between the types. What is often forgotten is that goals are incredibly powerful for:

■ breaking down, translating and distilling often fuzzy visions and strategies into hard, well-bound, deliverable packages
■ providing strong motivational frameworks that harness people to a common purpose and drive high performance (see also Chapter 6, Psychology).

There are three types of goals commonly used.

First, **outcome goals**. These goals refer to a desired state, e.g. to win an Olympic rowing gold medal, win a Masters Tournament or become a Fortune 500 company. They are generally more long term. Of concern for an organisation seeking to align many people to a common purpose is that they are more aspirational than motivational. Even more problematic is that they also tend to be outside the full control of the individuals or teams charged with achieving them. This has added significance when you read the section on stress in Chapter 6. Tying people and their work (and often their rewards) to outcome goals which are often succeed/fail or win/lose tends to move work pressure to the realms of work stress, especially as such goals generally tend to be beyond the direct control of the individuals. When pressure becomes stress, performance suffers. However, outcome goals can be helpful in the first stages of breaking down visions and strategic direction into elements more easily understood by the organisation.

Second, **performance goals**. These are really powerful drivers for individual and team/group performance. This is because they tend to be independent of external elements and are almost entirely, if not totally, under the control of the athlete, the coach and the team (or leader and followers). Performance goals can be adjusted and tuned by coaches/leaders and at any time. Any number of intermediate performance goals and check points can be built in. It is important to structure short-term performance goals as key milestones on the way towards the final performance goal and achieving the outcome goal(s). A typical performance goal in rowing might be 'improve on your previous 2,000 metre Ergo test'. While the outcome goal of winning an Olympic gold rowing medal is long term and outside the control of the individual athlete, improving their 2,000 metre race time is immediate and directly under their control. An example in business is where the leader may impose an outcome goal of 'securing a 10% increase in market share' but the follower's goals are focused on things such as 'develop and implement a customer retention programme'.

There is a further and fundamental importance in performance goals and that is in the area of psychological development. Achieving properly planned and pro-grammed performance goals effectively, progressively and steadily builds confi-dence in athletes even though they may not yet be anywhere near the ultimate outcome goals they have set. This aspect of a steady build up to stable levels of confidence is crucial in high performers. Confidence levels that are mercurial, that rise and fall with each setback or each success, create the wrong mindset required for sustained high performance. This mental conditioning is similar to that required of high performers in business.

Finally, **process goals**. Process goals have an important part to play because they focus athletes and teams on the actions, techniques and activities required to secure the performance targets. There is no point in a rower achieving 2,000 metres in 6 minutes 30 seconds on the rowing machine if his rowing style is idiosyncratic and not the same as the rest of the crew. Process goals might include: 'hold body angle in first part of the drive' or 'ensure only the inside hand feathers the oar'. An equiv-alent business example might be 'design and benchmark the customer retention programme to ensure it is a "best in class" system'. Therefore the way in which a process goal *conditions* a performance goal is critically important to both perform-ance and technique improvement, especially in team environments. Just as for per-formance goals, the psychological importance of process goals is similar in terms of building the athletes' confidence and state of mind. In this respect, Chapter 6 out-lines those psychological elements that are important in sport and which translate meaningfully into the organisational sphere.

In terms of highlighting the importance of performance goals, the following may resonate:

> Don't aim for success – the more you aim at it and make it a target, the more you are going to miss it. For success, like happiness, cannot be pursued; it must ensue as the unintended side effect of one's personal ded-ication to a course greater than oneself.
> **Viktor Frankl, Psychologist, Man's Search for Meaning, 1946**

In order to achieve high performance it is recognised in the sporting world that using all three types of goals together in a well thought through and intelligently interconnected fashion is a significant tool in driving high performance. The per-formance triangle, especially when used in its dynamic mode, employs all three goal types in seeking to improve performance in individuals, teams and organisations.

THE PERFORMANCE TRIANGLE

One of the cornerstone models I developed some years ago to guide my rowing coaching and my businesses, particularly with respect to organisational alignment issues, is the performance triangle. See Figure 4 below.

In sport, this model is used at individual athlete, team and squad levels. In organisations it may similarly be applied at the level of the individual, the team, the business unit or even the whole organisation, as we will see in Chapters 9 and 10.

It is a simple way of depicting the key elements essential in both individual athletes and teams to achieve high performance. As shown in this chapter it can be applied statically at any point in time. However, its real value is when it is applied dynamically over time to achieve long-term goals. This chapter introduces the model in its 'static' use. Chapter 5 looks at the model in its dynamic form. As with all models, while the concept is straightforward it is the interpretation and detail that is key to its success. (Note: the word fitness used in sport would be replaced by the word skill when used in the business and organisational context).

The usefulness of this model when applied to business performance is threefold.

1. Applying the model to a business helps reveal new insights about the organisation, how it views its people, how it characterises and segments them (often unconsciously), how it develops them and how it motivates them. Quite often in firms there are deeply embedded cultural mores and norms in place from previous eras that are still selecting people against outmoded 'attributes', applying inadequate 'skills' (fitness) regimes and coaching old-fashioned

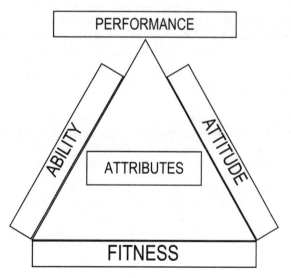

Figure 4: The performance triangle.

'technical abilities'. The 'This is how we have always done things around here' syndrome is alive and well in all organisations!

2. The model provides a detailed and structured way of recruiting, assessing and developing people with the attributes, skills, abilities and attitudes to take on the roles that will drive the desired high performance in all of the areas it is required.

3. The model provides clarity and guidance for developing people in order to achieve high performance. It also helps frame the creation of the performance environment and setting the targets, goals and measurement regimes that will check it is working. It should also be obvious that the model cannot be applied properly unless and until the desired targets, process performance and outcome goals are fully articulated and clear direction set out.

Training and development in the context of the performance triangle

At this point we need to address the words 'training' and 'development' because business organisations in general (and the HR department in particular) use them a little differently from how they are used in sport.

Training and development as applied in sport

Sport looks at the athlete (and teams) in a holistic way. In sport all aspects of the athlete and team (attributes, fitness, technical ability and attitude) must be developed in a coherent way if the athlete and team is to progress and be successful.

Attributes and attitude, for all intents and purposes, come as a given with each athlete. They can be enhanced and reinforced but this will be through programmes that are more psychologically focused. Basically if the desired attributes and attitude are not intrinsically part of the individual's make-up and psyche then even the best coach cannot put in what nature has left out. If, for example in a rower, the 'power and strength' component of attributes or the 'will to win' component of attitude is missing then, at a certain level, physical training will simply become too tough for the athlete and they will drop out of the team. This will either happen naturally or require the coach to remove the athlete. If neither of these occurs the team will become dysfunctional and it will be the coach's fault!

Of these two elements, depending on the sport, attributes is the least problematic as explained a little later in this chapter (see p.43). By far the more critical component is attitude. If there are deficiencies in attitude then this is where any blockages to high performance will most likely manifest themselves.

Training and development in sport combines both fitness and technical ability. In order to make a simplistic distinction training can generally be taken as focusing on fitness. Training (fitness) is commonly designed to build the total physiological capacity to undertake the sport at the competitive levels targeted by the performance requirements. This includes the biomechanical, musculoskeletal, cardiovascular and neurological capacities.

Development can generally be assumed to be about developing technical ability. It is the taking of the fit, prepared bodies of the athletes and teaching them the technical, mechanical and physical movements (and eventually the mental skills components) required to perform at the competitive levels targeted. Clearly these will be an overlapping and progressive series of programmes. As the body is trained and becomes fitter over time then its capacity to cope with increasingly tougher and longer technical ability development programmes improves.

While for clarity I have, in the sporting analogy, separated training from development there are obviously areas where these overlap closely. One such area for example is in mental skills where training and development are fully integrated. This aspect is more clearly illustrated in Chapter 6 (see p.73).

Training and development as understood in business

In business there is often little distinction made between training and development. In addition, training in business (when compared with development) generally has even less of a clear identification of what is trying to be achieved. How training programmes across the organisation integrate into the long-term direction and plans for the business is often completely neglected.

The distinction between training and development is often similarly vague and without direction, i.e. is it fitness for the role or increasing the competence in it? An example might be deciding that someone might benefit from a Finance for Managers course. Undertaking the programme could be likened to undertaking a fitness programme in sport to improve, say, flexibility. Gaining increased flexibility in sport would immediately be applied by the coach to learning the next level of technical abilities. In business, rarely does the returning manager with his new found finance skills come back to a boss who immediately starts work with him on applying them and developing them further. Just because the manager has a certificate saying he has passed the programme, i.e. is skilled (fit), does not mean that he is competent, i.e. has the technical ability to apply his new found skills. With this explanation in mind we can now examine the performance triangle model and its adaptation to business.

Attributes

This element of the model refers to the natural, predominantly physiological requirements that any particular sport requires of its athletes. Different sports require different attributes, e.g. speed, power, agility, co-ordination and size. There are exceptions to every rule but generally, as a rule, someone who cannot coordinate hand and eye will not be a Grand Slam tennis champion. Someone who has to lever themselves up a flexible stick to clear a six-meter pole vault bar is unlikely to look like an American football defensive guard. And your typical Sumo wrestler is unlikely to be much of a threat in the 400 metre hurdles.

If you study most sports and the specific requirements they demand of their athlete types it will be clear that there are varying degrees of natural selection involved centred around some basic, key attributes. For example in my own sport of rowing the controlling body, GB Rowing, runs a programme called World Class Start. This is

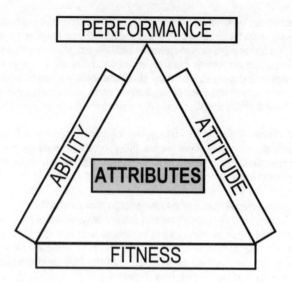

Figure 5: Performance triangle: attributes.

where talent scouts tour schools looking for young, potential world-class rowing athletes. Their initial selection criteria is quite simply twofold, namely 'levers' (otherwise known as physiology) and what I call 'grunt' (or raw power). Over time GB Rowing have assessed the best size and shape for a top rower. They therefore seek out young individuals with the right length arms, backs and legs and basic power that fit the current idealised physiological template. The philosophy is that if coaches can be given the right bodies (attributes) they can train and develop the right skills and secure the highest levels of performance.

This last point is important for anyone reading this and thinking that high performance in sport is hereditary and primarily about DNA, and that any links to business this book seeks to make are tenuous. It is obvious that for some sports there are attribute selection criteria that are clearly too narrow to be of much use for adaptation to business. Even in sports coaching circles it is recognised that certain sports are more about DNA than coaching and training. There is even a well-known aphorism that states 'If you want to be a 100 metre world record holder first choose your parents carefully'! The good news is that the more complex a sport is in terms of its technical, biomechanical and physiological requirements and the more team oriented it is, the less important the hereditary attributes are and the more critical good coaching and great attitude become. The adage that success is 10% inspiration and 90% perspiration is never truer than when applied to complex sports. Future Olympic champions do sometimes walk in to their local sports club off the street with no prior exposure to a sport.

Business is all about complexity and therefore many sports that work with complex technical, biomechanical and physiological requirements are relevant as comparators for business. As an example this can be seen in developing an America's Cup sailing team, with all its technology, highly sophisticated equipment, management complexity and the requirement to develop the athletes (as individuals and crews) to combine bodies and minds and equipment. It is the ways in which the performance triangle and other models introduced in this book are adapted and used in a business context that make them useful and highly relevant to a business seeking high-performance outcomes.

To show how the attributes element of the model may be adapted for use in business it will be useful to look at some examples. First, let us look at a comparison between rowing and a pharmaceutical company. Both the rowing crew and the pharmaceutical business compete in relatively well-defined arenas. In both the rowing crew and the pharmaceutical company there are a number of identifiable key roles. In this example we will take the stroke position in the rowing team (the number eight or sternmost position) and the R&D specialist in the pharmaceutical company. From experience over the years it is known that to be a successful stroke rower you must be able to set and adjust the race pace, respond cleverly to competitor attacks and still maintain a calm, flowing rhythm. In the same way there will be some critical attributes that predominate in making an above-average pharmaceutical industry R&D specialist. As an example (and at the risk of some inelegant stereotyping) I have assumed what some of these might be – see Table 1 below.

Table 1: Attribute listing – sport v. business

Key attributes for stroke rower	Key attributes for pharma R&D specialist
Effective body levers	Well above-average IQ
High aerobic capacity	Tendency towards introversion
Good raw power	High task orientation
Natural rhythm and control	Strong powers of focus and concentration
High powers of focus and concentration	High need for order and control

It is important to note that this is not looking for comparative attributes between the rower and the R&D specialist or seeking some form of matching. It is purely to show that, just as a sports coach is looking for certain attributes in each athlete and role in the team, a business leader can also employ a similar approach with this model to aid the best possible business team selection. Further examples that show how you can identify and list attributes are shown in Table 2.

Again I stress this is not about making comparisons between each pairing. It is about showing that if we think carefully about the attributes required in any role, whether in sport or in business, they will be better performed by people who are already naturally more suited to them. This does not rule out the exception to the rule but it does make candidate profiling for a selection exercise a more rigorous, detailed and thoughtful process.

Table 2: Further attribute listing – sport *v.* business

Key attributes of . . .			
Football striker	**Salesman**	**Quarterback**	**Finance manager**
Agility	Empathy	Fast thought processes	Good facility with numbers
Balance	Stamina	Excellent and rapid decision making	Pleasure in detailed tasks
Speed	Self-interest	High self-confidence	Good powers of concentration
High energy	Good actor	Action oriented	Adaptive mentality
Selfishness/ greed	Articulate	Agility, balance and speed	Need for order and control

Applying the attributes element of the performance triangle to a business may help leaders and organisation development staff think much more about the fundamental attributes they should be looking for in potential employees. The process of getting to the position where they know what these attributes are will invariably be extremely valuable and revealing in many ways.

It can be seen that attribute listing identifies both 'hard' (measurable and quantifiable) and 'soft' (qualitative, even psychological) characteristics. In the various stages of the selection process it will be possible to use and/or devise methods of testing individuals against desired attributes. This is not to say that there cannot be exceptions to an attribute template for a role. However, if there are certain personal attributes that are known to lead to more successful individuals in a role, then this part of the model can provide a useful filter at the initial screening stage. How good exceptions are managed is solely dependent on the openness and flexibility of the recruitment system and the skill, ability and experience of the recruiting personnel. If anything, having clearly identifiable attributes makes attractive exceptions easier to identify, perhaps even leading to a modification of the prevailing norm. Any system or process should be dynamic and designed to have the requirement for continuous improvement in-built.

Fitness/skills training
Fitness is a fundamental component of success in sport. It is a foundation requirement in any athlete, especially if they are coming new into a sport. Unless and until a basic level of fitness is attained, it is difficult to begin real work developing technical ability beyond a very elementary level, especially in power, endurance, strength and physical contact sports. Where the creation of a team is required then substantial complexity is added to developing the training programmes. Different roles and positions will require different strengths and physiologies.

Skill (fitness) most closely equates to what business organisations normally term 'training'. In many of the organisations I have worked in (and in most of the ones I

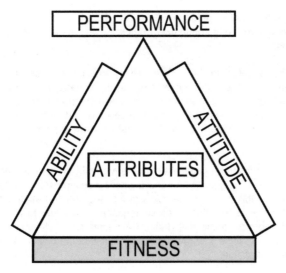

Figure 6: Performance triangle: fitness.

have worked with) training has been an unplanned lottery as far as the organisation is concerned. Training in business is almost always an individual preference without any clear idea of what is good for, or required by, the organisation overall. More worryingly, in my experience, only once have I seen training intrinsically linked to the primary strategic intent of the organisation. It is more often left to line managers and heads of department to decide on the training needs of the business areas under their control. Usually this is agreed on an individual basis, mostly at appraisal time. More often than not individuals are asked (if line managers are poor) what they would like to do for their personal development. With training budgets often limited and arbitraged by the HR department the lottery-style outcome is exacerbated. Favouritism and even personal prejudices on training type often prevail and questions as to the suitability of the training for the organisation and its strategic direction rarely if ever get asked.

With respect to training, the difference between sport and business could hardly be greater. Fitness training in sport is built around highly designed, highly technical programmes carefully constructed to deliver very clear outcomes and results. In team sports the programmes are tailored to each individual athlete, taking account of his current state of fitness, his current physiology, the demands required by his sport and his specific position or role in the team.

This aspect of highly designed training programmes, at all levels of the organisation, intrinsically linked to the desired strategic outcomes which is so fundamental to high performance in sport, should be no less the case for organisations. Depending on their role and position in the corporate hierarchy, employees will need to display some basic fitness characteristics required of that role. The more pivotal or critical their role to the delivery of high performance, the greater should be a) their fitness for the role and b) the attention paid to their training programmes by the organisations leaders.

In sport, fitness refers to the athlete's ability to cope with the physical demands placed upon all of the body's systems during the intensity of competition. It is the coach who takes full responsibility for the development and shaping of the various training and development programmes, albeit with his numerous specialists and discipline experts, to ensure his athletes and his team are fully prepared for these demands.

In business, I have rarely seen leaders take any significant (and, as importantly, sustained) interest in the training and development programmes for the people in their organisation. In this respect it may be useful to see how this might be achieved by looking at a few of the fitness aspects required for a rower to be successful and what might be comparable skill (fitness) elements for a sales manager to deliver high performance. Table 3 below outlines just a few of the fitness/skill requirements that might be desirable.

Table 3: Fitness requirements in sport v. skills requirements in business

Sport fitness – example: rowing	Business skills (fitness) – example: sales manager
Cardiovascular – general	Management of people – individuals and teams
Cardiovascular – specific: aerobic capacity	Time management
Cardiovascular – specific: anaerobic capacity	Organisational skills
Cardiovascular – specific: lactic acid threshold	Communication skills
Musculoskeletal – general	Managing meetings
Musculoskeletal – specific: core strength	Statistics and analysis
Musculoskeletal – specific: power release	Decision making
Power	Financial skills
Strength	Product knowledge
Flexibility	Handling pressure

Depending on your business, its structure and the nature and division of roles and responsibilities, you may have read the list for the sales manager and said to yourself that certain elements seem more like an ability rather than skill (fitness) items.

This is both understandable and positive. It means that you are already questioning and adapting the model to suit your organisation's character. It means the model is already beginning to help frame your thinking about just what it is your business requires of each of its key roles and thus the people in them. My simple rule is that the skill elements in business are the basic, underlying must-have functional skills required to carry out that role. They are basic 'skills' rather than the more advanced, full competence, 'abilities' we will address in the next section. In the case of the sales manager above, fitness may be said to focus more on the functional aspects of being able to sell. The abilities section that follows may be said to focus on the more advanced sales competences as shown in Table 4.

Ability development

As fitness builds, an increasing amount of attention can be given to developing technical ability. This means the coaching and development of the movements and techniques, even strategies, tactics and game plans, required to be successful in any sporting endeavour. Complexity increases when it is a team sport. Integrating several athletes into a team and trying to secure coordinated activity in order to beat another group of athletes is extremely demanding of a coach. The challenges increase still further where equipment is employed.

Skill, ability and prowess continue to be an interesting area of debate in sport. Rather like the perennial question regarding whether leaders are born or made (nature versus nurture), the same is often posed for athletes. Is ability and sporting prowess innate or can it be developed? The answer in my view is very definitely both. There are without doubt some people who have natural skills, abilities and bodies that give them a starting advantage in particular areas of physical endeavour. Examples might

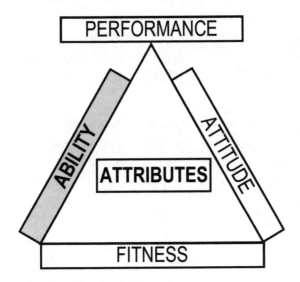

Figure 7: Performance triangle: ability.

be those with superb hand–eye coordination or those with the musculoskeletal and cardiovascular attributes that lend themselves towards speed or strength or endurance. However, even if these natural attributes are present it does not mean the owner of them is a natural for a sport.

Most sports require the development of abilities that have to be taught, trained and embedded. They have to be made part of a body's muscle memory. You only have to look at an American football team or a rugby team to see that the highest levels of sport can be attained by a considerable variation of body shape or size. Similar to the section on fitness it is helpful to look at an example as set out in Table 4 below.

I hope that the natural parallels in terms of ability can be seen between a complex team sport and a business environment. If in an organisation you have your squad of players who have been selected thus far for having the right attributes for their role and who have embarked on the company skills (fitness) training programmes they become ready for the development of their abilities. The reality of course is that, especially for the more senior roles, people in business already come with some skills and abilities. The point here is that in seeking to achieve high performance, organisations need to have a way of:

- assessing if the people in the various roles are actually as good as they seemed at the time of recruitment
- developing people to reach the levels of competence and excellence required to achieve the performance the organisation is seeking
- using formal development programmes and sets of measures to identify when to promote high performers (and help succession planning)
- removing consistent low performers who are unable or unwilling to improve.

Table 4: Ability requirements in sport v. ability requirements in business

Sport technical ability – example: rugby fly half	Business technical ability – example: sales manager
Ability to read a game as it unfolds (also part attribute)	Opportunity identification
Ability to pass with both hands	Structuring and crafting offers and proposals
Ability to pass accurately	Selling techniques, styles and behaviours
Ability to kick accurately and long	Negotiating and closing deals
Ability to manage on-field tactics (also part attribute)	Personal awareness and customer interaction
Ability to command those around him (also part attribute)	Personal awareness and team interaction
Ability to tackle	Coaching individuals and teams
Ability to evade tackles	Ability to adapt offers and proposals to suit circumstances

This last point is critically important and has driven me almost to despair in my business life. In general, organisations are absolutely hopeless at removing poor performers from any role, let alone key ones, and the reason is not employment legislation. It is important to note that I am not talking necessarily about getting rid of poor performers. Often they are potentially good performers – just either poorly led, poorly managed or in the wrong role, or all of these things. The reason poor performers are left in role is because, more often than not, businesses do not have a clear idea of exactly what levels of performance they need from their people. Nor do they help them develop what they need. Nor do they monitor or measure the progress and effect of that development. And even if businesses do detect performance that is sub-optimal rarely do they take steps to address the situation. I have seen average (even well below-average) performers remain in key posts while the business falls apart around them. I am sure this will not be an unfamiliar story to most of you reading this.

An example is a project-based company whose business grew hugely. Over a two-year period projects increased by 60% and it 'successfully' delivered five significant contracts worth a total of £420m. Despite all the self-congratulations it was known by a few that all had not gone well. An in-house audit discovered that over £60m of what would have been bottom-line income had been 'lost' due to simple things such as: inadequate record keeping that would have supported successful claims for extra work and variations; significant errors of judgement and decision making by poorly skilled, inexperienced people with poor abilities; deployment of the wrong equipment; poor project programming and inefficient use of resources. The list of errors, poor judgement and bad decision making was extensive. However, the fundamental and underlying reason for all the performance failures was that people had been rapidly promoted into critical positions for which they did not have the skills, ability and experience. The leaders were asking them to deliver performances they were not capable of achieving. Every one of them had been competent in lower positions but almost incompetent in these new, higher intensity ones. It was the sporting equivalent of putting a good club runner in a race with Usain Bolt. The reality is that this was not a failure of the individuals but an absolute failure of the leader and leadership. The individuals were inadequately prepared by the leaders, i.e. the organisational processes for which the leaders are responsible, in terms of their ability. Did the leaders take the blame? I leave you to draw your own conclusions!

Attitude
Whilst innate skills and abilities may give a starting advantage and subsequent taught ones improve those advantages, it is an individual's attitude that will realise the ultimate results. For those without a full set of natural skills, attitude is most often enough to achieve the same outcomes. It is attitude that ensures that athletes push the limits of their minds and bodies to achieve high performance. As noted above, in those sports where there is a high degree of technical complexity to master, attitude has an even greater propensity to achieve success. It is attitude that drives the commitment to push the limits of fitness and the development of technical ability that attains the highest performance outcomes. By way of an example, in Table 5 we can compare elements of attitude between sport and business.

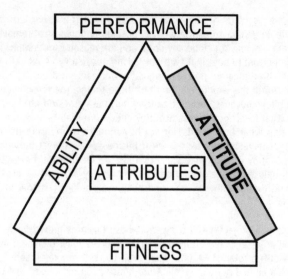

Figure 8: Performance triangle: attitude.

Table 5: Attitude requirements in sport *v.* attitude requirements in business

High performers' attitude in sport	High performers' attitude in business
High degree of intrinsic motivation	High degree of intrinsic motivation
Driving desire to win	Driving desire to win
Driving desire to be the best	Driving desire to be the best
Strives for perfection; desire for mastery	Strives for perfection; desire for mastery
Self-belief, self-confidence and high self-esteem	Self-belief, self-confidence and high self-esteem
Uses setbacks (even failure) as spur to increased effort	Uses setbacks (even failure) as spur to increased effort
Takes responsibility, for failure as well as success	Takes responsibility, for failure as well as success
Positive	Positive
Enthusiastic	Enthusiastic
Optimistic	Optimistic
Feels free to experiment and make mistakes	Feels free to experiment and make mistakes
Fully commits	Fully commits

I assume that it comes as no surprise that the attitudes needed to be successful at the highest levels in business are broadly going to be no different than those present at the highest levels of sport. The above will obviously be refined depending on the business type and the role envisaged, just as it would be depending on the type of sport and the athlete's position. For example, a rugby prop forward also has to have a high desire to feel pain, enjoy eating mud and a yearning for cauliflower ears!

While the attitude aspect of a person's character is critical for a coach to understand, there is only a very limited, and superficial, interest in it from businesses. There is certainly no real attempt to divine either what sort of attitude an organisation might need in general or what attitude candidates might need to have for specific roles. Attitude is part of an individual's psychological make-up – effectively it is in the genes. Individuals with the right attitudes can be developed to enhance them further, but those with the wrong attitudes are difficult to turn around, and organisations are not in the business of psychotherapy. Thus, selecting and recruiting for the right attitude is important in developing high-performance organisations. This is covered in more detail in Chapter 9.

It is difficult to describe just how broad, diverse and critical the impact of attitude is on people and their performance. Attitude is clearly about state of mind and an individual's psychological drivers. In the top performers in sport it transcends just committing to tough training and the dedication of time and effort. In the 2005 rugby Lions tour to New Zealand, Brian O'Driscoll suffered a substantial shoulder injury after being spear tackled into the ground by two New Zealand players. After surgery he used a cryogenic chamber in Poland to speed his recovery. The process is worth noting. The chamber is cooled to temperatures of -120^0C to -160^0C. Twice a day for a week subjects immerse themselves in the freeze chamber. Any longer than four minutes and the fluid in the eyeballs would freeze and five minutes in the chamber would mean death. In O'Driscoll's own words: 'it is a long three minutes'. In 2011 the whole Welsh rugby team underwent this process prior to the Rugby World Cup. In the very top performers, attitude will drive them to do extraordinary things to try and attain supra-normal performance.

In top athletes this aspect of positive attitude is clearly present to a much greater degree than in ordinary people but it is none-the-less present in almost all of us. With the right environment and the right triggers, guidance and support even low-level performers can have their game raised substantially by tapping into their natural desire to be better.

SUMMARY
By approaching each individual element with rigour and some imagination, the performance triangle readily applies to any organisation. However, at this stage, the performance triangle is useful only as a convenient, but simple model or tool to address the basic building blocks a coach or leader would look at when developing a high-performance individual or team. In this static mode it is useful primarily as a talent selection template and filtering tool. These in themselves are valuable

features. However, the model becomes far more useful and powerful, as we shall see in the next chapter. This looks at how the model can be made much more relevant across organisations, how it may be used over a longer-term period and how the focus changes over time. With the introduction of the time element we can derive a desired performance curve over time. With this dynamic form of the model we can plan and manage the drive for high performance in individuals, teams, departments and whole organisations.

CHAPTER 5
THE PERFORMANCE CURVE:
THE PERFORMANCE TRIANGLE
OVER TIME-

Poor performance comes not from setting high goals and failing to achieve them but from setting low ones and succeeding.

Eva Zaremba, Psychologist

The previous chapter introduced the performance triangle, describing its individual elements and how they may be adapted for use in business. This chapter takes the model a significant stage further by introducing how it may be used over time as a guiding framework. Timescales can be many years, including the period it may take a company to implement a strategy. It is a foundation model for developing and managing many of the concepts introduced in this book, especially those in Part 2. It is useful for guiding the development of individuals, teams and even whole organisations in achieving high performance. By using the model over time it is possible to manage performance goals, outcome goals, process goals, individual profiling, rates of progress, measurement, monitoring, evaluation and many other elements used in sports coaching. This is not to say that businesses are strangers to such concepts – most of those just listed are identical to elements required in any organisation. However, I have yet to come across the organisation that pulls together every aspect of people management as completely, as rigorously, as intensively and with as much sustained and meticulous discipline over long periods in the way coaching does for top teams in competitive sport, and this is where the performance curve can help.

At first glance the model is both simple and obvious, but it is in the application of the model at every level of detail that its true value is realised. Most importantly from a business perspective the performance triangle is strategically stable. This idea of strategic stability in models is an important concept and bears some further expansion. To have value to any organisation a model must be useful. Some models are helpful in providing an insight or a snapshot of a moment in time. Others provide a simplified overview that helps make sense of an otherwise complex situation – for example, the situational leadership model in Figure 2. However, if we accept that high performance can only come about through people, specifically people working together to deliver an effective plan or strategy, then there are very few models explicitly targeted at the management of performance of individuals, teams and organisations over time. There are even fewer that drill down to the levels of detail required to ensure strategy implementation occurs, while all the time holding true to the top-level direction or vision. In performance management terms the performance triangle seeks to be a little like the unified field theory in physics: unifying the very small (individual people and teams) with the very big (complete organisations). It is this cohesiveness between the big and the small, and the coherence in managing them over time, that creates 'strategic stability'. In addition to showing how it works towards achieving high performance this chapter will also show how strategic stability is embedded in the performance triangle model as it moves along the performance curve.

THE PERFORMANCE TRIANGLE APPLIED OVER TIME: AN OVERVIEW

Figure 9 depicts the performance triangle over time. The curve represents a typical performance development profile that we see not just in athletes or teams in sport but in individuals, groups and teams in organisations as well. You will also notice that different elements of the triangle are emphasised at different points on the curve. This chapter explains all this and more.

No model has value or usefulness unless the context in which it is to be used is clearly articulated and known to those applying the model. In the case of a business, the top-level context must always be the overarching vision and strategic direction, the strategy itself and how that strategy is to be implemented over time. The London Organising Committee for the 2012 summer Olympic Games (LOCOG) is a good example of this cascading of vision, strategy and implementation, since it had to address both sport and business in the same organisation. LOCOG's vision was 'to use the power of the Games to inspire change'. The strategy for such a complex project had a number of key strands, which included among others:

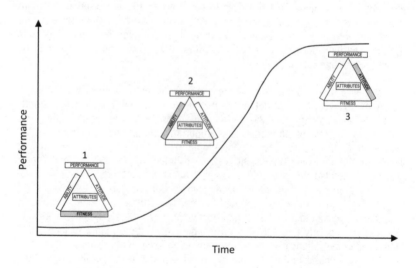

Figure 9: The performance triangle applied over time.

- delivering the Olympic Park and all venues on time, to specification and providing a suitable legacy
- maximising the economic, social, health and environmental benefits of the Games for the UK.

Sitting underneath the top-level vision and its overarching strategies were the detailed sub-strategies and plans, e.g. construction, marketing, communications, transport, health and safety, ticketing strategies, etc.

In any organisation, sporting or business, these top-level imperatives are always distilled into operationally applicable goals for implementation at the various levels within an organisation. Again, to be useful, a model has to be able to help derive these more detailed elements and apply them at whatever level is required. Where a model or management framework is used to help make sense of direction and goals, they must reflect and be aligned with the overarching strategy. If they fail in this they will at best be of limited value and at worst may create performance reducing fault lines in the organisation.

The most valuable benefit of the performance triangle when used over time is that it ensures corruption or drift away from the overarching strategy is difficult unless a conscious decision is made to move away. This is because the time imperative means:

- from day one the model is set up and its use designed to ensure congruence with the longer-term outcome and performance goals
- the individual elements of attributes, fitness, ability and attitude (and the desired values of each) are aligned, monitored and evaluated against top-level goal measures
- each individual's development and rate of progress, as well as those of the team, are visible with a frequency that ensures performance improvements are achieving desired and planned outcomes.

This book, especially Chapters 9 and 10 in Part 2, shows how this model can be directly applied in organisations and businesses. However, in order to see its effectiveness in driving high-performance cultures and behaviours and thus outcomes, it is first useful to see it at work in its sporting environment.

In approaching this section I first thought about using a scenario of an English rugby squad seeking to win the Rugby World Cup over a four-year period, but as English rugby enthusiasts are well aware, this would be too painful a journey! Instead we can look at a more modest sporting scenario. In this way we are using ordinary people similar to those you would find in the average business organisation. Let us take a typical, mid-level rowing club where the leadership has a vision of becoming a leading UK performance rowing club within five to seven years. As a strategic vision this is not dissimilar to an organisation saying it wants to be in the top three companies in its market sector within a given period.

Staying with the rowing club scenario, let us assume the club leadership has articulated this strategic vision in a way that most members in the club like and understand. The natural outcome of articulating a vision or direction is the questions it generates, even among those in full agreement and support. What does it mean for the club in performance terms? What does it mean to the individual athletes? What does it mean to the coaches and their crews? What does it mean to the men and women's first crews, or second, third and even novice crews? What does it mean to the masters squad or the juniors? What does it mean for resources, for coach numbers, boats, equipment, facilities, etc.? What volumes of increased activity (and success) can the club itself withstand before it fails to function under the load? Before answering these questions it may be helpful to have a quick recap on strategy.

A QUICK REVIEW OF STRATEGY

This book is not about strategy, but in order to place the performance triangle in context and highlight its value, a quick overview of strategy as it applies here may be helpful before we continue with the above scenario.

Vision into strategy

There are critical stages during the strategic process, of which the initial stage is having a robust, creative, yet rigorous way of originating an effective overarching strategy (or strategies) from the vision or direction.

The second stage is the translation of the overarching, top-level strategy into more practical, top-level, strategic goals and imperatives that the organisation can easily detail and articulate. This translation of the strategic vision into strategic goals has to achieve two things. Not only do the goals have to be real, but they also have to grab the attention of the people in the organisation; they have to be capable of being easily and engagingly communicated. They need to motivate and hopefully even excite followers.

Next, top-level strategic goals must be capable of being accurately translated down and across the various levels of the organisation, while remaining coherent and aligned to the vision or direction. You should be able to go anywhere in the organisation, examine the local strategic goals and see exactly how they contribute to the top-level goals. A surprising number of organisations fail in this very first translation and, without even realising it, have already built in the potential for strategic drift at best and complete strategic failure at worst.

Strategy into goals

The third critical stage is distilling these overarching strategic imperatives into strategic goals, targets and plans for the various levels of the organisation. This has to be done in ways that maintain organisation-wide strategic goal coherence and organisational alignment and provide strategic plans that can be understood and implemented at the local level. It is in this third stage that organisations often go badly wrong. It is this phase that most often accounts for the 70% rate of failure of strategies that is consistently reported. In our rowing club scenario, if the top-level vision of becoming a leading performance club was translated as, 'to become one of the top five clubs within five to seven years measured by the number of regatta wins each year' the seeds of failure are already planted.

On the surface, the strategic intent – 'to become one of the top five clubs within five to seven years measured by the number of regatta wins each year' – looks reasonable until you look at the detail. In this case, at least the top 15 slots are unobtainable without massive resources that are beyond most of the 550 amateur rowing clubs in the UK. In addition the 'number of wins each year' is the wrong measure from a performance point of view because not all wins have equal prestige. Unless the top management of any organisation is fully competent and intimately understands its competitive world then its strategic vision can often be seriously flawed in its conceptualisation and further doomed to failure by uninformed translation.

Monitoring and measuring strategy implementation

Compounding the problem of flawed translation is the fact that while a strategy may look reasonable at first glance, its tendency towards failure may not become visible for two or three years. When such failure does become apparent, competent leaders will grasp the nettle quickly, readdress the strategy and bring it in line with what is truly achievable. Unfortunately, in average organisations with average leaders what we are more likely to find is one of those self-fulfilling prophecies. First, the systems in place will be inadequate to identify strategy failure early enough. Second, strategy failure predominantly occurs because of a failure of leadership. Therefore, rather than admit they got it wrong, average leaders persist with their flawed implementation. Third, what they often do behind the scenes is to surreptitiously start altering the strategic narrative, its goals, and even the operational tactics being employed day to day to fit the failing strategy. When this occurs, not only are strategic coherence and organisational alignment corrupted and lost, but also, more dangerously, people across the organisation will know what is happening – that their leaders are seeking to furtively cover their tracks.

Engaging local leaders

At this point it is worth noting something that I always try to remember in day-to-day sporting and business activities. Within your organisation (especially if it is sizeable) there are people who are far brighter than you, more articulate than you, more engaging than you and thus with a more cohesive following than you. This means that at their organisational level they are true leaders and have far more influence than you. These local leaders are critical to ensuring organisational alignment to a strategy. If it is a bad strategy, they will spot it and will exert considerable influence as they denigrate it within their group. If it is a good strategy but not communicated effectively, local leaders may fail to buy in. Even if they buy in they may be unable to properly translate and communicate to their followers an already unclear story. If, as outlined above, the strategy is corrupted by the organisation's leaders in order to save face, then we have probably the worst situation. This cynical manipulation can galvanise powerful local leaders into condemnation and divisiveness as they lose respect for poor leaders they now believe are not just incompetent but deceitful. I refer you back to Chapter 2 and one of the key things people look for in their leaders: a need for leaders to be genuine and trustworthy!

Unintended consequences in strategies

A last comment on strategy before returning to our scenarios and the performance triangle is the issue of the 'unintended consequences' of strategies. Organisations often get themselves into trouble by developing a strategic vision and associated strategic plans that have outcomes they did not foresee. In the simple case of our rowing club scenario an unintended consequence of trying to be successful would be the need to attract a lot more members to increase the talent pool to achieve better crews. Better crews will achieve more success and consequently more success will attract more members, and so on. This initially virtuous circle of ever-increasing membership could become a vicious one outstripping resources leading to lack of boat and equipment availability, lack of coaches, disgruntled rowers, poorer performance and a stalled or even failed strategy within a couple of years.

A business example might be Tyco's telecommunications submarine fibre optic cable business. Tyco manufactured, installed and maintained global fibre optic systems for international telecoms companies and held about a 35% market share globally in these activities. During the dot.com crash in 2001 Tyco looked at its operation and decided that because it made all the hardware it would embark on a strategy of full vertical integration and become a network operator, thus effectively becoming a telecom company in its own right. Logically, it made sense to increase and control the whole value chain when existing customers were cutting back or squeezing prices hard. However, an unintended consequence was that Tyco's customers did not like their hardware supplier now being a telecom competitor. The resulting almost instantaneous loss of customers and painful contraction of their business was certainly an unintended consequence, but in reality entirely predictable.

Articulating and communicating the strategy story

Picking up our rowing club scenario and the application of the performance triangle again we know that the overarching strategic intent is 'to become a leading performance club in the UK within five to seven years', but this has to be given meaning to those in the organisation. A story that conveys significance to those who will have to deliver it has to be created. Assuming the committee is competent the next level of translation might be:

> The club's strategic aim is to be positioned within the top 20 UK rowing clubs within seven years based on consistent top performance of both men's and women's first crews at Henley and National Championship Regattas. Top performance means that within three years our first crews will consistently be quarter finalists or better and within five years will consistently be within 1% of the speed of the winning boats.

This type of rephrasing of the vision now begins to set primary performance targets that are internally specific but, more crucially, are tied externally to what competitors are doing. Even better is that it consists of both outcome goals and performance goals – both critical elements in any competitive environment.

The other thing that good strategies achieve is the ability to be distilled downwards while maintaining strong coherence and alignment with the top-level strategic intent. In this case the coaches of the squads from which the first crews will be derived have very clear goals. It is also easy to cascade down similarly clear goals for the second, third or any other squads that will drive high performance in these squads and give athletes a pathway upwards to the top.

THE PERFORMANCE TRIANGLE AND THE TEAM

Let us now apply the performance triangle to the rowing club strategy by assuming we are the senior men's coach charged with developing the men's first squad comprised of approximately 12 rowers and a cox into a 1st VIII capable of being top-level performers within three to five years. The coach needs to first understand what the strategic requirement really means at this level.

The overall top-level outcome goal as stated by the club leadership, 'To be positioned within the top 20 UK rowing clubs', is, in reality, of no importance to the coach at all. All he can work on as a coach are the club's performance goal requirements of 'quarter finalists' and 'boat speed'. At this point he will be in the phase of distilling the strategy down to his level of implementation, similar to a senior functional manager. He will have to develop performance goals and associated outcome goals relevant to his squad and team selection processes that remain tied into the club's strategic goals. He has to build a story that makes sense to his athletes that will both motivate and drive them to achieve the goals he as coach distils out of the top-level goals.

This is the stage where the best coaches get into the often mind-numbing detail of planning a competitive sporting campaign that will frame several years of squad, team and individual athlete development. The first stage in this long journey is working out as accurately as possible just what the targets mean. In the rowing club scenario the top-level strategic goal translates into a frighteningly simple requirement at the coach's level. To make the quarter finals of the selected events on a regular basis he needs to have a crew and boat that goes fast enough to be consistently challenging for a place in the finals. (Note: if you look at the data for most sports very little separates the top six teams or athletes in terms of performance.) So, all the lofty ideals espoused by the top management, all the visionary statements about where the club wants to position itself and its goals translate very simply into the figure:

5.75

Quite simply if the coach cannot develop a 1st VIII crew that within three years is able to row a boat faster than 5.75 metres per second then it would not be in contention for the last six places and the club's strategic goals would fail to be achieved. However, if it can be achieved it would also be close to the five-year goal of being within 1% of the speed of the winning crews.

You may also have noticed that the 'quarter final placing' which is an outcome goal for the top management (club committee) has been turned into a performance goal at the coaching level. Performance goals are extremely powerful because they are goals that are completely within your control. They are also goals that entice people with the right mindset to try to exceed them. Consequently, they provide the opportunity to motivate people much more readily than outcome goals. With performance goals it is also much easier to plan performance pathways that give regular checks and feedbacks to all concerned.

Now the work begins and this is where the performance triangle provides such a stable framework for the process. The coach has to turn the simple figure of 5.75 into a three- to five-year squad, team and individual athlete development strategy together with the associated plans. We can now take the model and start using it in earnest. In this case it is against a single performance goal but a number of strategic goals can be built into the model or multiple models with separate but still strategically aligned goals that can all run simultaneously.

PHASE 1: PLANNING FOR HIGH PERFORMANCE

For any coach in sport (and for any leader in business) it is the quality, the detail and the unremitting effort that goes into developing the high-performance-programme planning that will be the best guarantee of success. In *The Mind of the Strategist* Kenichi Ohmae clearly shows that in addition to the strategists' creative and intuitive abilities it is their attention to painstaking analysis and their intimate understanding of the detail that sets them apart.

In any competitive environment this high-performance plan is the foundation of the strategy story, and the vehicle for turning strategy into something deliverable for the people required to do the work. It is the guiding mechanism that turns the top-level strategic outcome goals into lower-level performance, process and outcome goals that, when aggregated across the organisation, deliver the total performance required to meet the organisation's top-level visionary and strategic aspirations.

In the case of our rowing coach, long before he thinks about squad selection or athlete training plans he must first map out what the performance and outcome goals really mean in terms of what has to be attained over what timescale. Figure 10 below shows how this thinking process translates into a top-level performance plan. The coach maps out the performance levels required to be reached to achieve both his performance goals and the organisation's outcome goals.

It can be seen from Figure 10 that even though this is a very straightforward overview it already captures everything required to develop the required detail around time-based, high-performance planning that meets the needs of both the coach/squad/team and the overarching strategic requirements of the organisation. In business terms it provides all of the SMART elements required of goals. In addition it provides two extra elements that I believe makes it SMARTER:

S Specific: the goals are tied into both the lower- and higher- level needs

M Measurable: not only measurable but coherent over time and create stretch

A Accepted: can be internalised, shared and be seen as desirable

R Realistic: are seen to be achievable and address all items that need to be captured

T Time-managed: goals are time-related and bound in to suitable milestones

E Exciting/Energising: the goals help motivate individuals, squads and teams

R Range: covers all the elements that need to be addressed to ensure success.

With this overview of the scale of the tasks ahead the coach is now able to break it down into more detail. In this he will need to consider a multitude of factors that will include, among others:

- squad selection
- athlete profiling
- the nature and structure of fitness training plans
- the nature and structure of technical ability development plans
- the nature and frequency of testing regimes and rates of progress monitoring
- periodisation of the training, development and testing regimes
- monitoring and measuring of competitors
- management of squad v. team v. individual needs and performance
- management of physiological training and development
- nutrition management
- mental skills and psychological management
- resource and equipment management
- logistics management and programming.

Most of the above elements can be directly managed within the framework of the performance triangle and other elements are at least informed by and keyed into the model. The four stages outlined below show how this model is used and develops over time.

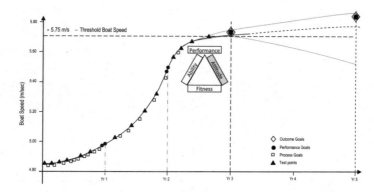

Figure 10: Phase 1: Planning for high performance

Stage 1: Squad selection phase

Stage one is to select the squad from which the eventual team will be chosen and in this process the model shows the critical elements we need to focus on. Figure 11 shows the individual athletes represented within the overall performance group.

As outlined in Chapter 4, in arriving at the initial squad selection the coach will look primarily at the attributes and attitude as the basic determinates of future high performance. On the basis that this is a squad being developed for eventual high performance the coach will certainly set a series of squad entry tests for the athletes – for example fitness, power, strength, aerobic capacity, etc. Only those that pass the attitude, attributes and entry fitness tests will be selected. This is a critical stage for coaches and they are quite ruthless in controlling this 'entry gate'.

Significant control of the entry gate is rarely the case in business. More often than not this process is managed locally: well down the line of management or even handed over to external consultants. At this level, managers and consultants often have only a vague template to work with to aid their selection criteria for recruitment. More concerning is that these consultants are not selecting for the initial pool, nor for the core development squad, nor even the team – they are charged with seeking a specific position within the team.

Unlike in business the selected squad needs to have considerably more than the number actually required for the eventual team in order to ensure a resilient squad and to foster healthy competition for places. It also ensures high quality back-up for injury, failure or unforeseen events. To make up the Rugby World Cup squad the England team originally starts out with 50 elite players, which is reduced over a period of months to 40 and then eventually to the final 30. Some who make it to the final squad, however, may still never play in a World Cup match.

What you find in sport is that even the athletes who failed to make the first squad have had their ambitions raised by the selection, training and testing processes.

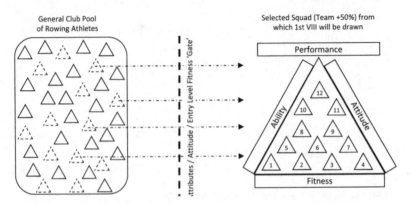

Figure 11: Squad selection.

Those that have the right mental approach become extremely strong members of the second team and because of their attitude remain future first-team prospects. Far from demotivating them, for those with the right attitude the initial non-selection for a first team position acts as a spur for their continued development and increases their determination to get selected next time. Competitive environments galvanise the best people.

In highly strategic team field sports such as football, rugby, hockey or American football, the squad size and attributes must also take account of enabling different game strategies to be played out, e.g. offensive or defensive, fast and agile, powerful and dominating or one of attrition.

The last crucial component to be completed at the outset of a sporting campaign is the selection not just of the athlete squad but also of the coaching one. The best coaches develop broadly disciplined coaching teams and also use all the tools at their disposal. In the last few decades this has increasingly seen the use of sports scientists, sports nutritionists, sports psychologists and many other specialists. In addition, the use of technology plays an increasing role in training and development programmes. For example at some top rugby clubs not only are athletes wired up with heart monitors that are tracked and recorded during training sessions, they are also fitted with individual GPS units that monitor their activity around the pitch.

Stage 2: The fitness phase

Chapter 4 showed the performance triangle in the static mode of simple athlete and squad selection. It now becomes more useful as we embark on delivering high performance over time. This chapter continues to use sporting scenarios as the vehicle for showing the development of the model. Part 2 shows it used exclusively in business and organisational contexts.

Back to our rowing club example. Figure 12 below shows the initial starting point for the squad and demonstrates that, for these athletes, their initial performance is low relative to the end requirement. All of the usual elements of new group dynamics will be exhibited here. The coach will have to pull this squad together as a cohesive unit as quickly as possible in addition to building a serious level of fitness as a strong foundation for the hard work that is to come. It can be seen that the plan has the highest number of test points in the first year and that the majority of these are concentrated at the front of the year. The positive aspect of this hard, fast start is that it is both a great filtering process and a strong bonding one for those that survive. It quickly filters out those who do not have the right attitude that the coach may have missed during initial selection.

In this phase of early squad development the coach will usually have a standard plan to achieve the initial fitness levels required. Despite having favoured approaches good coaches will be reviewing and amending even core plans by regularly keeping abreast of the latest research for their sport, attending new development seminars, listening to the grapevine and, most importantly, using their instinct. Very few of the best coaches are formulaic across the board. They try different things but in a controlled manner, testing new ideas in small areas of their overall development plans. In this

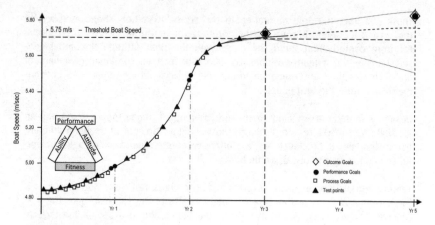

Figure 12: Focus on fitness (training).

way they avoid invalidating previous performance measurement results and thus losing sight of comparative progress and improvement. Quite often where a change is desired coaches will run the new test in addition to the old one for some time in order to be sure that it is both valid and an improvement in programme development.

In formulating his fitness training plans the coach must intimately understand the nature of the sport and its requirements of and demands on the human body. The wrong type of training (or even the right type at the wrong time) could render the goals unobtainable.

While the focus in this early period is on building high levels of fitness in all the key aspects required of the sport, some technical ability work will be taking place. In our rowing club example this will be limited because the coach will still be developing cardiovascular and musculoskeletal performance that will enable the athletes to do the advanced skills the coach will require – maintaining core stability, body rotation under load, increasing aerobic capacity, increasing lactic acid tolerance, and a myriad of other things.

Effective testing, recording and the processing of vast amounts of information are crucial at this stage – not just for checking on rates of progress and improvement but for motivating and spurring on the athletes. Performance information must be visible to all – competitive people enjoy seeing how they are doing relative to others. All sports at top level maintain detailed athlete profiles that closely chart quantitative and qualitative data and information. This aspect of constantly testing, recording and monitoring each athlete's performance development is critical to the overall development of high performance in teams.

In every single moment of squad and athlete work sessions the best coaches are consciously (and unconsciously) constantly assessing their athletes. Coaches will be appraising athlete's attitudes, their reaction to good and bad performance, how they work with others, what motivates them and how they drive themselves to improve and progress. Even though it is still a squad with no team selected the coach will be beginning to form preliminary opinions about roles and positions from what he sees of technique, style, character, etc. Most importantly he will be assessing the physiological and psychological strengths and weaknesses of the athletes.

Despite the predominant focus on fitness there will be an inevitable improvement of actual performance on the water. This will primarily be due to the increasing power and strength of the athletes but even in this early fitness phase some technical ability development will also be being undertaken. However, as the performance triangle model shows, performance gains will be modest until technical ability becomes the primary focus of the coach.

Stage 3: Developing and learning: the technical ability phase

Within a period of time the required minimum level of fitness is attained and the coach can switch the emphasis to applying the newly developed power, strength, flexibility, speed, capacity and endurance of his athlete into developing technical ability. In the case of this example it will be the athlete's ability to move the boat effectively by employing all his power efficiently through the oar in the water and minimising the effects of his body acting as a brake while returning to a position to take the next stroke.

Fitness training does not stop during this phase. It remains as intensive as ever but the athletes are now capable of both high levels of fitness training and long periods on the water to start honing their rowing technique. Coaches are well aware of the need to move athletes through the various phases of learning (cognitive, associative and automatic) as they develop ability in the mechanics of the rowing stroke. They are also aware of the different rates of progress achieved from athlete to athlete. Figure 13 shows this next stage of athlete, squad and team development. This phase of athlete and squad development is where there is the highest rate of improvement in performance.

Developing technical ability is also a painstaking process. It is not just about developing individual ability. It requires bringing the disparate and differently shaped athletes together to undertake a complex activity that requires incredibly precise timing and coordination.

Imagine eight athletes all approaching two meters tall each sliding a body mass of around 100 kilograms up and down a boat that is 20 metres long but less than half a metre wide. Imagine them doing this to move an oar 3.5 metres long through the water up to 45 times a minute. At this rate each stroke is less than one and half seconds. Less than half a second of that stroke is in the water generating boat speed. The precision required to get almost a tonne of human flesh moving backwards and forwards on a sliding seat in one and half seconds whilst still propelling a boat forwards at over 20 kilometres per hour requires teamwork, technique and technical ability of an inordinate degree.

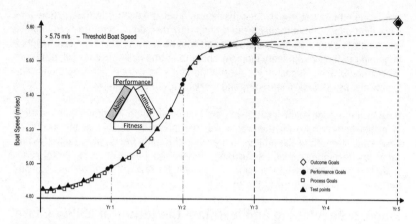

Figure 13: Developing technical ability.

The best coaches do not rush to judge at this stage. Most know that quite often those that seem slow to pick things up initially can become the most effective rowers when they do get it. Similarly someone whose technique is less than perfect may be supremely fit and powerful and have a fantastic attitude. I have quite often put athletes in a crew who are technically not the best but who succeed because of their other strengths. Conversely, I have never put an athlete in a crew who is not fit, regardless of how good they may be technically.

One other thing that has a dramatic effect on performance improvement at this stage of the development curve is the identification of weaknesses and fixing them. Towards the peak of the curve, as performance gains flatten out, you end up having to work extremely hard on minutiae. As 2003 Rugby World Cup-winning coach Clive Woodward says in his book *Winning*, 'we, didn't do one thing 100% better, we did 100 things 1% better'. These are teams working at the peak of the curve where the big gains are long in the past. The good news for those beginning the journey out of the world of average is that it is possible to find those single areas of large gains – and this is often in identifying a weakness and turning it around. In such cases the performance enhancement achieved is almost always greater than incremental improvements of strengths. This obviously changes over time, but in the early period look hard for weaknesses that can be fixed. Athletes with the right attitude understand the power of identifying and fixing weaknesses. The same is not always true of people in organisations.

At some stage, depending on the raw material that makes up the squad, there will be a leading cadre of athletes developing that begin to look like they can make a crew. The coach now has some difficult decisions to make as he thinks about selecting his initial top crew. Despite the fact that all the athletes in the squad have always known that the eventual selection process will split the squad into a 1st VIII crew and back-up rowers, it is always hard for those not selected. The best coaches will have been managing the athletes from the beginning to ensure he retains the motivation and support of those not initially selected. Again, the best coaches craft 'stories' that keep the supporting athletes engaged. The most positive element here is the general honesty of athletes about their own performance. Most will know why they have not made the selection at this stage, and for the best athletes, those with the right attitude and motivation, it will spur them to work harder to succeed next time. It is also one of the positive aspects of maintaining detailed and complete athlete profile records of performance data and making them visible. One-to-one discussions about performance and why one person is selected for the team and another is only in the squad become much easier and more focused on real issues. More importantly, because the focus is on real elements it is easier to talk about pathways to improvement that will provide further chances at eventual top team selection.

Putting a crew or team together is not just about technical ability. It will be about all of the aspects shown in the performance triangle plus that indefinable element of human chemistry between those that make up the team.

Stage 4: Attitude

As with most things in life, a person's attitude is a key determinate of the outcomes they obtain. For a competitive athlete, especially in technically complex and/or high contact team sports, it is the primary requisite for success at the top level of competition. While a strong and positive attitude is essential for all phases in the development of high-performance people and teams it becomes the most influential determining factor as performance levels begin to reach the top of the performance curve – see Figure 14.

As the team moves higher up the performance curve the rate of improvement begins to slow. The big wins in fitness and technical ability progress have been achieved. This is probably the toughest phase of any sports training programme.

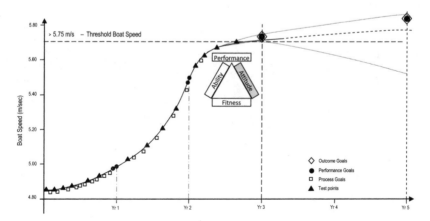

Figure 14: Attitude: small gains, large pains.

This is where gains are only incremental yet the effort required to achieve them remains intense.

At the top levels of sport, mental skills and mental conditioning are as crucial as physical conditioning. Most top teams employ sports psychologists to assist in this area of athlete development. However, these experts in their field can only work with what is there already. The mental fragility of athletes mentioned in Chapter 4 is less likely to be an issue at these top levels but their relative vulnerability when compared with their competitor's remains. What is meant by this is that although the athlete's attitude towards commitment to training, desire to win and sheer determination to improve his conditioning and technique, i.e. meet all his performance goals, remains inordinately high, any failure to turn this into results can create doubts about his ability to win. I am sure you will have seen some spectacular collapses in an athlete's performance once doubts creep into their mind. In these areas coaches and sports psychologists work hard on mental preparation and toughening.

Stage 5: Even more attitude

If you reach the top in any sporting endeavour there are two huge mental issues to deal with. The first is that all the competitors around you are probably at much the same level as you in terms of physical fitness and technical ability. The second is that if you are the sport's leading athlete or team every single competitor is seeking to beat you. As a result their attitude is highly positively driven. It is very often the case that challenging is easier than defending because as the challenger you have little to lose. As the defender if you relax even a little the only way is down. See Figure 15.

In his prime, it was arguable whether five-time Olympic rowing gold-medal winner Sir Steve Redgrave could get any fitter. It was also likely, after 12 or 16 years of honing his skills, that his technical ability was about as perfect as it could get. When you

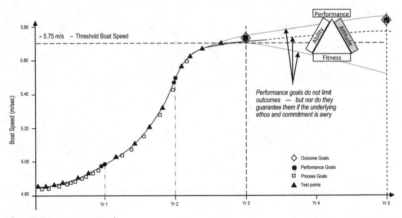

Figure 15: More attitude.

look at all the competitors at this elite level in highly technical sports it is also probable that they have all reached similar levels of physical conditioning and technical ability. In the 2000 Sydney Olympics 2,000 metre final, Redgrave's coxless IV beat the Canadians into second place by just 0.06 seconds. To put this into perspective it means that after four years of continuous training, the Great Britain IV won a 2,000-metre race by no more than the length of a mobile phone! What makes the difference at this level, when there is little more that fitness and ability can add, is attitude and having the mental toughness to want to succeed, whatever it takes. It is what drives the mental discipline to keep ultra-fit, to keep striving for the perfect performance – but most importantly it is that mental toughness that keeps the athlete going long after the body says stop.

At the ultimate level of sport competitions can be lost by the body, but they are won by the mind.

SUMMARY

This chapter has deliberately applied the performance triangle model to sport because in the first instance this provides the simplest and clearest way of describing its application and value. Sport and teams in sport are simple, well-defined environments. They are also environments where there is an overriding imperative not to be content with being average.

By contrast organisations are messy, fuzzy and comparatively unbounded. They are also institutions where most often there is little desire to be anything at all. This means that for most people organisations are little more than the vehicle by which they generate the currency that enables them to do something they really want to do once they leave work.

Part 2 of this book shows how this model and others may be used to help clarify the complexity and ambiguity in organisations and their competitive environment. It also shows how the models talked about in this book may be applied. I hope that by using the simple examples of how such precepts are applied in sport you are able to extrapolate (or better still imagine) how they can be adjusted and developed for organisations and businesses.

CHAPTER 6
PSYCHOLOGY IN SPORT AND BUSINESS: I THINK THEREFORE I CAN

To enjoy a mental activity, one must meet the same conditions that make physical activities enjoyable. There must be skill in a symbolic domain; there have to be rules, a goal, and a way of obtaining feedback. One must be able to concentrate and interact with the opportunities at a level commensurate with one's skill.
Mihaly Csikszentmihalyi, *Flow: The Psychology of Optimal Experience*

I rather hope that you have turned to this chapter and are either metaphorically, or even literally, scratching your head and asking yourself 'What on earth is a chapter on psychology doing in a business book about high performance?' I am confident that, if you were not aware already of the importance of mental skills when it comes to achieving high performance, you will be by the end of this chapter. As individuals reach the plateau at the higher performance levels it is predominantly psychological or mental skills that make the difference in achieving ultimate high performance.

I have to qualify this chapter by stating that this is a massive subject even in sport. Many of the elements raised here have generated multitudes of books in their own right. This chapter is absolutely not a learned treatise on psychology in sport. Its sole purpose is to provide a small window on some psychological aspects that many of you will already suspect are hugely important when it comes to achieving high performance. This importance is generally shunned by business organisations. By providing this brief overview of how mental skills are developed and used in sport I hope to open a window on:

- how important psychology is in both sport and business
- how it is a critical element in achieving high performance in any walk of life
- how these mental skills can be taught and developed.

Most business books I have read on this subject focus quite narrowly, e.g. on mental toughness or mental resilience. They do not address the all-encompassing benefits for achieving high performance organisation wide. This chapter seeks to provide a broad look into the mental skills and techniques that are used so effectively in sport to obtain not just high but exceptional human performance and relate them to the people and environment found in organisations.

WHY BUSINESS AND ORGANISATIONS NEED TO PAY ATTENTION TO MENTAL SKILLS

The importance of mental skills

The business community's reaction to psychology and its application in organisations is ambivalent to say the least. A great many of the business people I talk with believe it is all 'touchy-feely' nonsense. At the other extreme there is a danger of incense and chanting breaking out. If you are more towards the 'nonsense' end of the scale – and before you flick to another chapter in exasperation – let me highlight some key areas that psychology in sport deals with (see Figure 16 below).

I hope you will recognise at least a few areas where a high proficiency in such skills would provide considerable performance-enhancing benefits. If the word psychology puts you off, use mental skills – most sports psychologists do! In this diagram psychological elements that enhance individual performance and that have some positive correlation with the business environment are identified. In this chapter I only address those elements relevant to organisations. When it is possible to see first-hand the power of the mind in sport and its effects on athlete performance I am amazed how little we formally address it and harness it in business.

My last point in this opening pitch for the importance of understanding the power of mental skills in business relates to the leader. The very best sport coaches, especially those who utilise psychological training in a major way, have a very clear philosophy or vision that pervades the total environment they create for their athletes. Almost exclusively it is a performance goal-based environment and they use mental skills training not as a gimmicky, stick-on plaster but as an integral part of their coaching model. There is unlikely to be a single international class athlete alive today who does not have a mental skills development programme, or who

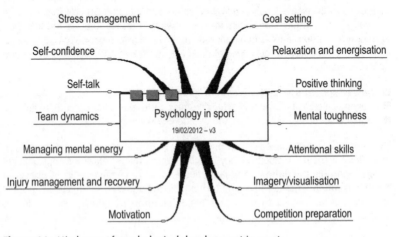

Figure 16: Mind map of psychological development in sport.

does not use a high order of mental skills ability to reach the rarefied levels of the highest human performance.

> *It is the mental power that separates the exceptional from the very good. When they line up for the 100 metre sprint there will be nothing to choose between them, talent for talent, training for training. What separates them is what goes on behind the eyes.*
>
> **Frank Dick, Director of Coaching, British Athletics Federation, 1979 – 1994**

Sport psychology as an intellectual discipline and area of study has been around for almost 100 years. However it is really only in recent years that the importance of psychology and the training of mental disciplines by sport psychologists and coaches have come to the forefront of athlete and team development and training. It has been clearly recognised that psychology plays a very large part in the success of top athletes and, more relevantly for businesses, in the success of top teams. In the past, the very best coaches and athletes were intuitively aware of the criticality of mental preparation and used a few, often individually developed, ideas and techniques for going about such preparation. By the 1980s the beginnings of a more widespread recognition of the importance of psychology in sport began to emerge leading to top sporting bodies often creating formal positions for sport psychologists. Today almost every high-level sport, club, athlete and team either has its own, full-time sports psychologist or uses consultant psychologists on a regular basis. These days every coach who goes through their formal coaching training and accreditation programme is made aware of the importance of the mental approach to performance.

The use of mental skills is an everyday activity

At the human and individual level we do mental skills pretty much every day and on a very frequent basis. I am sure that many of you when faced with a complex task, difficult problem or situation will talk to yourselves about it. Things such as the following.

- 'I am not looking forward to this meeting, I know Dave is going to be really difficult.'
- 'Okay, team talk coming up in 30 minutes. I have to nail these three key issues – if I can do that I will have done really well.'
- 'Why on earth did I press "send" on that email? This is going to mean real trouble.'
- 'This is going to be a really tough contract to deliver – but I have done it before and I have a great team. It just means committing to some hard work and making sure everyone is really disciplined.'

In sporting terms this is called self-talk and human beings do it all the time. You will notice from these examples that two are positive and two are negative. Unfortunately the brain is wired to work better with bad news and with negatives more readily than with positives. Athletes use mental skills techniques to train themselves to engage in highly structured and highly positive self-talk and block out the negatives. This mental skill is no less useful or important for business athletes and teams. This chapter will provide more information on self-talk later.

How many of you, when are you about to do something important, find yourselves imagining the situation in your mind and picturing how you might approach it? Mentally seeing scenarios and planning how you will deal with them? I bet that when you have just done something dreadful or extremely embarrassing you agonisingly play the scene over and over again in your mind. I bet that in doing this you also visualise how you could have done it differently, how you could have said something else or just wished that, by doing this constant mental rewind, you could somehow go back and erase the event entirely. Finally, I also bet that the mental picture in this negative event is far clearer, starker and more controllable in your mind than any positive ones you might have. Don't you just hate the way we are negatively wired! What you are experiencing in these situations is imaging. The use of imagery is something sports psychologists and athletes use extensively and it is incredibly powerful.

Lastly, how many of you take a big, deep breath, or several, just before you step into a room for an important meeting or confronting a difficult situation? If so you are engaging in what sport psychologists refer to as arousal control. Again, athletes take this to incredibly high levels of sophistication. They practise techniques for relaxing, energising, psyching up, psyching down, getting into the zone, etc. The ability to adjust states of mind at will are skills whose benefits to business, teams and individuals will, I hope, be obvious.

Almost without exception, in the course of normal training routines, every top sporting athlete and team devotes a considerable amount of precious training time to psychological techniques and exercises to enhance mental skills. For the top sports performers and their coaches mental skills development is viewed as being just as important as physical conditioning and technical skills training. In fact, for many at the very top levels of their sport the mental aspects are considered to be the major factor in securing success.

> *The importance of psychology in sport is far greater than many people believe. In some ways it's an obvious asset to any sportsman. Athletes train their bodies to incredible levels. Everything is put into physical training. Yet very little is done mentally. Most of the time the limiting factor is the mind, not the body. In an Olympic final there is very little difference between the athletes in percentage terms. What is the factor that makes someone better than their nearest rivals? Most of the time it's their mental state. He [a psychologist] told us about the skills of visualisation and everything fell into place. I had been developing ideas like that myself naturally over the years. It would have been useful if someone had told me seven or eight years before, at the start of my career.*
> **Sir Steve Redgrave, five-time Olympic gold-medal winner (1984, 1988, 1992, 1996, 2000); nine-time World Championship gold-medal winner; 16-time winner at Henley Royal Regatta**

By way of framing this whole aspect of psychology in sport and demonstrating its relevance in business we can again tie in it very directly with the performance triangle. See Figure 17.

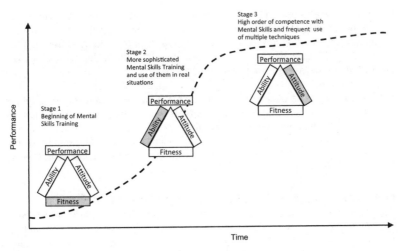

Figure 17: Progressive development of mental skills.

In the early fitness (skills) and technical ability development stages, mental skills are important and need to be trained and developed just as physical fitness and technical abilities are. Their use will be practised as part of training programmes and in real competitions as well to continually build ability. However, it is as athletes reach their peak of fitness and ability that mental skills become critical. It is the enhancement of these particular skills that leads to high and exceptional performance.

I use many of these mental skills techniques in my sport coaching activities and I work with my athletes in helping them develop these skills. I see the positive results almost on a daily basis. In my business activities I am still surprised at how careful I am about even introducing such topics to the leadership teams of organisations. However, given the slowly increasing awareness of the power of mental skills to make a huge difference to performance – and just how formally and methodically they can be developed in everyone – I hope I have expanded their potential with more enlightened leaders.

There is one significant distinction or difference in how athletes in sport and people in business use and apply mental skills. Athletes use the majority of such mental skills at low levels of intensity during normal training and development, only bringing them to a peak just before and during competition. People in business are quite often under competitive pressure (both internal and external) for the full working day, every day. The mental skills provided by programmes similar to this used by athletes would seem to be even more critical for the business environment – not less.

MODELLING AND WORKING WITH MENTAL SKILLS REGIMES

Given the complexity of all the elements that comprised the introductory mind map in Figure 16, how do we make this subject useful and usable for organisations? How do we present a compelling story to show there is something worthwhile in this area of mental skills? In taking a practical approach I have developed a goal-focused model (process, performance and outcome) in Figure 14 to try to make sense of the mental skills elements that could apply to organisations and to depict how they can be applied to achieve high-performance results.

In this model the main processes or tools that make up mental skill development are goal setting, relaxation and energising, self-talk and imagery and visualisation. By working on personal development using these process tools the skill and ability in the performance elements is increased. If application and ability in the performance elements is increased then success in achieving the outcome goals of superior mental skills will naturally flow from this.

Outcomes: what well-developed mental skills deliver
The point of undertaking any development programme is to produce an enhanced and more successful outcome of whatever the position was before you started. Embarking on a mental skills development programme to help the drive towards high performance should be done in conjunction with all the other elements this book refers to. If you are seeking to develop mental superiority, resilience, toughness and ultimately better mental performance throughout your organisation there are a couple of key things to bear in mind. The first is what is the quality of your raw material – your people – to undertake such training and development? Second, what is the quality of your competition's people and how far are they into such programmes? In an age of average it is quite likely that they are no different from you, and thus there is an advantage to be had by embarking early on such a programme as this. As always, this comes down to the selection of the right people for the totality of the high-performance endeavour you are about to embark on. This is covered in more detail in Chapter 9.

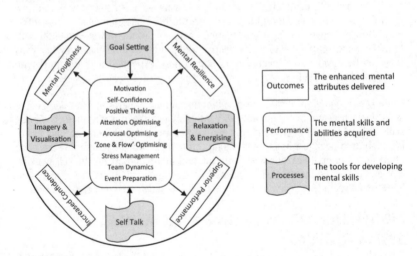

Figure 18: Mental skills development model.

Performance elements: the mental skills we can train and develop

Countless books have been written about the elements shown under my general grouping of performance. Often a whole book will address a single element. This chapter seeks only to capture the essence of why they are important with respect to delivering high-performance results from people.

Motivation

Without motivation even the most naturally talented people would fail to achieve anything close to their potential. What is motivation? Is it an attribute that coaches or leaders can develop? Is it an attitude innate to an individual? Does it respond better to rewards or punishment? Is it finite or can it increase and decrease? Do you either have it or not? Some definitions may help:

> Motivation can be defined as the 'drive to strive' and is often inferred by the apparent effort and intensity directed towards a targeted behaviour.
> **Dr Joan Duda, Professor of Sport Psychology,**
> **University of Birmingham**

> Motivation is the arousal, direction, and persistence of behaviour.
> **Dr James Franken, Dean and Associate**
> **Professor, Troy State University**

It may simply be summed up as being the desire to do something that is important to us; the will to undertake all that it entails and the persistence to see it through to its conclusion.

Motivation is easy to recognise. It can be seen in the following ways.

- The choices people make, i.e. the things they choose to do (training, extra work, extra learning).
- The effort people expend, i.e. the commitment they give or sacrifices they make to succeed.
- Their persistence, i.e. the time they commit, the obstacles they overcome, the determination they bring to succeeding.

Motivation is both intrinsic and extrinsic. Intrinsic motivation comes from within the individual and is often expressed (or even visibly seen) as a driving desire to succeed in some task, event or other element important to that individual. In seeking to achieve that success the individual will strive extremely hard to develop all the things they need to succeed: skill mastery, competence, control, etc. In sport it is often just the sheer love of the game and the exhilaration of knowing you are doing it well.

Extrinsic motivation is that which is provided by something outside the individual and can be best summed up as the 'carrot and stick' approach. They are things that are generally termed 'reinforcements' and which either increase or decrease the likelihood of particular behaviours occurring. On the carrot side of the equation they may be financial rewards or trophies, praise, promotion and enhanced recognition (tangible rewards). On the stick side of the equation it may be loss of money, demotion or some degree of humiliation. Also part of the modern theory surrounding motivation is that of regulatory focus and the notions of promotion and prevention. People with a promotion focus tend to concentrate on securing gains or as psychologists phrase it, 'seek to avoid the absence of positive outcomes'. By contrast, those with a prevention focus are seeking to avoid negative outcomes or losses. Examples of each motivation driver might be the 'promotional' person who enjoys the feeling of winning for the sheer pleasure it engenders, whereas the 'prevention' person seeks to win because of the fear of loss of status or recognition. Both promotion and prevention focus have a motivational impact but one is the fear of losing something whereas the other is the desire to achieve something.

Coaches and leaders are aware that intrinsic motivation and promotion focus tend to be the most powerful drivers and the ones that sustain maximum effort for the maximum time. They are also fully aware that motivation is not something that they can 'give' to their athletes or followers. However what they do know, whether intuitively or through learning, is that they can create the environment within which people can build increasing levels of motivation. In this regard in Figure 18 the four process 'tools' for developing enhanced mental skills work predominantly on increasing intrinsic motivation levels.

Self-confidence

It is unlikely that anyone would argue with the statement that self-confidence – defined as the belief in one's own abilities, not to be confused with over-confidence – improves performance. There are any number of examples from sport and business of confidence breeding success and success breeding confidence. Quite apart from both the intuitive and anecdotal evidence there is also scientific evidence in sport to support this conventional wisdom. Self-confidence is also known to improve performance because of its relationship with three other mental traits – anxiety, motivation and concentration. See Figure 19.

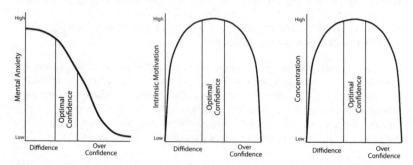

Figure 19: Relationship between self-confidence and anxiety, motivation and concentration.

Reprinted with permission from D. Burton and T. D. Raedeke, 2008, *Sport Psychology for Coaches (Champaign, IL: Human Kinetics),* p.189.

As may be deduced from these diagrams, self-confidence can be a double-edged sword. Top athletes understand that self-confidence needs to be modified with the concept of 'realism'. They recognise that when it becomes unrealistic it is misplaced confidence. This can lead to failure and indeed into a spiral of ever-increasing failure. The four tools combine to provide techniques for building, sustaining and managing confidence levels.

Positive thinking

Closely allied with self-confidence is the trait of positive thinking. Positive thought patterns enhance performance; negative ones detract from it. Positive thinking is important not just because of the obvious impact on confidence and motivation when things are going well. It also helps creates the optimal level of arousal which can lead to 'flow' and help achieve what athletes refer to as the 'zone'. Even more critically a strong mental ability to manage positive thinking is a major determinant of how well athletes (or anyone) manage failure and bounce back. The key mental skills tool that helps develop positive thinking is self-talk and this is explained below.

Attention optimising

What is attention and how do we recognise it? Maybe definitions will help.

Attention is the taking possession of the mind, in clear and vivid form, of one out of what may seem several simultaneously possible objects or trains of thoughts ... It implies withdrawal from some things in order to deal effectively with others.

William James (1842–1910)

Attention is the ability to focus selectively on a selected stimulus, sustaining that focus and shifting it at will. It is the ability to concentrate.

Anon

Perhaps looking at the opposite end of the spectrum may prove even more useful. Below is a description of the symptoms of attention deficit disorder (ADD/ADHD).

The brain seems to be unable to filter the huge amount of stimulation we receive every minute of every day from the world around us. So the person is bombarded with all sorts of information and cannot pick out what is relevant and what should be ignored. Rather than giving things too little attention they may pay too much attention to too many things, and so lack focus. The main six brain functions affected are:

- *flexibility: changing from one topic or idea to another*
- *organisation of thoughts and ideas*
- *planning: thinking ahead, setting goals*
- *using memory effectively: taking in, storing and retrieving information*
- *keeping emotions separate to logical reasoning*
- *appropriate inhibition: acting after thought and consideration.*

BBC health website

Quite simply, high performance cannot be achieved without high attention skills. In sport the ability to focus and concentrate on the task in hand to the exclusion of everything else is critical to success. Research has shown that the most successful athletes have an ability to maintain focus and concentration for the duration of the competition. They are shown to be able to exclude irrelevant stimuli. Crucially, if they do become distracted, they are able to regain focus rapidly and with little effort. Just to put that in perspective the longest period an individual batsman in cricket has faced the bowlers is 16 hours 10 minutes: that's two days of concentration with bowlers hurling a 160 gram missile at them at around 150 kph approximately every 60 seconds. Attention skills are critical to good performance. The ability to develop high (above-average) attention skills helps lead to above-average performance.

The effects of a loss of focus and concentration are easily apparent. How many times have you watched a sport and seen a mistake made or the flow and momentum of the game change to the other side. Often this occurs because the focus has been lost. How often in business do you see poor attention skills and loss of focus, either by individuals or teams, resulting in poor work, mistakes and even injury on occasions.

How often have you heard someone shout at a person who is not performing well 'pay attention' or 'you have to focus'? I often hear coaches in sport (bad ones) yelling at their athletes when things are going wrong 'You guys have to focus, you have to concentrate and pay attention to what's going on out there'. This always makes me wince. It is like telling someone who can't read music they have to get the tune right! If you have not been taught how to focus, how to concentrate and how to develop your attention skills so they can be brought to that sharp focus then just yelling the words will make no difference at all. Actually that's not quite true. In order to please the person yelling you get to see some interesting facial expressions as people try and do the things they think go with trying to concentrate – gritted teeth, squinty eyes, clenched jaw. I am sure you get the picture.

It is clear that attention skills are essential when performing at critical moments such as championship finals, making an important presentation to a customer or when doing open heart surgery. However, the ability to pay attention, to concentrate and focus is critical for the learning process itself. In sport, because athletes train so hard physically, good coaches are acutely aware of the mental alertness of the athletes. Coaches know when trying to teach a new move or new plan will be a waste of time because of the lowered mental state of their athletes.

Given all the above affirmation of the importance of attention skills how can they be developed and increased such that they become a positive factor in securing high performance? The four process tools in Figure 18: namely goal setting, relaxation and energising, self-talk and imagery and visualisation are used.

However, these tools must be given something to work with. In this regard athletes and coaches address the following areas and create plans, strategies and techniques for developing and enhancing mental skills for dealing with them:

- distractions: external and internal
- attentional cues: verbal, visual and physical
- performance routines: preparation phase, focusing phase, execution phase
- error parking
- simulation: e.g. bad luck training.

Arousal optimising

Arousal is a critical element in the performance of almost any meaningful activity or task. Arousal is essential for the activation of the body and mind, for stimulating the physiological and psychological responses required to perform even at a basic level. Arousal is the catalyst that fires up our energy systems. Clearly the level of arousal varies enormously, even naturally throughout the day let alone through activity. The following simplified description of the physiological changes caused by arousal in sport is interesting.

> *When you are faced with a stressful competitive situation, the cortex of the brain is stimulated triggering the activation of the autonomous nervous system, which controls most of the body's automated systems (e.g. organs and glands). The autonomous nervous system pumps adrenaline, noradrenaline and cortisol into the bloodstream and these hormones spur physiological changes that prepare the body for action: heart rate, blood pressure and breathing increase and muscles begin to develop tension in anticipation of the work to come. Glucose is released from the liver to provide extra fuel for emergency response, while blood is shunted away from the digestive system and directed to the large muscles of the arms and legs which will be needed for major physical response. Decreased blood flow to the digestive systems causes athletes to experience 'butterflies' in their stomach, while reduced blood flow to the extremities can leave hands and feet feeling like ice cubes. Kidney function is limited and the bladder is emptied making for plenty of trips to the restrooms. Brain activity increases enhancing alertness and athletes begin sweating, a sign that the body is cooling itself in preparation for vigorous activity.*
>
> **Zaichkowsky and Baltzell, 2001**

All in all there is a lot going on in the body and brain during states of high arousal. You have no doubt worked out that if the physical and psychological effects are this dramatic then it is logical to assume you can become too aroused and that 'over arousal' can be detrimental to performance. I am sure you have at some time been in situations where the pressure has been so intense that arousal has moved to an extreme level. Instead of excitement and anticipation the situation has become one of high anxiety and stress. When this occurs the ability to perform becomes severely impacted. Even skills and abilities that appeared to be in the autonomous category can become impaired. Again, when talking of sport you may well have heard the terms 'psyched up' and 'psyched out' and these have also crept into everyday parlance. Figure 20 shows this more clearly.

Coaches of high-performance athletes and the athletes themselves are well aware that getting the state of arousal just right and being able to control it over the period

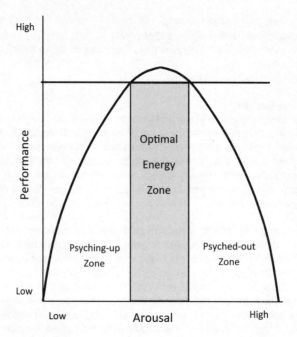

Figure 20: Arousal optimising.

Reprinted with permission from D. Burton and T.D. Raedeke, 2008, *Sport Psychology for Coaches (Champaign, IL: Human Kinetics)*, p141.

required is a key element of high performance and eventual success. It can also be seen that different sports (or different activities in business) will require different states of arousal: for example high for short durations (100 metre sprint) or lower but more sustained (five day, test match cricket). The other key point to note is that in team sports there is the added complexity that each member of the team will have different levels for the point of optimum arousal. These last two points (different activities and multiple people) are especially important in the business environment.

Stress management
In modern times stress in the workplace gets talked about a great deal but I believe rarely do leaders and managers understand stress in the same way that most sports coaches will understand it. Good sports coaches know that a lot of the things they will do with and to their athletes in terms of training and development are going to stress them. You may cast your minds back to the terminology 'progressive overload' that we mentioned in earlier chapters. Coaches and athletes alike are fully aware that stress, if not recognised and managed positively, will prevent athletes and teams achieving anything like their potential. Not only does it reduce performance and satisfaction in the activity but more damagingly it can destroy self-confidence and undermine months and even years of dedicated and committed training and development.

What is interesting is that the symptoms denoting an increasing state of arousal can be both the trigger for high performance or abysmal performance depending on how the athlete is mentally prepared and ready to manage the physiological and psychological stimuli arising from the competitive situation. The old expression 'one man's drink is another man's poison' was never truer for athletes and stress.

It is important to note that this section is making no attempt or claim to deal with chronic or acute stress and the medical conditions arising from it. This is the pre-serve of clinical psychologists. This section is looking at those lower levels of stress that occur from time to time both in sport, e.g. during competition, and in work, e.g. deadlines, critical meetings or serious decisions.

It may also be useful to have a working definition of stress. In 1970 Joseph McGrath defined stress as 'the perceived imbalance between the demands placed upon us and our response capabilities when failure to meet the demands is deemed to be important'. Clearly if demands placed upon us are deemed to be important and if we perceive ourselves as incapable of meeting those demands our stress levels increase accordingly.

We can take this a stage further by looking at how we address or appraise stress as organisms. Richard Lazarus was one of the most influential psychologists pioneering the study of stress and the use of appraisal theory. He showed that when faced with a stressful situation we automatically appraise it via three types of information: the demand being placed on us, the personal control we can bring to bear and the coping strategies available.

1. In evaluating the demand being placed upon us we look at the importance of that demand and the certainty or uncertainty of succeeding in achieving it.
2. Personal control relates to our skills, capabilities, experiences and how well they will assist us in addressing the demand. Critical to this is the degree of freedom within which we are able to utilise these personal elements.
3. The coping strategies that each individual can bring to bear are personal and derive from the individual's abilities, experiences, emotional balance, and learned techniques from programmes such as mental skills training. Coping strategies fall into three main areas.

   i.   The first is problem management whereby stress can be reduced or even eliminated through the use of problem management techniques. These can be as simple as planning, use of routines, issue listing, etc.
   ii. The second is emotion management. Stress can be reduced or eliminated through the use of techniques such as relaxation, positive thinking, self-talk, energising routines, etc.
   iii. The last coping strategy is termed maladaptive coping. It is no doubt obvious that these will be negative coping strategies. I am sure most of you can think of any number of individuals who on occasions use maladaptive strategies as a method of coping with stress. Example of such strategies would be loss of temper, undue aggressiveness, use of drugs, etc.

I'm pretty sure you can all think of business leaders whose only coping strategy seems to be the maladaptive one. Clearly the best coaches and the best leaders focus on the two positive coping strategies both for themselves and for those for whom they are responsible.

When seeking to obtain high performance good leaders and coaches take positive steps to prepare and train their followers and athletes to deal with stress. In addition they keep themselves sensitised to the situations that they are placing their followers and athletes into and are constantly scanning for signs of stress.

Zone and flow optimising

I am sure that most of you reading this chapter will have heard the expression that he or she is 'in the zone'. It is also quite likely that you will have heard this applied most often to sportsmen and women. Psychologists refer to this as being in a state of flow and it has been the source of extensive study both inside sport and in society as a whole. It may surprise you to know that over 8,000 interviews have been conducted around the world investigating just this effect. When people talk about being in the zone or in a state of flow they invariably talk about being outside themselves, with enhanced focus and concentration, with greater clarity and a sense of timelessness with the things that they're doing happening almost of their own volition.

In modern times this state of flow seems to have been appropriated almost exclusively by the sporting fraternity. However, it is also widely experienced by people in many other areas of human endeavour. People in business have spoken of critical situations where they just seemed to know what was coming next, when problems were arriving thick and fast and knowing instinctively which ones needed dealing with first, coping with ease under difficult situations, seeing ways ahead with remarkable clarity and having the mental capacity to take them in their stride, even to the extent of being able to second-guess questions being put to them. Always in these situations is the feeling of timelessness, of having the space and time almost without any pressure to make the necessary decisions.

Professor Mihaly Csikszentmihalyi is perhaps one of the leading psychologists most associated with the study of flow and has established the following features of people in a state of flow or in the zone:

- completely involved in what they are doing: focused, concentrated
- a sense of ecstasy: of being outside everyday reality
- greater inner clarity: knowing what needs to be done and how well it is being done
- knowing that their skills are capable for the task
- a sense of serenity: no worries about oneself and a feeling of growing beyond the boundaries of ego
- timelessness: focused in the present and where hours seem to pass like minutes
- intrinsic motivation: whatever produces flow becomes its own reward.

It is all very well talking about being in the zone or in flow, but how do individuals reach a stage where such states of being can occur on a regular basis? One thing that is known is that they cannot be forced. Another thing that is known is that training and preparation and being an expert in the field of your endeavour is likely to produce states of flow more frequently. Key to this training and preparation is not just in the skills and elements of the sport or work but in the mental skills training that will help create the optimal mental conditions for flow to occur. Csikszentmihalyi also recognised that for flow to occur the individual will be in a situation where both his or her skills and the challenge to which they must be applied are at an optimum level. Figure 21 depicts the state under which flow is most likely to occur.

What sports psychologists know well is that by using mental skills training to develop the acquisition and use of the elements described in this section there is an increased likelihood and frequency for athletes to enter such states of flow and be in the zone.

> *That day I suddenly realised I was no longer driving conscious [sic] and I was in a different dimension. The circuit for me was a tunnel that I was just going ... going ... going and I realised I was well beyond my conscious understanding.*
>
> **Ayrton Senna, during the 1988 Monaco Grand Prix**

Process elements: the four tools for building mental skills

Having outlined seven mental skills performance attributes that will assist athletes and people in business in achieving the highest level of performance, how can we

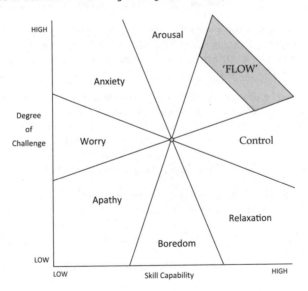

Figure 21: The state of flow.

Csikszentmihalyi, *Finding Flow: The Psychology of Engagement With Everyday Life* (Basic Books), reproduced with permission

deliver programmes that will develop these mental skills to the same high order that we expect in terms of fitness and technical ability? Most texts that deal with enhancing performance through sports psychology focus on the four tools or techniques described below. As emphasised at the very beginning of this chapter these are very large subjects in their own right. They are powerful, they are proven and they are instrumental in delivering high performance, not just in athletes but in any walk of life. The reference section of this book provides any number of authors who would make a great starting place for people interested in understanding, developing and using the mental skills covered in this chapter.

Goal setting

I first raised goals in a formal way in Chapter 4 with a view to showing the effect of goals in helping to secure high performance in organisations. In this section we will look at the effect of goals on the individual, especially in relation to developing mental skills. In this regard the benefits of goal setting can be seen as follows:

- goals enhance focus and concentration
- goals boost self-confidence
- goals help manage and even prevent stress
- goals help create a positive mental attitude
- goals increase in intrinsic motivation
- goals improve training
- goals enhance skills, techniques, strategies and tactics
- goals improve performance.

Burton and Raedeke, *Sport Psychology For Coaches*

Goals will clearly work best when the person (or team) to whom they apply understands them and is fully committed to them. So the key element in goal setting is understanding how to increase people's commitment to them. In this regard the following elements are key:

- goals must be directly relevant to the individuals or team
- the individuals or team must participate in setting their own goals
- coaches and leaders should help individuals and teams shape their goals
- coaches and leaders must provide support to help individuals and teams achieve their goals
- individuals and teams should be encouraged to make their goals visible and open
- goals should be challenging and stretch the individuals or teams
- goals should tap into the core of the intrinsic motivations of the individual or teams
- the individuals/team must understand the benefits, rewards, etc. in achieving the goals.

Burton and Raedeke, *Sport Psychology For Coaches*

In sport, goal setting is a highly formal process and the best coaches tend to focus on performance goals. They use process goals to condition and deliver the required improvements but it is the performance gains they are seeking. Success in achieving outcome goals is a by-product of designing great processes that achieve the desired performance requirements. If the coach or leader has mapped out the performance path he requires his people to attain over time and if he has judged the competitive environment correctly then the outcome takes care of itself: they will win.

Athletes' goals will be set out formally in individual development charts: their current level of achievement against each goal is recorded as are the desired levels and progression over time. Goals will include fitness goals, technical ability goals and in the best coaching environments, mental skills goals. Goal-setting skills themselves can also be developed and this is done through a formal process of education, skill acquisition and skill implementation.

Goal setting: education

The education stage is about helping individuals to understand what goals are and the difference between effective and ineffective goals. For athletes with great dreams and aspirations who are new to goal setting this can be a difficult stage of learning. The purpose of the education stage is to create a permanent goal-setting mindset in an individual or team. This requires them to think about their goals on a daily basis in a formal, systematic way with written goal management frameworks that chart progress. At first this can appear a time-consuming and laborious process. However, effective goal setting not only identifies the things that have to be done, it also identifies problems and obstacles and thus what can be done to avoid or overcome them.

Goal setting: acquisition

To achieve the highest levels of performance athletes in particular need to break down aspirations into short-, medium- and long-term goals. They must also critically assess their skills and abilities and identify where they are now and what they have to do over time if they wish to achieve their dreams and aspirations. This is the acquisition stage and it is here that an athlete will set out their three or four long-term objectives (outcome goals). With the help of a good coach these will be distilled into a number of key performance goals addressing short-, medium- and long-term timeframes. They will be formal, written down and monitored regularly.

Goal setting: implementation

The implementation stage requires an athlete to work on achieving their goals, which generally translates into achieving rates of progress on a number of broad fronts. It requires athletes to appraise honestly such progress and either on their own or with their coach make whatever changes are required. Good coaches will work continuously with their athletes on their goals, providing feedback, adjusting the goals as required and ensuring the goals are continually challenging and stretching their athletes.

Goal setting and goal management are highly dynamic and critically important elements in setting and achieving high performance. Good coaches in sport and good leaders in business are fully aware that they have to remain as engaged in the goal-setting and goal-achievement process as the people they are responsible for.

Relaxation and energising

In sport psychology, relaxation and energising are subjects that have seen a huge and well-documented amount of research. For high-performing individuals, whether in sport or business, the ability to be able to relax or energise themselves, at will, is an extremely important skill. We have seen that the inability to control things such as arousal, attention, focus and stress will lead to a significant falling-off in performance. The individual who has the mental skills and ability to control arousal and stress in particular will be particularly well positioned to deliver sustained high performance.

I won't dwell too long on the elements of relaxation and energising because for anyone interested in developing the mental skills to use these techniques there are a number of excellent books already available. In short, however, there are effectively two elements to each of relaxation and energising, namely 'total' and 'rapid'.

Relaxation

Total relaxation is a process that will take 20 minutes or longer and can be used to overcome high levels of stress, recover from high-intensity activity and even help in injury management. The techniques required to achieve total relaxation include diaphragmatic breathing, muscle tensioning and relaxing, scripts and cue keywords. Clearly total relaxation is not much use in a live, competitive stressful situation. It will generally take too long or be impossible because of the nature of the situation. In such instances rapid relaxation can be used. By learning the correct techniques and training in them, individuals can develop the mental skills required to achieve rapid relaxation in around five seconds. The benefits of being able to control arousal and break the stress spiral so rapidly are obvious. I am sure it is obvious that, quite apart from athletes in critical competitive situations, both techniques for relaxation at will would be extremely beneficial to business people in high-pressure situations.

Energising

The benefits of being able to apply both total and rapid techniques to energising oneself are similarly obvious as will be some of the techniques. With regards to total energising, specific breathing techniques, imagery, music, cue words and even the visioning of sources of power are all used as techniques for achieving total energising in an exercise that takes around 10–20 minutes. Total energising is used for psyching-up in a controlled way before the start of an intensive or competitive activity. Apart from physically speeding up the heart and respiration and stimulating brain activity it controls arousal, builds concentration and boosts confidence. Similar to relaxation above, there will be times when rapid energising is required and this can also be achieved in around five seconds by developing the appropriate mental skills.

Self-talk

As human beings we talk to ourselves often and about everything under the sun. How we talk to ourselves depends upon our mood, our environment, what is going on around us and the way in which we are being affected at any particular time. I think anyone reading this book will be aware of just how powerful – both positively and negatively – talking to ourselves can be. I am sure you have often seen athletes, either prior to or during competitions, talking to themselves, 'hyping' themselves up or berating themselves. This can extend even to the extent of athletes physically striking themselves as reinforcement for the things they are saying. Positive talking to ourselves reinforces positive thinking and if we do it consistently enough and in the right way, such positive thinking can be become an ingrained habit that positively affects the performance.

There is, however, a significant fly in the ointment. The human brain is wired to react more strongly to negative information than positive. Research has shown that when volunteers are shown a series of pictures the brain displays higher levels of electrical activity when looking at negative pictures than at positive ones. The brain seems naturally wired to use its cognitive processing more actively when assessing negative or potentially threatening things than positive ones. As a survival strategy this would seem to be a fairly sensible piece of genetic programming but it is not a great enhancer of non-survival-based high performance. In simple terms, negative thoughts fixate the brain's attention much more effectively than positive thoughts.

From the above, while it is apparent that positive thinking will have a significant effect on achieving high-performance outcomes, the natural tendency of human beings is to fixate on negative thinking. In sport, psychologists and coaches have long recognised that this tendency to fixate on the negative can be overcome by training athletes in the techniques of self-talk. These techniques are also evident in many other arenas: life skill coaches, motivational/self-motivational speakers, self-improvement gurus and even, occasionally, in business.

In order to be useful as a tool self-talk has to be a technique or a skill that can be taught and developed into a high order ability. There are many ways of doing this but most methods generally involve the careful analysis of a situation and the creation of a self-talk log, leading to the development of a self-talk script. These logs or plans will look at the positive elements of a particular event or situation, assess the predominant emotions generated and create a list of the positive thoughts arising. They then look at the negative elements of that situation and the negative emotions and thoughts derived. Finally, both the positive and the negative aspects are synthesised into a script that accentuates the positive aspects and reframes the negative elements in a positive way. This script is then the basis of a self-talk programme that can be used prior to the event and by taking parts of it at any one time, during the event.

While there are a number of ways of carrying out this synthesis of the positive and negative, most subscribe to eight strategies as follows:

1. be an optimist
2. be realistic and objective
3. focus on the present not the future or the past
4. assess problems as challenges not threats
5. view success as replicable and failure as surmountable
6. concentrate on the process not the product
7. concentrate on the things you can control not those you can't
8. detach your performance from your feelings of self-worth.

Burton and Raedeke, *Sport Psychology For Coaches*

Imagery and visioning

There probably isn't a single high-performance athlete on the planet that does not use imagery and visioning to aid their performance. Whether we realise it or not we all use imagery and visioning every day in very creative and powerful ways. What we do not do is formally develop and practise these mental skills and attune them to enhancing personal performance.

It is important to understand that imagery is an extremely powerful tool that significantly aids performance. It is important to appreciate that imagery is a skill that can be developed through training. I personally use imagery both with my athletes in sport and for myself in business. For those in the business world who are yet to be convinced of imagery's efficacy I would point out that athletes apply it to the improvement of neuromotor skills. Let me repeat that in a different way. Athletes use mental imagery to improve and perfect a physical, biomechanical skill without going anywhere near a piece of equipment or a facility. If imagery is powerful enough to improve the performance of physical skill it is pretty much a given that it can improve mental skill performance in areas much more relevant and exciting for business. Table 6 lists some of its uses in sport.

Table 6: What imagery is used for

Skill learning and practice	Skill learning or acquisition Skill practice Error detection and correction
Tactical and game skills	Strategy development Strategy learning Strategy practice Problem solving
Competition and performance	Familiarisation of competition sites Mental warm-up Pre-performance routine Preview Review
Psychological skills	Managing arousal Anxiety and stress control Improving concentration and attention Increasing self-awareness Building confidence and self-efficacy Increasing motivation Controlling psycho-physiological response Developing interpersonal skills
Coping with injury and any training	Coping with pain and injury Dealing with a long-term injury Recovery from injury Recovery from heavy training

Reprinted with permission from T. Morris, M. Spittle, and A. P. Watt, 2005, *Imagery in Sport* (Champaign, IL: Human Kinetics), 215.

It may be seen that almost all of the elements in this table would be just as performance-enhancing in business as in sport.

Coaches, athletes and of course sports psychologists all attest to the critical importance of well-developed mental skills and imagery as one of the key areas that helps deliver success at the highest levels of performance. Good business coaches are beginning to bring such aspects into their portfolio of coaching techniques.

When training for any skill it is important to have an understanding of just what it is you are trying to develop, how you are going to train and what is the plan for doing so. In undertaking any training for imagery skills the two key elements that are critical for development and recur time and again are vividness and controllability. Vividness means not just the image's visual clarity but also its sensory richness. The most effective use of imagery is when all the senses are used: visual, auditory, olfactory and especially kinaesthetic. Controllability refers to the ease with which imagery can be generated and the accuracy with which images can be manipulated and transformed by the mind. While vividness and controllability are the key dimensions for imagery development, others include exactness, perspective, orientation and duration. Of these, perspective is an interesting one since the individual can take either an internal or external perspective when imagining themselves performing some skill or task. Clearly for certain elements of training being able to 'stand outside of oneself' is a powerful way to see yourself performing a difficult or precision exercise.

There are a number of strategies or plans for imagery training programmes (ITP) but in general the key components tend to focus around those outlined in Table 7.

Table 7: Key components of an imagery training programme

Prerequisites for ITP	Performer's characteristics Performer's knowledge and understanding of the task Performer's knowledge and understanding of imagery Performer's goals Performer's psychological and physiological state
Environment for ITP	Quiet and distraction-free Performer should feel comfortable Imagery should be incorporated into both training and competition environments
Content of ITP	Stimulates imagery vividness and control Progresses from simple to complex situations Involves all the senses Uses images that emphasise kinaesthetic situations Uses images that are dynamic and realistic Uses both internal and external perspectives Imagery should be performed in real-time Operates from a positive focus Involves memory for creation and recreation

	Imaging includes both the complete skill and the outcome of the performance Script should contain stimulus, response and meaning Content should reflect real performance meets
Rehearsal routine for ITP	Requires scheduled practice sessions Practice should be systematic Practice should be short, frequent but high quality in initial stages (15 min/day) Increased duration as proficiency develops Practice to be fully integrated with total training regime Tailor to individual preferences Encourage athletes to practice on their own Team sports can involve group imagery practice sessions
Enhancements to ITP	Build and incorporate cues and triggers to facilitate imagery process Cues may be visual, auditory, language based Audio and/or video tapes may facilitate imagery Video tapes of expert performers Use of technical aids: flotation, bio-feedback, etc.
Evaluation of ITP	Performers should maintain a log Athletes should evaluate performance after each imagery activity Feedback should be immediate, especially in early phases Changes in training and competition performances should be monitored Regular reporting on the effectiveness of the ITP is required

Reprinted with permission from T. Morris, M. Spittle, and A. P. Watt, 2005, *Imagery in Sport* (Champaign, IL: Human Kinetics), 183.

SUMMARY

Psychological factors remain one of the most untapped areas for performance enhancement in business. This chapter has briefly introduced the key components of mental skills training that is undertaken in sport. It has addressed only those concepts that may be more applicable to business and hopefully has provided suffi-cient information to convince you of the benefits and effectiveness of the use of mental skills and the training of them. I have long found it strange that while there is so much evidence from the world of sport of the real high-performance benefits of properly applied psychological programmes, astute leaders in business have not taken up the challenge. The good news is that those that do will have an almost clear run for a number of years.

PART 2

ADAPTING AND APPLYING COACHING CONCEPTS AND MODELS FROM SPORT INTO BUSINESS

A practical guide to synthesising the high-performance principles used in sport with already-established business concepts

CHAPTER 7
SETTING THE SCENE: DO AVERAGE
ORGANISATIONS NEED LEADERS?

To be anything other than average will necessarily entail the leader and their people doing something that is different from the herd. If at this stage you believe there is some magical set of ideas, techniques or cunning strategies that, once learnt and applied, will catapult your organisation to the top I am afraid not just this book, but all business books, will disappoint you. The 'magical' thing that will take you and your organisation into the high-performance zone is quite simply pure and unadulterated hard work once the direction and strategy is established. This is the grinding, detailed, sustained and directed application of effort across the whole organisation over the long term.

While hard work is absolutely essential and high performance cannot be achieved without it, on its own hard work is no guarantee of success. In the same way that just being the fittest athlete in a sport does not automatically result in gold medals, neither does just working hard mean success in business. To result in high performance and success the work must be applied intelligently, cleverly and where it will be most effective. Most importantly it must be carried out by people with all the personal elements we have seen in Part 1 as being critical to achieving high performance.

This opening chapter of Part 2 seeks to explain why most organisations never move far from the pack that makes up the world of average performance. It also promotes and examines a somewhat radical notion: that in average organisations leaders are not as important as we have been led to believe.

In looking at why most organisations (and their leaders) are average this chapter also sets the scene for the remainder of Part 2 which is: what can you do about it to be become a high performer?

AVERAGE IS AS AVERAGE DOES
The only thing we can say with any certainty is that the vast majority of modern organisations are average. It is after all what the word means. Average means typical, normal or usual. If you take a statistically relevant sample of the workforce in the average organisation then it will be average. A statistically relevant sample for a national population is about 1,000 people. On this basis, if a company has a workforce of 1,000 employees or more it is a good bet that it will be average. Very large organisations with tens of thousands of employees cannot help but be extremely average, if you get my meaning. Even a workforce of a few hundred will tend towards average.

Very few organisations actively select across the board for high performance. In fact very few organisations consciously select for performance-related elements at all – even when they think they do. Education, qualifications, previous experience and 'do we like you' are generally the broad criteria for acceptance into most average entities. Arguably this is current best practice for setting and assessing acceptable entry criteria. I am sure you will have seen many leaders, especially lower-level leaders such as department heads and line managers, often fail to select the best candidates unconsciously, or even worse consciously, so they will not be threatened by someone more competent.

At the top of the organisation (even with better than average leaders) little interest is shown in selection and recruitment below the next level down from the top leadership, and often not even that. The leaders generally approve budgets and headcounts and then just assume that the HR and recruitment process is working. It probably is working but not in a way that will drive high performance. It is more likely to be working in a way that is guaranteed to sustain average performance at best. The only way a high-performance 'blip' might occur is if the market or competitors inadvertently cause it.

There is also the generally held belief that leaders have the vision for the organisation, give it its direction and set the top-level strategies and goals. Certainly as organisations become larger this seems less and less the case. Where companies are large and have shareholders the primary and fundamental focus of almost all such organisations is on shareholder value and 'meeting the numbers'. Since shareholders are generally numerous, diffused and relatively powerless and it is the organisation's leaders who 'set the numbers', then getting away with average performance is achievable, often for many years.

With short terms of tenure (on average around four years) a leader, even if they were exemplary, would struggle to make any meaningful impact on a large organisation through their own brilliance. More often improvement in performance occurs through normal market movements, new products or services already in development, the day-to-day actions of employees or just plain serendipity. Visions often remain just dreams. Directions become incremental adjustments on a well-trodden path. And the reality is that most 'strategies' are little more than year-on-year financial plans managed by the chief financial officer to ensure the leadership team hits the expected numbers.

THE SELF-DESTRUCTION MYTH

Highly relevant to this discussion about average versus high-performance organisations is the debate you often hear that goes something like this:

> If organisations have too many thrusting, ambitious, driving and aggressive individuals it will tear itself apart. People will start leaving footprints on each other's backs, politics will be rife and the organisation will disintegrate.

I have even heard figures quoted for the maximum number of such ambitious individuals organisations can withstand: ranging from 3% to 15%. Where people get these figures from ·I have no idea but there is nothing more exact, nor more vociferously defended, than the statistics quoted by a threatened leader. In sport the reality is that in high-performance teams every single individual is a high-performance person and wouldn't be in the team if they were not. There is no room for passengers in a highly successful team. The key to building and maintaining a high-performance endeavour is to have high-performance people working in a high-performance environment getting high-performance support.

HOW DO AVERAGE ORGANISATIONS SURVIVE?

If workforces in normal organisations are only average how do they survive and prosper? Surely it must be the leadership? Vicky Wright, past President of the Chartered Institute of Personnel and Development in 2011, stated: 'The average tenure of a CEO is approximately 4.5 years'. This comment led Richard Goff, Head of Client Engagement at the Chartered Institute of Personnel Development, to speculate in *People Management* magazine:

> *It certainly means CEOs tend to be on their way before the five-year plan reaches full bloom, or ignobly fails . . . It's also an average; meaning, of course, that a good proportion are in roles less than four years. If you square this against the average tenure of workers in organisations . . . and the time it takes to change culture at organisations . . . this means most employees tend to outlive CEOs.*

You will no doubt have spotted that the word average crops up quite a lot in the above observations. What is really interesting is that, given most employees are in their organisations far longer than their leaders, they will know far more about their business than the leadership. A key element that Goff mentions in passing is that four years is not enough time to change the culture of any substantial organisation. Which brings us back to my question: if organisations may generally be considered to be populated with average people led by average leaders (who may be considered to be short-term appointees), how do they survive? What is it that, if it were done better than average, might make an organisation a better performing one? To answer this question it may help if we look at the primary elements that make up the average business organisation and see if, for various sizes of entity, we can postulate some broad theories.

ARE LEADERS IMPORTANT?

In any organisation that is only performing averagely I would contend that the leader and leadership functions must be close to superfluous. As we will see in Part 2 and particularly in Chapter 9, much of the winning business and delivering it is carried out in the middle of the organisation. The organisational 'doers' are predominantly middle managers and their staff plus a few senior managers overseeing rules, processes and procedures. Therefore if a company is only performing averagely and that average work is being carried out quite adequately, what are the leaders doing? This section sets out in more detail what is happening in organisations and why average leaders are redundant.

In general all organisations are an arrangement of the following six basic elements that make up the combined internal and external environment it operates in:

1. the product(s) or service(s)
2. the leadership
3. the market (for the sake of this exercise this is the total external environment not just customers and competitors)
4. the people (the workforce)
5. the rules, processes and procedures
6. the culture.

Organisations survive through a mix of these elements combining together in ways that provide customers with what they want at a price they are prepared to pay. How they combine is not the same in all organisations and it is important to understand how these elements can be ordered differently by their relative importance in different organisations.

By way of showing just the broadest examples let us take four different categories of organisation, namely small companies, medium-sized companies, large companies and global, multinational companies. For small, medium- and large-sized companies I use the European Union definitions. There is no agreed global definition for a multinational company other than being one that operates in more than one country. The multinational definition used here can be considered to be a very large, global company.

Small company (revenue <€10m/employees <50)

For the purpose of this scenario let's assume a profile for a post-start-up company, five years old with around 30 staff, most of whom have been hired in the last two years. This will probably look and feel like your average entrepreneurial entity. The ordering of the six elements in order of importance to the organisation will probably be as shown below.

1. **Product/service.** The company would have been created and formed around the original idea for the product or service and its development programme. It is the 'utility' of the product or service that creates the business not the leader.
2. **Leader(s)** will be the original and probably entrepreneurial founder(s) with the original idea and the initial energy. Leaders will manage people and company very directly, hands-on, with little delegation of authority.
3. **Market.** Simultaneously with the product/service development the market would be developed.
4. **People.** As the product or service moves from idea to prototype to production and delivery the workforce (followers) get recruited.
5. **Rules, processes, procedures.** Very few in company's embryo years. Founders are in direct control of all key functions and responsibilities.
6. **Culture.** This is the last element to begin developing in the organisation. It begins to develop with the arrival of the first employees and the telling of stories of the embryo years.

In this small company scenario it appears initially that things happen through the expertise, innovation, drive and enthusiasm of the founders. These founders become de facto leaders whether they are good leaders or not. However, more usually, while the founder may have invented or innovated the original product or service and brought it to market, it is the attractiveness of the product or service itself which provides the business momentum rather than the brilliance of the leadership. The founders' talent will have been identifying the opportunity and bringing the product or service to the market. These qualities do not automatically ascribe great leadership qualities to the founding entrepreneurs. What is often seen, unless the product or service idea is very good and sustainable in the first place, is that the entity fails and usually quite quickly. There is a strong case for arguing that if the product or service is excellent it is that which ensures the company survives not the founding leaders. In fact we very often find start-ups, even with brilliant ideas, either failing or being bought out by larger organisations.

Medium company (revenue <€50m/employees <250)

Medium-sized companies that have survived to this stage of growth have usually been around for a while, generally greater than 10 years and will have therefore developed some longevity and presence in their market. Because of this they will have naturally developed some market scale and reach. To have survived this far they will also have established, as a minimum, an acceptable reputation for product or service quality and delivery. In such a case the fundamental elements in average, medium-sized organisations will likely be ordered by importance as shown below.

1. **Product/service.** The medium-sized company has been around for a while. There will be a strong focus on making sure the product or service is optimised for cost, price, quality, etc. Probably also some product development/extension.
2. **Market.** The same reasons apply for market focus being high as for product and service. The organisation has the beginnings of market momentum and is competing based on a mix of product, scale, familiarity with customer base and relationships and its environment.
3. **People.** Because the organisation has been around a while people know what they have to do. It is still small enough for people to know each other and pass on knowledge – but myths and legends now form part of the 'reality' (often promulgated and romanticised by the founders).
4. **Leader(s).** The organisation now has sufficient scale and functional management capability that its people are now able to deliver despite their leaders. Leaders may or may not have delegated more tasks and authority.
5. **Rules, processes, procedures.** More formalised management rules are in place to govern and control routine activities. Leaders still control the formulation of these rules, plus key responsibilities and authorities.
6. **Culture.** An adolescent corporate culture is in place and growing rapidly. At this stage it may be considered something akin to a teenager emptying the student fridge: it devours the good bits as well as those that are potentially lethal. The resilience of youth absorbs both and somehow keeps going.

It is certainly possible to argue a variety of juxtapositions of the six elements because medium-sized companies cover a wide range of entities and operating conditions. However, my main point here is to indicate that the leadership is neither the most important element nor the least.

Large company (revenue >€50m/employees >250)

Large companies tend to have been around a long time. Longevity will have been achieved through a variety of means, organic and non-organic (and often just plain good luck) but all geared to generating increasing revenues and profits though successful product/service development. This will consequently have delivered recognition (brands) and increasing market position and share. Strong market position generates an increase in income that in turn provides the opportunity to increase scale, both in resources and market reach. All of these things create market mass which, when coupled with the application of the associated organisational resources, provides massive corporate momentum (or viewing this more negatively, inertia). As a result, in average organisations we can order the basic elements as shown below.

1. **Market.** The scale, position, reach and product/brand penetration have reached a market acceptance level that ensures the organisation's momentum can be maintained with just average application of average talent.
2. **Product/service/brand.** The nature of the product or service itself has achieved sufficient ubiquity or utility that continues to ensure it will be purchased by the market with just average application of average sales talent, e.g. company scale and market presence ensures access to customers and investment/finance.
3. **Rules, processes, procedures.** Rules and procedures now govern every aspect of corporate life in every department and for every function.
4. **People.** When we look at large organisations with workforces of over 1,000 people the way in which they are organised is a mix of the norms and mores provided by the organisation's culture, plus the rules and procedures set out by each department's functional requirements, plus the overarching HR rules and regulations and lastly whatever impact the leaders might be able to exert during their short tenure.
5. **Leader(s).** In large organisations leaders are generally selected either by peer group and/or influential shareholders and/or their own network of influence and connections. They are usually selected because they are seen as a safe pair of hands, in theory as stewards of the organisation but more probably as stewards of the dividend flow! With an average four-year tenure their strategic impact is generally low and in most cases new leaders change the old leaders' strategy.
6. **Culture.** The organisation's longevity has seen the development of a strong culture (not necessarily the best one) that a) dictates 'the ways things are done around here' and b) ensures they would continue being done in this way regardless of whether there was a leader or not. An example might be a strong bureaucratic culture such as a civil service or public sector organisation.

Leaders are now more distant from operations. In any event the organisations will be weighed down with formalised ways of doing most functional activities such that leader interventions are not required under normal operating conditions. The layers of the organisation have begun to establish a life of their own.

Very large, global, multinational company (operating in more than one country)

As companies reach leviathan proportions the importance of people in general and leaders in particular seem to diminish significantly, see below.

1. **Market.** For the global multinational the market now has significant multi-layered complexity as well as huge scale, position, reach and product/brand penetration. Leaders are generally very distant from relevant contact with the organisation's market environment.
2. **Product/service/brand.** Multiple products/services will have global ubiquity, huge volume and scale. Other than a market or industry collapse it would take gross strategic/leadership incompetency to fail.
3. **Rules, processes, procedures.** Rules and procedures now govern every aspect of corporate life in every department and for every function. Quite often at this stage of the life-cycle even quite small decisions have been pulled up a level or two during procedure manual writing. Processes and rules dominate.
4. **Culture.** Organisational culture will have built up a scale and momentum of its own that, coupled with rules, processes and procedures, will have displaced many of the creative, individual decisional aspects of running the company/operations.
5. **People.** In the worst cases in global entities most levels of employees become ciphers. Most aspects of everyday corporate life are codified. People are absolutely human resources – just units of production, despite the rhetoric of leaders.
6. **Leader(s).** Generally relegated to being a steward for their period of tenure, with maybe some resource direction and allocation. The only time they may have a truly critical role to play is in either averting a disaster or recovering from one but only if they are not average and did not cause it in the first place.

This aspect of corporate momentum and the ineffectual role that most top leaders play requires a little more explaining. How many times have we seen major companies with ridiculously highly paid leadership teams not just sleepwalking toward a cliff but positively sprinting towards it with eyes ostensibly wide open?

Large organisations can survive the most incompetent leaders, their decisions and their failures. BP experienced over 10 years of worldwide safety, environment and quality failures culminating in the Deepwater Horizon oil spill. Tony Hayward, BP's CEO, appeared simply inept in handling almost any aspect of the Gulf of Mexico disaster and as a result may have increased BP's liability by billions of dollars. In a BBC interview Hayward himself said that he would probably have done better if he had had an acting degree from RADA (The Royal Academy of Drama and Art) rather than one in geology, when dealing with the fallout from the Gulf of Mexico disaster.

Another example is Goldman Sachs and the Abacus mortgage scandal. Goldman Sachs were fined $550m by the New York Securities and Exchange Commission who alleged Goldman had packaged up mortgages into Abacus and then sold the collateralised debt obligation to investors without telling them one of its powerful clients, the hedge fund Paulson, had been taking a trading position intended to profit from a fall in the value of US house prices. Despite the venality of the leadership and the fine, the company's share price rose immediately – by almost 5% – on news of the settlement. No doubt you can immediately call to mind several very large companies in any number of industries that have continued plodding along quiet happily regardless of the inept leadership displayed either in causing problems or averting them.

LEADERS AND THEIR RELEVANCE

From the hypotheses in the scenarios above how do average companies with average leaders survive? They often survive despite their leaders not because of them. They survive because they have people working in ordered environments who know what to do in their roles, at their level and just get on with it.

From all of the foregoing it would appear that this is saying that leadership is irrelevant as organisations reach a certain scale. Certainly if you accept the four scenarios outlined above then leadership, as we generally know it and see it exercised, becomes increasingly irrelevant with company size; but with one critical proviso. It does so only in the average performing company. Most organisations, especially large ones, provided they have a good product, a willing market and average employees will potter along quite happily even with poor leaders. This is for all the reasons given around the six organisational factors set out above.

I most emphatically do not believe that leaders are irrelevant. Far from it! For a company to be a high-performance organisation it absolutely requires great leaders and excellent leadership. What I am saying is that if you have great leadership and it is able to move an entity towards high performance then the opportunities are significant because the majority of the competition and its leaders is only average.

SUMMARY

The above is not meant to be depressing. It should, to the right mindset, be positively exhilarating. It means that in a world of average companies and leaders the opportunities to be a high performer abound.

To create a high-performance organisation you have to be a good leader but not necessarily a great one. You do, however, have to couple leadership with great understanding of your business (domain knowledge) and be prepared to do hard, detailed and sustained work. Having a clear idea of how you are going to apply that knowledge and hard work is also critical. Guiding frameworks (of which the models and ideas in this book are some) are essential in order to govern your direction and recognise you are on track.

Regardless of the size of the organisation, good leaders want to be at the top of the order, having an impact, making a difference and enthusing their followers. They work hard to ensure this is the case and they generally work longer than four years in the role. The following chapters set out how leaders can make this difference within their organisations and how to avoid being just average.

CHAPTER 8
SETTING THE TONE: CREATING THE HIGH-PERFORMANCE ENVIRONMENT

Dream no small dreams for they have no power to move the hearts of men.
Goethe

How do we go about achieving the high-performance organisation? What is it that good leaders can do to create an environment within which high-performance habits can flourish? If, to paraphrase Archimedes, you can move the world with the right lever and fulcrum, what are the levers available to leaders to move an organisation and its people away from average performance towards being the best?

This chapter provides a new model and a new way of looking at organisations along two critical dimensions. The first dimension deals with organisational factors. These are 'indirect' factors as far as the followers might perceive them. The second dimension addresses people factors and these are very definitely 'direct' factors as far as the followers are concerned.

It is important to note that in the context of this book when talking about the organisation's environment we mean its 'internal' environment. In terms of creating a high-performance environment the internal one is the one that leaders and followers can most directly modify and influence.

DRIVERS OF PERFORMANCE
The first aspect any leader must confront and accept is that they can only achieve sustained success though people or, to be strictly accurate, through their followers. Leaders are the enablers, the developers. They may even be the creators of ideas, but no matter what they are, leaders can only secure high performance through helping others achieve and succeed. In this regard the great leader, the high-performance leader, must also be a great coach.

The next statement is obvious but worth making none-the-less. In sport, coaches do not run the races or play the games; their athletes and teams do. Once their athletes take to the field then the coach's ability to affect the outcome of the competition reduces to zero, or close to it. Both he and his athletes have to believe they have the right strategy, are fully trained and properly prepared for the competition. However, the performance and the outcome are now entirely in the athlete's or team's own hands. This is not so different from business. Leaders do not go out and sell and win each contract or compile the successful tenders or negotiate and close day-to-day deals or even make and deliver the product or service. They have to trust that their followers can do this and that they can do it competently. It is in this day-to-day activity that we again come back to the fact that most organisations are only average and that leaders must do something that makes their followers want to achieve higher than average performance.

Leaders have to take a vast array of hard and soft organisational elements and synthesise them in a way that creates an 'incubator' for the development of high performance. I deliberately use the word incubator because the seed bed for delivering sustained high performance lies within the totality of the organisation. Leaders cannot single-handedly drive (or drag) an organisation kicking and screaming into the high-performance zone on their own. Or more correctly, they may be able to, but only for a limited period. A very high-energy leader using either coercive, charismatic or other attributes and abilities may well drive or drag an entity into some form of above-average performance but it is unlikely to be the highest it could achieve. Unless they have applied broad and deep leadership competences to harness all the people in their organisation then even that modest above-average performance is unlikely to be sustained over the long term.

When leaders embark on a programme to move an organisation from a low performance level to a high one it is not too much of a stretch of the imagination to say that they are trying to manipulate the very DNA of their organisation. In seeking to create an environment conducive to achieving high performance it is first necessary to be clear about the organisational 'genes' that will need to be adjusted and modified.

Figure 22 (showing organisational factors as high-performance drivers) depicts in graphical form the complexity that has to be addressed. There are two main strands of an organisation that leaders can change and adapt, namely **organisational factors** and **people factors**. By modifying some or all of the elements in these two areas leaders will affect the totality of the organisation's internal environment. Get these modifications right and an environment in which high performance can take place will result. How long it takes will depend upon the skill, ability and experience of the leader. It is also important to reiterate that creating the high-performance organisation is also hugely dependent on the talent that the leaders have at their disposal. As we will see in later chapters this aspect of the talent pool is extremely important.

I hope it is clear from the model that what we really mean by creating a high-performance environment is imbuing an organisation with a culture that ensures all the elements that make up the organisation can do nothing else but seek to deliver high-performance outcomes. As the model indicates, all the elements that comprise an organisation's 'culture' can be influenced only indirectly by modifying organisational and people factors. Carrying the earlier DNA analogy a stage further this is not unlike trying to manipulate genes to achieve a specific result, e.g. blue eyes or red hair.

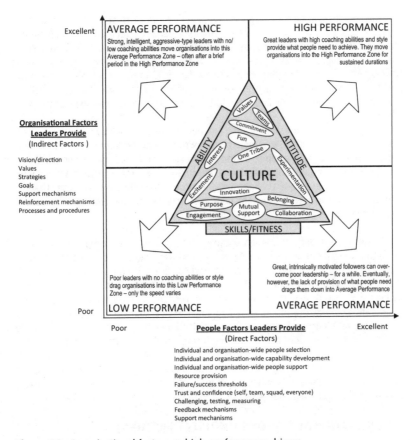

Figure 22: Organisational factors as high-performance drivers.

INTRODUCTION TO DIRECT AND INDIRECT FACTORS

The two elements of organisational and people factors may also be viewed as 'indirect' and 'direct' factors in people and performance terms. What is meant by this is that the organisational factors are a part of the organisation's fixed frame-work as far as the employees are concerned. They are set by the leadership and are generally long-term strategic and planning elements. In the short term individuals, teams and groups have limited influence over them. As a result of having little immediate influence over them, organisational factors may be termed indirect factors from a follower's perspective. People factors are elements which, on a day-to-day basis, leaders are able to use to influence the totality of the psychologi-cal relationship with those they hope will deliver high performance. Thus from a follower's perspective these will feel much more immediate and thus may be termed direct factors.

The leadership can get the organisational indirect factors so badly wrong that, regardless of how good the people are, they cannot overcome the debilitating effects of the structural environment in which they are being asked to deliver. However, this is rare. Having average organisational/indirect factors is far more common. Having only average organisational factors has less impact on high-performance people (and therefore the high-performance outcome) than you may think. High-performance people usually find ways to overcome average organisational factors.

It is I hope evident that leaders cause far more damage to achieving high performance by getting the direct or people factors wrong. High-performance organisations need to have the right people, in the right places and properly resourced. These people can also require supporting mechanisms that energise them, reward them, enable them to develop and allow them to do the best they possibly can. Leaders who are unable to create the right people structures and motivating environment will be doomed to failure.

The leader's job is difficult enough when coming into the leadership role of a well-established organisation that is only performing averagely. It becomes significantly more difficult when a new leader is required to turn a failing organisation around. You will remember from Chapter 2 that more often than not the first (and often formulaic) response of leaders in this type of turnaround situation is the metaphorical equivalent of firing the athletes, selling the training equipment and doing a very clever sale and leaseback deal on the stadium rather than working out what really needs to be fixed. It's very easy to arrest a losing streak if you stop playing the game!

Whatever the situation being confronted the leader who truly desires to create a high-performing entity will have to address the organisational and people factors and make the necessary changes.

ORGANISATIONAL FACTORS (INDIRECT FACTORS)

It is in the area of organisational factors that leaders will generally feel most comfortable. It obviously feels more leader-like to be creating missions developing sweeping strategies and producing headline-grabbing grand visions. While these may be the more grandiose things that appeal to leaders they are unfortunately not the things of automatic success. If they were then 70% of strategies would not fail, as is often reported. However, they are without doubt important and we set out here the precepts for ensuring these elements stand the best chance of success in creating the high-performance environment.

Leaders tend to be the ones who have an idea of where they want to take the organisation: the 'vision' in modern parlance. It is the leaders who frame the vision and the strategies to achieve it. In terms of the organisational factors only leaders tend to have the power to change these to suit their vision.

Clarity of vision/direction

You don't have to read too many books on business and leadership to understand that the ability to have a vision or direction for an organisation is a key requirement of leaders. What is less often written about, and certainly less discussed, is the importance of that vision also having meaning for the followers within that organisation. All too often bright and intelligent people are placed in the role of leader, apply their intellect to the problems they perceive the organisation faces, then derive their vision, direction and often even the top-level solutions that fit their view! More crucially, the leader's vision, direction and even initial solutions are usually very individual. They derive from the leader's own particular background, education, experience, mindset and world view. This would not be so much of a problem if the person is a true leader. Real leaders, great leaders, either instinctively or through learned behaviour, have the ability to recognise that they must modify and translate their vision into one that their followers can understand and adapt to. Followers have to (and will) integrate the leader's top-level vision into their own world view, especially as it is reflected in their particular role in the organisation. Unless the vision is fully accepted and integrated into people's psyches (internalised) its chances of success, at any level of performance, are limited.

Unfortunately, as discussed elsewhere in this book, many modern leaders may more accurately be described as very senior managers. In the majority of cases their ability to translate and adapt their vision into a compelling story that followers can understand is often very limited. If you cannot communicate your dream and instil in your followers even an approximation of your passion for your vision its chances of success are limited.

It may well be that because of the leader's knowledge and mastery of the business they perceive that the organisation must embark on a programme of change. Their vision may require the organisation and its people to do different things in different ways and to stop doing many of the things they currently do. We all know how the majority of us feel about and react to major change. Thus, the leader's vision in a situation requiring major change must be even more brilliantly positioned in the minds of followers.

The easiest change situation to communicate is the emergency. Sometimes known as the burning platform or sinking ship scenario this is where the reasons requiring change are blindingly obvious to everyone. The most difficult situation under which to inculcate a vision requiring change is the one where, to the average follower, there appears to be no immediate emergency or requirement for that change. While most followers want some stimulation and excitement, the big change situation, without any signs of a sinking ship, tends to be rather too much stimulus for most.

In creating visions and directions the best leaders are able to weave compelling stories that engage their followers in any situation. Great leaders have the ability to subtly shape the same story to suit different audiences, to use language and create pictures each audience understands. Lastly they take the right amount of time required to tell the stories so as to ensure their followers have sufficient time to assimilate them and engage with them. This requirement to provide time for assimilation is one of the key areas overlooked or ignored by leaders, especially in Western-biased organisations. There is a desire to rush to action which often turns out as a rush to failure.

In an organisation I worked with in China the requirement was to take what was effectively a domestically focused state-owned enterprise (SOE) and turn it into an internationally focused, high-quality competitive company. This required reshaping the entire organisation: redundancies, recruitment, new working practices, old asset sales, new asset purchases, changed terms, conditions and rewards, etc. Before this fundamental reform could even be broached a 'visionary' story had to be framed that would clearly draw a picture that would not only help the company's people understand why change had to happen but one that would positively engage and excite the whole organisation. It took three months to craft a story that would make sense to most if not all of the people. It then took a further six months of continual repetition of the story (and minor rephrasing for different group interests) to secure full understanding and engagement in the direction of the company. However, those nine months of effort and careful attention to people's needs and fears paid dividends in the speed, accuracy and effectiveness of the whole change programme. By the end of Year 3 the company was the seventh best-performing joint venture in China securing not just high-performance but government awards.

Where the change requirement is taking place under a non-urgent scenario (or a different culture from the Western one) effective leaders have clear ideas on vision communication. Most importantly they try to allow sufficient time for dissemination and assimilation by their followers. The vision is the overarching device that harnesses strategies, plans and goals into a coherent whole that drives direction and performance. The failure of leaders to secure organisation-wide understanding, acceptance and engagement is a key reason why organisations fail to achieve their strategies and goals.

Storytelling is something that the best leaders recognise as being a powerful mechanism for getting the attention of their followers, engaging them in the narrative, involving them and making them part of the story itself. It is the clarity, the repetition, the rephrasing and the constancy of the stories that ensure the continued engagement of the followers. Provided the leader's actions match what the narrative is saying then all four of the elements that followers desire (those described in Chapter 2) can be met:

- sense of purpose
- sense of belonging
- sense of excitement
- authenticity of the leader.

Superficially, the above all sounds very rational and sensible. However, it rather glaringly fails to address the possibility of an existing culture within the organisation and the impact of that culture on anything that remotely looks like change. Peter Drucker once said: 'Culture eats strategy for breakfast'. Good leaders recognise the challenges that established cultures create. They cleverly take approaches that superficially appear to accommodate the more intractable requirements of the existing culture but they subtly begin to alter it in those areas that are less resistive. In the non-emergency situation a little more time can be taken in the early stages to create the small changes that will begin to impact on the inertia that culture can often impart. Eventually these changes mount up over time and alter direction with ever-increasing rapidity. In emergency situations, especially where disaster is imminent and visible to all, the task of creating a compelling story becomes a little easier for any leader, good or bad. On the sinking ship, when the pumps have failed and water is lapping around everyone's neck the leader does not have to create a very sophisticated story to get people to believe the situation requires a bit of attention.

Values

Values can be incredibly powerful in harnessing the organisation to an ethos or philosophy that can govern almost every aspect of how (and how effectively) an organisation does business or achieves its aims. However, in the vast majority of organisations' values are at best a waste of time or at worst viewed cynically by everyone in the organisation. This is because followers often see them as a box-ticking exercise geared to some external corporate governance requirement. In most cases they are little more than a comfort blanket for the leadership, something they can show shareholders and include in the annual report.

These statements are pretty damning for an aspect of organisations that can and should be highly positive and performance enhancing. Consequently, the statements need a little explanation. I work with organisations on leadership, strategy and performance and the question of values comes up in almost every single case. When I ask the participants 'Does your company have values?', I have rarely had a negative answer. I then ask them to tell me what they are. The response is always similar. Some people can recite one or two, some will know a few more but are not clear on the details. Most say yes, we have some values but I can't remember them. My last question quite simply is: 'Have these values been created by the people in the organisation or have they been "handed down" by leaders who just expect people to follow them?' In well over 95% of all organisations I have dealt with values are a list of platitudes dreamt up by the leadership in isolation from the followers. Quite often they are not even formally 'handed down': they just seem to suddenly appear. The lack of involvement and engagement of the followers means that values tend to be viewed as just another piece of corporate fluff with no harnessing or performance-enhancing effect whatsoever.

The encouraging thing is that it does not need to be this way. If leaders take the time to involve people across their organisation in the values-creation exercise they may be pleasantly surprised. One organisation I worked with was in project engineering for large and extremely complex infrastructure development. The leadership devolved the responsibility for creating the organisation's values to a large group of approximately 50 people from across the organisation. Within two weeks they developed five core values that they believed represented what the organisation stood for. These five values were then promulgated more widely to see if they resonated across the organisation. They did.

It is worth pointing out that at least two of the values caused the leaders of the organisation a considerable degree of consternation given the nature of the company's business. If you are in a complex, high-value and often difficult infrastructure and project execution business, the value 'we never walk away' can be pretty daunting! But this was exactly how the engineers, project execution and support staff saw themselves as they worked for their customers. There was a huge amount of pride in the fact that they would 'never walk away' until the job was done and the customer happy. This single (and arguably very difficult) value had an interesting effect on the organisation. With this clear understanding now wildly articulated throughout the business the detailed thinking, engineering and commercial work that went into proposals became much sharper and more effective. The value 'we never walk away' created a cultural shift. Once people realised that they would not be able to walk away from a problem they began working much harder at the front-end solution to ensure they removed or minimised any problems during eventual project execution.

Leaders who fail to properly develop the incredible potential that values can bring to the organisation are failing to harness a powerful and influential tool that can help develop the high-performance environment.

Clarity of strategy

Visions are the easy part of setting the direction for an organisation. Much is written about the importance and impact of visionary leaders. In reality the impact of visionary leaders is close to zero if they are unable to turn those visions into strategies, plans, instructions, guiding principles and deliverable requirements that will ensure an appreciable part of the vision actually materialises in the real world. Not only this but these strategies and plans must be able to withstand (and be resilient enough to adapt to) the turmoil and buffeting found in any competitive environment.

The leader has to inspire confidence in his strategy, not just his vision. He has to demonstrate that he has thought through the ramifications of the journey and provided the resources to cope with the challenges along the way. It is relatively easy to create the initial energy and enthusiasm but it is the totality of the strategic planning over the long term that will ensure that energy and enthusiasm does not dissipate or turn dangerously corrosive a short distance into the journey. This is a fundamental requirement in creating the right high-performance environment and enabling followers to raise their game, increase their individual performance and thus collectively increase that of the organisation.

Slightly different from leaders in business, coaches in sport first have to derive the vision *from* their athletes. It is the athlete's or team's aspirations that are the drivers of the programmes. The coach then looks at the athletes (talent) he has to work with, the facilities (resources) available and the competitive environment to assess whether the aspirations are realistic and achievable. At this point the coach will recognise one of two situations. The first is that the aspirations are sound and the talent available has the capability of being developed to achieve them. The second is that the aspirations are unrealistic for the talent available. In this second situation the coach must either lower the aspirations of the team or recruit better athletes for it. However, once these fundamental issues are resolved the coach moulds the vision with the athletes and then gets to work on the goals and how to achieve them. He sets out strategies, plans, programmes, instructions and many of other detailed frameworks that will guide almost every waking moment for these athletes and teams.

It is this commitment to an incredible level of detail in every aspect of strategy setting and planning that sets apart high-performance leaders in any sphere of life. The coaches of high-performance athletes and teams have strategies and plans for all elements of individual and group development. They use the best experts, take advice and keep up to date with all the latest ideas and techniques – plus they are prepared to experiment. Along with these detailed strategies and plans, great coaches spell out clearly what level the competition is at and what each athlete and team needs to do if they want to succeed in their competitive environment.

If leaders in business want to create a high-performance organisation then they must take the time and make the effort to provide real strategies and plans that properly address the challenges that the organisation's aspirations will create. These strategies and plans must be intellectually rigorous, 'battle-hardened' and have a degree of flexibility to cope with situational changes. This aspect of strategic flexibility has to be approached very carefully. Strategies that are fully flexible are rarely successful as they can flip-flop and change from one thing to another. Strategies that are locked down, rigid and unbending also have their problems as they prevent organisations reacting to changing situations and opportunities. This means that the best strategies will have a strong core of plans and objectives that ensure directional stability and vision delivery but that also provide the organisation with scope to take advantage of opportunistic situations or withstand pressures and threats.

Perhaps the most critical aspect of great strategies (after securing full and unequivocal organisational alignment and engagement of course) is the degree to which they have been battle-hardened. For any organisation and environment any number of bright young things with degrees and/or MBAs will be able to develop perfectly reasonable strategies to achieve some desired outcome. However, the one thing that you can bet your life on is that those strategies will not happen as intended. To paraphrase military theorist Carl von Clausewitz, strategies never survive the first gunshot of battle. Great leaders, especially great strategic leaders, test their strategies and the underpinning assumptions to a very high degree. The use of scenario planning, sensitivity stress testing, gaming, etc. will expose flaws and add robustness to strategies. However, these require a strong commitment of time, effort, resources and intellectual rigour that most leaders and organisations seem reluctant to provide. As we have seen in Part 1, coaches in top-level sport do this game plan designing and testing to an extraordinarily detailed degree. Such testing is not designed to make the strategy 'environment' proof because this is impossible. It is designed to alert and sensitise the leadership and especially the followership to changes in the key parameters that will impact on the strategy. With this sensitivity they are much more likely to make faster and more highly informed adjustment and change decisions.

Regardless of the detail, a strategy or plan must make sense to the followers, many of whom will have been in the business longer than the leaders. Failure to align people with the strategies being proposed means that those strategies will at best fail to achieve the outcomes envisaged and may even cause the organisation to fail.

Clarity of goals

If the vision sets the direction for the organisation and the strategy sets out the detailed plans and requirements required for undertaking the endeavour, it is the goals that provide the motive force that gets everyone moving along the road together. The role of goals is critical to making sure that progress accelerates at the pace required.

The three different types of goals (outcome, performance and process) have been covered at various points in this book so I will not dwell on these again here. What is important for leaders to recognise when seeking to create the high-performance environment is that different parts and levels of the organisation will have very different goal-oriented requirements.

Staying with the road analogy, not only will different parts of the organisation be moving at different speeds, they may also be using very different vehicles designed for undertaking different tasks. Some may be ranging far ahead carrying out reconnaissance, others may be providing the maintenance to keep the whole convoy running. The important thing for the leadership is to make sure that every part of the organisation has goals that are relevant to its role. These goals must ensure continued improvement in the fitness and ability of the applicable parts of the organisation to deliver the strategies and plans at the rate of progress required. It may be seen that goals play a number of key roles in driving an organisation and its people towards high performance.

How goals influence high performance

Organising role. Goals, especially process goals, can be used as the fundamental building blocks of activities, plans, task forces, etc. When properly integrated across the organisation they harness effort, guide people and their disparate activities, and maintain the direction of travel.

Monitoring role. Performance and outcome goals are the direct measure of whether the strategies and plans are a) being followed and b) working. Using goals to monitor and measure the effectiveness of the strategy and the organisation's ability to implement it enables early visibility of problems and the need to adjust.

Motivating role. Goals, especially performance ones, have extraordinary power to motivate people. The goals not only need to be designed to deliver the strategies but to tap into the needs and desires of the people themselves. They must also create a degree of 'stretch' for people causing them to improve and strengthen their skills and abilities.

Rewarding role. Without goals, without the ability to measure performance effectively and transparently, it is impossible to create a visibly fair system of rewards for delivering high-performance and the associated successes that go with it. Without transparency and fairness, appraisal and reward mechanisms may even become counter-productive if people believe them to be biased, worthless or maybe even corrupted.

Clarity of reinforcement mechanisms

For many, the topic of reinforcement (enforcement) mechanisms is a difficult one to broach and is often avoided. More often than not any talk of reinforcement mechanisms is seen only in its negative connotations. The most important and by far the most effective reinforcement mechanisms are the positive ones.

Any successful coach of a high-performing team will tell you that if your view of securing high performance is based predominantly on the use of the stick from the carrot and stick school of management you are unlikely to secure the performance you desire. Even if you do achieve performance through heavy use of the stick it is unlikely to be enduring (or endearing!). Performance achieved through the extrinsic motivation of fear is fragile. When it falls apart it does so spectacularly quickly.

If you have the right people, i.e. those who are driven more by intrinsic motivations rather than extrinsic ones, then positive reinforcement mechanisms are the primary requisites that will deliver improved performance. This generally means mechanisms that:

■ provide recognition of people's contributions
■ value people and their skills and abilities
■ enable people to influence the elements of work and organisation that affect them.

Unfortunately, not all organisations are populated by highly-motivated people with the attributes and attitudes the organisation needs to achieve high performance. Therefore, if the leaders of an average organisation wish to take it on a journey towards high performance they will, at an early stage, need to deal with a significant percentage of people who just plain fail to respond to the challenges of raised performance expectations. It is even more critical when dealing with these difficult issues that the reinforcement mechanisms are clear and inextricably linked to transparent and unambiguous measurement and monitoring processes and goals.

In high-performing sports teams athletes know very clearly when they are not up to the mark. Their training performance is so well measured that it is very clearly and quickly visible. Top athletes, because of their ethos, also have a tendency to put the team first and know when they should not be on it. The same is not true in organisations. It is the responsibility of the leaders to ensure that not only are the mechanisms in place to identify poor performance but take measures to deal with poor performers if they are unwilling to take the required steps to improvement.

This last point of poor performers being unwilling to respond to the new circumstances is an important one. Through experience I have found that very few people in organisations who appear to be 'difficult' are beyond redemption. More often than not their difficult behaviour is a result of stress caused by the changes being required of them and their inability, not their unwillingness, to deal with them. On many occasions I have had situations where, with a little empathetic attention, good communication and some supportive development, an apparent 'no-hoper' has been turned around and become highly effective. In several cases it was also an issue of round pegs in square holes and by changing roles the desired increased performance from the individuals was achieved. Before rushing to get rid of apparent poor performers, it is important to first check whether they are unwilling or refusing to change or just unable to do so without help.

However, on the other side of the equation, it never ceases to amaze me how often appraisal systems identify significant numbers of poor performers who are the same individuals year after year and where the only form of censure is to not award a performance-related bonus. They still get an incremental, cost of living pay rise, they still deliver substandard performance and they still create a visible reminder to all around them that substandard performance is clearly acceptable by the leaders. As a result, poor performers are left in place or, even worse, left to 'wither and die'. They may have previously been promoted into key positions and everyone will know that they have subsequently been sidelined, are no longer relevant and have no organisational power. This sort of failure by leaders to deal honestly and decisively with such people-problems creates negative outcomes on at least three counts:

1. it leaves an ineffective person in place, which acts as a motivational black hole for those around them
2. everyone can see the leader's failure to address the problem, thus he will be seen as a weak and ineffectual leader
3. the poorly performing individual will know they are viewed as having been sidelined and will suffer as a result and/or may engage in disruptive activities.

It is also instructive that organisations seem only to promote people. Rarely, if ever, do they demote people. The reasons for this are fourfold.

1. Leaders (including managers) are generally very poor and/or weak at having to make these difficult discussions and handling the interpersonal situations that arise.
2. There are very few demotion precedents in organisations and so they do not know how to deal with them.
3. Employment legislation makes it too painful: creating potential for constructive dismissal and employees will go to a tribunal and/or sue.
4. Leaders and managers are too nice.

In canvassing organisations I have worked with in my consultancy role, the minimum figure I have had quoted as being the percentage of below-average performers in an organisation is 5%. The most frequent one is 10%, but 20% is not at all unusual.

Of all the elements preventing a company from becoming a high-performance entity, the deadweight of having a workforce with a high percentage of consistently below-average performers is a significant one. Not only are they detrimental to performance through their own failure to contribute but they also have a negative impact on a significant number of other people around them who are well aware that non-performers are not being dealt with.

Leaders who do not grasp the nettle of dealing with poorly performing individuals will never be able to create a high-performance organisation. If a leader does not have the luxury of building an organisation from scratch and inherits a typical, average entity then the initial cull of poor performance may be frighteningly high. Even when the leader thinks he has optimised the workforce there will always be a baseline percentage that fails to meet the requirements of a high-performance company. If you follow the Jack Welch dictum (former CEO of GE) then you get rid of this bottom percentage and refresh with new recruits. If, however, you follow the squad approach favoured in high-performance sports teams you take the time to improve the lower-performing athletes. If you and they have already invested time and energy in reaching a certain level of performance it should not be written off too lightly or quickly.

Clarity of processes and procedures

Every organisation from the very smallest start-up to the largest global conglomerate has processes and procedures. Processes and procedures are an important part of governing and controlling the activities throughout an organisation. Developed wisely they may be the repository of the knowledge within the company and the way things are done all the way through to crises and disaster management. Developed wisely they are incredibly valuable.

Unfortunately, there seem to be two laws of the universe when it comes to processes and procedures. The first states that the volume of processes and procedures increases exponentially with the size of the organisation. The second law states that the usefulness of processes and procedures decreases exponentially as the size of the organisation increases.

Observation of the development of processes and procedures in organisations indicates it is almost exclusively an additive exercise. As organisations get bigger and/or more widely distributed in terms of location the more processes and procedures seek to increase control. In the worst cases they become constraining rather than enabling frameworks and thus act as a brake on performance. Leaders need to put in place a mechanism and/or a task force to assess all the rules and procedures and remove, adjust or change completely anything that does not lend itself towards enabling high performance.

PEOPLE FACTORS (DIRECT FACTORS)

It is in the area of people factors that leaders can really make a huge difference by using properly applied, high-order coaching skills. If, as is so often stated, people really are the most important asset for organisations then understanding how to coach them for high performance is the best chance for securing the high-performance levels desired.

The previous organisational/indirect factors may almost be considered 'hygiene factors'. This means that most organisations can create a vision, a strategy and some management frameworks and mechanisms that will do the job. What makes the difference between average performance and high performance is how all the people in the organisation are excited, motivated, developed and supported in driving the company onwards and upwards. The more intelligent, more capable and more intrinsically motivated the workforce then the more a coaching approach is required.

There is a simple diagram that links in with the people factors shown in Figure 22. This diagram is Figure 23 and it shows just how important these people/direct factors are when seeking to create an environment for high performance.

It is the leader's responsibility to ensure that the right people-related factors are in place, namely those that first move people into the optimal energy zone and second, draws them up into the high-performance zone.

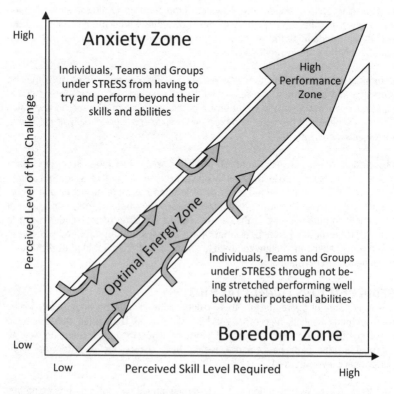

Figure 23: Why the capability of people and challenge of the task must be in balance.

Reprinted with permission from R. Martens, 1987, Coaches Guide to Sport Psychology (Champaign, IL: Human Kinetics), 93.

Individual and team capability development

Chapters 9 and 10 discuss in more detail the selection and development of people in high-performance organisations. The key thing for leaders is to understand that once they have the raw talent with the potential for delivering high performance it is essential that they have clear plans for developing all that talent. These plans must project into the future and create the career path for people within the organisation. If you have intelligent, highly capable and intrinsically motivated people the failure to provide them with continuous personal development and challenges may create a worse situation than if you had average people working averagely in an average organisation. Highly capable and self-motivated people will become bored (and even stressed) if they do not have the challenge and stretch to continuously hone their skills and add to their abilities.

Just as coaches at the top levels of sport go to extreme lengths and meticulous detail in constructing their training and development plans, so too must the leader who wishes to develop the high-performance organisation. These plans must be fully integrated with everything that the company is doing with respect to direction, strategy, goals and the various timescales that these elements create. If there are significant anomalies or differences between the development plans for the company and its people's aspirations and needs, then there will be the potential for performance-reducing tensions.

There is substantial complexity in developing such integrated development plans. The needs of each individual, each group of individuals and specific teams within those groups or the organisation as a whole will all be different. What marketing people need will be different from what service delivery people will need and that will be different again from say finance, product development, commercial, sales, etc.

Integrated people and organisational development planning

Thinking through and drawing up a fully integrated people and organisational development plan is a considerable intellectual and resource-consuming exercise but failing to do it is the first step towards failing to achieve high performance. It would be rather like a Formula 1 team boss stating 'We will be Constructor's World Champions in three years time', and then doing nothing to develop his design crew, engineers, technicians or mechanics but still expecting them to come up with a world-class racing machine based on only their current skills and abilities.

This is where a people and organisational development group or department (as opposed to the modern HR organisation) becomes an essential part and key asset of the company. Instead of being just a 'pay and rations' department this part of the organisation would be fully integrated into the business. They will have the skills to help distil the strategies and goals into long-term development programmes tailormade for each part of the organisation. They would have the abilities to structure and design the programmes with little or no third-party, consultancy intervention since they would know far more intimately how all the elements combine to drive goal achievement and thus the performance levels required. All this is a far cry from the average organisation, many of whose leaders think training is development and that outside agencies possess the best answers.

Individual and team support

In order to give their best every individual, every team and every group must understand why they are in the organisation and be clear about how their roles contribute. This is not about a job description. It is about people having an absolutely clear idea of why they exist in the organisation and why they are valuable to it. There is an anecdote about a president of the US (Kennedy, I believe) who on a visit to NASA asked a janitor who was sweeping the floor what his job was. The answer was immediate and clear: 'I am helping to put a man on the moon'.

Support starts right at the very basic level of helping everyone to understand just how they fit into the story, how they contribute to it and the breadth and depth of support available to them to help them do it to the best of their ability. What is required is a highly effective people and organisational development group with the breadth and depth of business and people skills to be fully aligned with the organisation's business drivers, goals and delivery requirements. These are not just people professionals but staff with a grasp of what a high-performance business needs and who are high performers in their own right.

Resource provision

Everyone knows instinctively and intellectually that, quite simply, if you do not provide the right type of resources, in the right numbers, in the right place, at the right time the chances of any sort of performance, let alone high performance, are close to zero. In our private lives we do not embark on any endeavour or journey without first working out what we need, what extra we might require if things go wrong, how we can obtain what we need and when we must have it by. So, what is it that goes wrong in organisations? There are any number of academic, business school and consultancy papers and studies that prove time and again where failures in strategy (and thus performance) can be directly attributable to a failure of leaders to provide the resources required and in the way required. Conversely, there are papers and studies proving that in those organisations where the leadership get resource allocation right and in line with their strategies they achieve markedly superior financial performance. Therefore, to create a high-performance environment leaders must ensure they pay attention to getting the resourcing equation in line with the vision and its strategic needs.

People can overcome lack of resources and produce a great result – once, possibly twice. If the failure to provide everything that is required to execute the task or programme is a continual issue then even great individuals and teams will become demotivated and their performance will decrease over time. This is not a linear performance reduction. As the evidence mounts that the leader does not see their efforts as being sufficiently important to warrant the proper resources, a tipping point will suddenly be reached and the level of performance will fall off a cliff. At this stage organisations lose their best people.

This does not mean that leaders have to meet every wish or whim of a high-performance individual or group. Meeting just the reasonable resource requirements sufficient to do the job well is entirely acceptable, provided the resource decision making fully engages the individual or group undertaking the work. Every organisation has constraints. These may be financial, people, organisational and even political. Regardless of what the constraints are, the leader must ensure that the individual or group required to deliver is fully educated about what those constraints are and included in discussions about what is possible and what is not. If you have the right people and involve them seriously they will recognise the validity and reality of the constraints and once aware of them will a) be far more positive about not getting all the resources they wanted, and b) will probably be highly motivated, even excited, in rising to the challenge to find creative ways to do the task with less.

As in all things involving very capable, self-motivated high-performance people, it is 'how' the leader does things much more than the 'what' that will maintain the drive and commitment of such individuals.

Failure and success thresholds
Organisations in general are incredibly poor at setting and managing what I call failure and success thresholds. Typically, organisations set a few top-level company targets which are predominantly financial and then leave heads of department, line managers or anyone else with direct reportees to deal with lower-level target setting and objectives. Sometimes these lower-level targets and objectives are built around hard, quantitative measures. More often they are soft, qualitative targets. Regardless of whether they are hard or soft, the worrying thing in most cases is that they are set (even self-set by managers) at levels which reflect average rather than high-performance requirements. The way in which some token account is addressed for securing better than average performance is generally the inclusion of targets that are typically called stretch targets.

If a leader is trying to create a high-performance environment in their organisation the setting of average targets, even if he has recruited high-performance people, will not achieve the performance levels they are capable of. High-performance people are self-motivated by stretching themselves and seeking to achieve that next level of performance. The 400 metre hurdler is not going to be very satisfied with achieving a personal best time if he later finds out the hurdles were set 10 cm lower than that required by champions. In fact, he is going to be highly depressed and one can envisage an extremely interesting discussion between him and his coach shortly after he finds out. Conversely, setting the thresholds unreasonably high will also have a debilitating effect on the performance of individuals.

Getting the balance right is the responsibility of the leader. Setting a few top-level company financial targets and then leaving the rest to managers across the organisation is an abrogation of this critical responsibility. This is where a proper people and organisational development type of department fully engaged at the strategic level as well as the operational would be extremely effective.

Trust and confidence

In all my time in corporate life and from all the reading and studying I have done in business related matters, the aspects of trust and confidence receive scant attention. I think we all know intellectually that these aspects are important but the reality is that in corporate life they are not elements which the leadership, personnel departments or line managers spend any time worrying about, let alone developing.

It is only since I have been coaching in sport that I have begun to understand the significance and impact trust and confidence have on performance. More critically it is the impact that collective trust and confidence in those around you has on a group or team's performance. I am sure you can all think of top-level teams in sport where the trust and confidence the players had in each other was non-existent and the impact that had on their performance. In high-pressure situations you can even see a team initially performing well and then completely disintegrating when a few mistakes are made and the trust in each other evaporates.

Conversely, you can no doubt think of teams that were initially underdogs and given no chance of success suddenly performing brilliantly and doing things no one ever thought they were capable of. This sort of performance, especially on a sustained basis, is unachievable unless people trust each other and have confidence in the skills and abilities they bring to the team will group.

Leaders are absolutely responsible for creating the environment that fosters and builds trust and confidence, both in the individuals and in the collective. It starts by ensuring everyone knows where they fit, what their role is and what everyone else's role is. Without this clarity, especially in individuals' immediate environments, it is difficult to develop trust and confidence.

I do not make light of the fact that this is a difficult and complex area. If we look at a definition of what trust really means it highlights the challenges leaders face. **Trust is the releasing of conscious control over something, especially something that is important to you, and giving the responsibility for it to someone else**. To take this step is no small matter. If you consider that most organisations are populated by many and varied individuals each with their own drivers, desires and ambitions it is immediately apparent that organisations can be highly politicised environments. Unless some positive steps are taken to create a trusting environment it will not happen on its own.

I have found that, generally, talented, high-performance individuals are less concerned about trust issues than average performers because they have confidence in themselves, their skills and their abilities. They are comfortable in their own skins. Provided leaders send the right signals and recognise and reinforce the right behaviours then high-performing individuals generally respond well. A key role for the leader in developing such an environment is clearly, immediately and visibly censuring any behaviour that undermines the development of a trusting culture. Unfortunately in many organisations today leaders and their acolytes, far from censuring such behaviours, are often the fomenters of it.

Trust and the subsequent confidence in others, comes about through disclosure. For disclosure to be successful and aid the development of a trusting environment it has to be a two-way process. Developing trusting relationships especially in organisations has an element of risk for individuals. It will only develop if this two-way disclosure is both open and balanced. Organisations that recognise the importance of trust and confidence people must have in each other will have people and mechanisms specifically geared toward to helping this happen.

Reward structures

When it comes to rewards, carrots, and especially sticks, tend not to work! When talking of carrots and sticks I am specifically referring to extrinsic rewards such as bonuses, higher salaries and other material rewards. The whole subject of rewards goes to the heart of human motivation in general and is even more relevant when talking about high-performing, intrinsically motivated individuals. Particularly for these types of individuals, extrinsic rewards not only fail to produce the expected outcome, they can actually minimise performance.

These statements are not a belief, a personal feeling or an ideology. They are in fact supported by scientific testing and a raft of experimentation with groups across skill sets and across nations and cultures. Extrinsic rewards do not work. Actually, this is not quite true. Extrinsic rewards can work but really in only two ways.

The first way in which extrinsic rewards can work when related to performing tasks is when those tasks are simple. By this I mean the tasks have simple rules, a narrow focus and simple goals. In simple, mechanistic environments extrinsic rewards can work. The moment that tasks or goals become complex, requiring thought, creativity, collaborative working, application of skills, ability and knowledge, extrinsic rewards have been proven not to work. Even worse, they have been proven to have a negative impact on performance.

Second, if the inducements are big enough, we can get people to act in ways in which they would not otherwise act or which are not natural for them. In terms of performance, if individuals are not being themselves they are unlikely to perform to their full potential. Big enough rewards, like big enough punishments, do not produce high performance; they produce only compliance.

Despite what has been said above about extrinsic rewards the salary structure must pay some attention to meeting the needs of the individuals and be comparable to market norms. Bearing in mind that in creating a high-performance environment the leader is seeking to attract high-performance individuals, the market norm for the salary structure will probably be towards the upper range of the percentile. The leader should also be seeking to create an environment that is open and transparent and this should extend to 'pay and rations'. Having a transparent salary structure removes a lot of the uncertainty, unhealthy perceptions and discontent that secrecy can create. It removes the propensity for favouritism, compensation creep and politicisation of pay and rewards.

Challenging, testing and measuring

Just as in sport, high-performance individuals and teams thrive on challenge. High-performance individuals are internally driven to continually improve their own performance through the development of their skills and abilities. Having put in the hard work to achieve improvements in key areas they need to see that they are having the desired effect. In sport this is easy because there are so many hard or quantitative tests and measures and competitions for doing so. It is less easy in business where hard measures are difficult to come by.

It may help in this regard to look at the key areas where testing and measuring can take place. There are basically three.

1. The individual, team or group against himself/themselves – this means progress and development measured against some previously attained level or against the plan.
2. The individual, team or group against their internal peer group.
3. The individual, team or group against external elements, i.e. competitors.

The individual, team or group against himself/themselves

The first of these can be very effective and motivating if done properly. However, designing appropriate and effective testing and measuring regimes, especially around soft measures, is not easy. Even where such regimes are well designed, the way in which they are implemented can render them not just useless but even have a negative impact on performance.

By way of example, let's assume you have someone in the commercial department who has high potential but requires the development of their knowledge of insurance to reach the next stage of effectiveness. A development programme is designed and in due course completed by the individual. If in the annual appraisal all that happens is that a tick is placed in the 'insurance objective box' then the regime has failed.

What should happen is that the regime should have at least three stages. Stage one is to undertake the skill or knowledge development. Stage two is to have that knowledge tested under controlled conditions, assessed with learning feedback provided by an individual that the recipient deems relevant, i.e. an acknowledged expert. Stage three is for the organisation to put the individual into a position where they have the responsibility to employ the newfound knowledge or skill as part of their increased role and importance.

We can see from this that the development aspect of improving individuals, teams and groups is the easy bit. Even the second stage of knowledge and skill acquisition assessment is relatively straightforward. Where it almost always breaks down is in the fact that most organisations fail to then place the individual into positions early enough where they can use their newfound knowledge or skills in real, performance-affecting situations. Where this type of failure occurs the knowledge and skills atrophy through lack of use.

The individual, team or group against their internal peer group

The second area listed above is without doubt the most dangerous from an organisational point of view but it is amazing how frequently organisations do this badly. In a sports team environment athletes generally form a squad. Everybody within this squad undergoes fitness and ability training and development and everybody is fully aware that their performance is comparative. They all know that for whatever position they play in the team there will be others competing for it. They know that in the four broad areas we have already covered (attributes, fitness, ability and attitude) they are being compared against each other.

When handled well by a good coach, this approach can create not only a highly competitive atmosphere but also a supportive one. In a good squad the quality of the selected team becomes the prime focus rather than the individual needs of each athlete. This does not mean that the needs of each athlete disappear. It means that they are recognised, discussed and taken into account but in the context of the squad and team rather than just at the level of the individual. When this works well it is generally because everything of importance to the team is open. Performance scores from training regimes are posted for all to see. Everyone can see how they are doing relative to others in the squad.

Coaches communicate widely and openly about how they select for teams and the criteria used. More importantly where someone in the squad is not selected for the team for a particular competition, coaches take the time to communicate not just why but how the individual can improve their likelihood of future selection. A lack of openness or a lack of transparency as to how things are done creates dark corners and shadows wherein discontent begins to breed.

In most companies, internal comparative testing and measuring is done badly. There are not just dark corners and shadows but whole rooms where the lights are off. The causes are many and include the following.

- Poor frameworks and guidelines at top level that fail to integrate the organisations direction and needs with department level plans and people's personal aspirations.
- Inappropriate and unmonitored development programmes at local level.
- Lack of transparency of development budget allocations, development needs, programme quality, results achieved, assessments, individual performance, etc.
- Different levels and quality of measurement at local level when comparing division by division or group by group.
- Favouritism and prejudice.

The individual, team or group against external elements

The third and by far the most powerful form of testing and measuring for high-performance individuals, teams or groups is doing so against external competitors. For organisations, this is also the most difficult to do. It is relatively easy to measure the overall organisation against a similar competing one, i.e. change in market share, change in profit per employee, financial returns, etc. It is much more difficult to achieve at a group, team or individual level. It can be done but usually requires more effort and creativity than most leaders are prepared to apply.

Just as in sport, the visibility of competitor performance in business can act as a spur to high-performance individuals, teams and groups if they are the right sort of people and if their organisation has clear ways of identifying their performance.

Feedback mechanisms

In high-performance environments, for example in top-level sporting teams, feedback is critical to the performance. Feedback is the way in which high performance is encouraged, reinforced and even rewarded. It is critical to understand that feedback is all about communication. It may also be counterintuitive to realise that feedback is as much, even more, about listening and observing as it is about transmitting. What I mean by this is that feedback has to be based upon solid information about what is being discussed. You cannot 'get' information if you are the one who is doing most of the talking. Great leaders tend to be great listeners.

Feedback can be general or specific and of the two, specific feedback is by far the more effective and motivational. Just saying things like 'well done' or 'great job' has little significant effect on individuals, especially high-performing ones. Being more specific and more descriptive shows both your understanding of what has just been performed and that you value it. For example:

> I think the way in which you all solved the cable performance problem was brilliant. Until your team came up with the Arena software solution the company had been struggling for months. Congratulations and very well done! I cannot thank you enough. Would you like to present a paper at this year's Technology Council Forum in Hawaii?

This piece of feedback provides understanding, context, appreciation, recognition (of the task, the work of the individuals and the value) and reward (that has value and meaning to the receivers).

Great coaches and great leaders provide high-quality, descriptive feedback as a matter of course. It seems to be part of their DNA that they walk around with their eyes open and ears attuned. They are excellent at seeing and hearing what their people are doing and achieving and saying thank you for that work. Leaders seeking to create a high-performance environment must make sure that everyone in key positions responsible for elements of performance are trained to become excellent at providing feedback if it is not something they do naturally.

SUMMARY

The key points in this chapter may appear obvious, but in almost every organisation it appears that this isn't the case, or if it is, little or nothing is done to make the changes required to achieve high performance.

There is a very good reason why such changes do not occur. The reason is that addressing all of the elements covered by the model and this chapter is not only hard work, it requires that hard work to be applied over long periods of time. There should be no surprise in this. Top athletes, top teams, and even the best performing companies can be seen to be applying themselves to that hard work. How do they manage to do this? They do it because their coaches and their leaders manage to create an environment that meets the key needs that we have identified in other chapters. The other thing that tends to be seen in organisations where these needs are being met is that there is a sense of enjoyment, even fun, across the whole organisation.

The very best leaders and coaches are able to draw together the huge complexity of direct and indirect factors in ways that positively impact on the organisation and all the people in it. They are able to provide desirable drivers around both the formal and informal needs of the organisation and its people that give impetus to delivering high performance. Great leaders and coaches seem to do much of this naturally but they still display a huge work ethic and work hard at the detail, especially that which falls outside their natural talents. Leaders and coaches who are less 'natural' may have to work that little bit harder and on more areas but will still be able to achieve increasing levels of performance if they stick with it. Not surprisingly, like any skill and ability, leadership responds to hard work and practice.

CHAPTER 9
TALENT SELECTION: SECURING HIGH-PERFORMANCE PEOPLE

Innovation has nothing to do with how many R&D dollars you have. When Apple came up with the Mac, IBM was spending at least 100 times more on R&D. It's not about money. It's about the people you have, how you're led, and how much you get [from people].

Steve Jobs, Apple Inc.

We now need to address the lifeblood of any organisation: its people! If leaders are required to be excellent at one key aspect of their skill set it has to be in the area of working with people. Without good people around them to execute and deliver no leader can realise their vision or their plans.

So, the question is, apart from the leading, motivating, visioning and strategy-setting aspects that leaders have to engage in, is there something else leaders can do related to people that will better ensure they achieve high performance? The answer very definitely is yes! In the highly competitive sporting world coaches do not take a group of people at random and hope that by some incredible piece of good fortune the group just happens to contain some top-level, gold-winning athletes. Or that out of 30 individuals off the street a world-beating, championship-winning team just happens to exist.

If you take a group of people at random they are most likely going to be average. As we have seen previously at the beginning of Chapter 7, the bigger the sample the more likely that they are going to tend towards the average. It is important to recognise that great coaches and great leaders can and do manage to achieve much greater than average performance from average groups – but this is rarely sustained. Rarely are such groups able to withstand the pressure from the talent they are exposed to at the top levels of competition. It is usually fleeting glory. How they are led, how they are fired up and how they are organised are all critically important things, but who are selected and how they are chosen is where it all really starts.

Given the above, how can we ensure that we create organisations that are better than average and that remain so for sustained periods? Quite simply, if we wish to develop a high-performing organisation for the long term we must start in the same way that a good sports coach starts and that is through very careful, very thorough and well-screened selection.

The rest of this chapter provides some ideas and frameworks using the performance triangle that will help the leader who is passionate enough about high performance in the shaping of their organisations and their people to achieve it.

TALENT SELECTION PROCESS

Talent selection in the modern era seems to be fraught with difficulties especially when a leader is seeking to be highly specific in who is selected. Employment legislation seems to place a straitjacket on the thought processes of business leaders. Reality, though, is rather different because it is easy to be highly selective in recruitment and select for high performance. There appear to be two primary causes why this does not happen: the quality of the leader and the quality of the organisation's recruitment processes.

The first reason companies tend to be less than successful in recruiting is because leaders often lack the rigour, energy and attention to detail that ensures organisation-wide selection helps meet that leader's vision. Such leaders, whether through laziness or lack of competence, tend to abdicate their talent selection responsibility in its totality to the HR function. This does not mean leaders have to oversee every hiring and firing but it does mean that their requirements and interest are well known and that they display such interest overtly.

The second cause of failing to select for high performance is of more concern. This is the failure of the organisation's own recruitment processes and procedures to achieve a quality of people advantage. It is the biggest contributor to ensuring the company is populated with average-performing staff. Often even the language used when talking about people is dehumanising. People throughout the organisation often refer to staff and staff numbers as 'headcount'. Referring to people as human resources and headcount places them not far above a bolt on a car or a circuit board in a piece of electronics. We will know without any shadow of doubt when people really are a company's most important asset because that will be the day they are referred to as people.

An illustration of the recruitment process

In the recruitment situation what generally happens is something along the following lines. A manager somewhere in the organisation decides that they need one or more new staff. Internal procedures probably require that the manager makes a case to increase their staff. This request will be submitted up the hierarchy to a point where it splits and goes to the decision-making line manager or director, the personnel department and quite often also to the finance department for a headcount and budget check. Eventually word comes back down from on high that the recruitment request is approved. At this point the manager concerned may work with someone in the personnel department to develop a description, create an advertisement and maybe decide how, when and where advertising will take place. If the role is senior enough it may even involve the engagement of a specialist recruitment company. The CVs from applicants are screened. Depending on the size of the organisation, this may be done by the recruitment company, the personnel department or the manager responsible for the recruitment. A shortlist is drawn up and a number of applicants are interviewed. A decision-making interview is eventually held with the recruiting manager and the person or people required are appointed.

So far so good you might think. The problem is that very rarely in this typical process is it informed and guided by the organisation's medium- to long-term cross-company goals and objectives. Even more rarely is it keyed into and directed by the organisation's overarching long-term strategy and direction. It's also rare that the vision of where and what the company is seeking to be guides the process. More often than not the process is driven by an individual manager's immediate workload and staffing requirements. Even worse, the individual manager and the personnel department will rarely have been given the imperative to recruit the highest capability individuals as part of a drive to raise the overall standard of people within the organisation. Often it is the opposite with cost minimisation being the key driver.

There will almost always have been little or no recruitment training for that manager. Unless the 'people' department has been included at the top level of strategic direction setting, staff will not know the details of the long-term plans. Even if they have been included, rarely are the staff in that department qualified or experienced enough to undertake proper organisational development because this is not what modern HR in most companies does. Consequently the organisation's 'people' people are not properly equipped to assist in this deliberate, positive selection of high-talent, high-performance new entrants.

The situation can be considered to be even worse when an outside recruitment agency is involved. They are even less likely than internal staff to have a clue about the long-term directional, strategic and high-performance drivers. They will be working to a simple job specification and some form of briefing without intimate knowledge of the organisation's high-performance imperative and detailed requirements. This does not mean they are not useful and needed. It does mean the people with that knowledge in the organisation must expend a lot more time and energy getting into the details with the recruitment agency to ensure the gene pool is strengthened in ways that are desired, rather than diluted at best or polluted at worst. This dilution/pollution effect becomes more pronounced the closer you get to the top of the organisation because senior level appointments tend to be externally managed by recruitment agencies.

Selectivity is important

If an organisation is serious about becoming a top-level, high-performing entity for the long term then not only do the leaders need to be above average but so too do the people. A top-level coach in sport knows that top-level success will only come if he is able to build a squad of athletes that are capable of delivering the high performance required for that success. They may not all be at the height of their powers and abilities at the time they are chosen. Nonetheless, the good coach will not only see the right things in the people they choose but be able to put in place the training regimes, ethos and structures that will draw out the very best in their people. Building this squad starts with selection and this is tough and incredibly detailed. Selection is inextricably linked not just with aspirations and goals but the speed at which they are required to be undertaken. Business leaders who fail to give the same degree of attention to the building of their high-performance organisation will always languish in the lower echelons of their league.

Many of you may now be saying, 'Hang on a minute, there's a big difference between recruiting five, 10 or 30 people for a sports team and recruiting thousands for a multinational company.' The answer is emphatically, 'Yes, absolutely.' In a sports team the livelihoods of thousands of people do not rely on the outcome of winning and losing games! In the multinational company, in fact in any business, the outcome of winning or losing is far more important than in sport which is why I am always amazed that leaders generally make so little effort to get the quality of the people as right as possible. I am not making light of the fact that this is a very difficult endeavour especially in a company that employs thousands around the world. The challenges of changing the personnel profile of a large, established organisation are enormous but that is no reason not to embark on the journey. In some ways, for the right leader it is even easier in large organisations to start that journey because every day there will be people leaving and joining somewhere in the world. It is up to the leader to use their energy, enthusiasm and intelligence to ensure they get the people who can bring their vision to life. There is an aphorism that says 'Nothing worthwhile ever happened that did not have a passionate man at its centre'. What I see generally in organisations is that very few leaders have the driving passion for high performance that triggers the energy, stamina, attention to detail (the right details) and sheer persistence required to make it happen.

ORGANISATIONAL COMPLEXITY AND SELECTION

Start-up organisations and smaller, single-location entities will have far less compli-cated personnel situations than large organisations. In smaller companies of a few tens to a few hundreds of people, leaders will have a much easier task on their hands when it comes to recruiting and releasing people in their drive to reshape an organisation for high performance. Large organisations, especially multinational and global ones, are incredibly complex organisms. Figure 24 seeks to depict the prob-lems that an organisation faces when it comes to selecting and recruiting personnel.

Replicate this organisation structure in multiple locations around the world, each with its own local leaders and leadership teams and it can be seen that the selection process can become even more unwieldy and highly parochial. Regardless of the existing shape, size and complexity of their organisation leaders must get to grips with, and be involved in, setting the selection rules that will guarantee the quality of their people (and of course their development) if they wish to create a high-performing entity. From military memoirs and histories we often read how top-level commanders know their troops and their leaders to such a fine level of detail that they know who they can trust to lead the charge and who they can't. In the Second World War, Field Marshall Montgomery had 220,000 troops scattered across North Africa but still managed to have this fine level of knowledge as to their capability and therefore just what he could achieve with them.

Getting to grips with this challenge means having to address the detail of just what it is the leader and the organisation require at each level and in each area in order to achieve high performance. Of course this does not mean that top-level leadership will be interviewing junior-level staff. What it does mean is that top-level leadership must think about the requirements that the direction, strategies and goals of the organisa-tion create at all levels. Not only must they think about the requirements but they

Figure 24: Organisational complexity from a recruitment perspective.

must also stipulate in some detail what they require at each level in terms of the quality of the people being recruited. These requirements must be translated by the people experts in the organisation into very clear frameworks and guidelines that anyone undertaking a recruitment exercise is able to understand and apply. Recruitment ability and quality of personnel recruited could even become a performance appraisal item for key line managers.

This attention to detail with respect to the quality of staff and their ability to achieve high performance is not only about new staff coming into the organisation. If leaders do not assess and address the quality of existing staff then the impact of any high-talent recruiting policy will be reduced if poorly performing existing staff remain in place. This is a much more difficult area to deal with. Leaders must ensure that a robust and effective performance management system is in place that quickly and clearly identifies high, average and poorly performing staff in the existing workforce. The problem with most performance management systems is that they appraise on very narrow and very simple performance measures. The next chapter address these issues in more detail.

Regardless of the performance management system, what is required of leaders and the organisations they lead is the will to deal with poor performers and the support mechanisms to develop average performers upwards. Very few people in organisations are beyond redemption if their underlying motivators are identified.

As an example, some years ago, I inherited a salesman who was patently hopeless at selling. My sales director and I did everything to try to help him improve his performance. Appraisals (quarterly) proved to be difficult sessions: the salesman was adamant that he could turn things around while his boss kept saying he would have to get rid of him if he didn't. Understandably the salesman was an unhappy and stressed individual. At the eleventh hour a position came up in the proposals department that suited this salesman's background knowledge. He knew he was close to being fired when he was offered the new job on a six-month trial, but he still wanted to turn it down. He eventually took the new job and quite literally became a changed person and a star performer in the process.

Some time later he confided that he had hated sales, that having to go out and see customers on his own terrified him and that he had been stressed for a long time. His reasons for staying in this desperately unhappy role were numerous. They included fear of change and fear of what others might think. However, the worst aspect from the organisation's point of view was that because of his background in sales he thought he would only get another sales job so he might as well stay in the company he knew and where he had friends. So here we had a stressed, unhappy person, doing a job he hated, performing it badly and minimising the organisation's performance as well as his own. In the right role he flourished to a degree no one thought possible. The ability to identify such things is a skill and ability that should be integral in the people department of any organisation that seeks high performance.

THE PERFORMANCE TRIANGLE AND SELECTION

Regardless of the level, discipline or role that is being recruited for, the performance triangle provides a robust model or framework around which recruitment (and as we shall see later, even development) criteria can be built. This section sets out a few examples in order to show how the model might be used. First, it is useful by way of contrast to examine the more usual methods employed when setting out recruitment criteria. This will normally be little more than a job description that includes:

- description of the role
- who it reports to
- responsibilities of the role
- authority levels
- experience required
- qualifications required.

As shown above the responsibility for setting out all these elements usually remains with the person doing the recruiting and seldom has any hurdle heights imposed by the leadership deriving from the organisation's vision, strategy and top-level goal requirements. All of the elements described are targeted at the job itself, i.e. what is specifically required to perform the role and its tasks. Little or no account is taken of what other aspects might be required to drive the organisation towards high performance when carrying out this role.

Normal recruitment processes select with a focus on past experience and current competence and matches them against the requirements of the role. By comparison, recruiting for high performance selects not only on these traditional, role-based skills but also on personality traits, attributes, development potential, performance potential (in addition to basic role competences) which are all matched to the organisation's top-level drivers. This is a not-so-subtle difference. When driving to reshape an entity for high performance we are not seeking just to continue performing the existing roles competently and adequately. We are doing nothing less than seeking to change the DNA of that entity. At the risk of mangling the metaphor, to achieve this fundamental genetic change you have to work at the cellular level. Leaders cannot afford to leave such a critically important aspect to chance. They have to spell out very clearly what characteristics they want to see in their gene pool. Failure to work at the detail level could see the desired tiger turn out to be a domestic cat.

Whatever has to be changed or improved, whether it is, metaphorically, the organisation's intelligence quotient (IQ), emotional intelligence quotient (EQ), attributes, attitudes, skills or ability, it must be done. The only thing that may be negotiable is the time taken; but even this may be driven by external events. There must be significant rigour in any selection and recruitment process and there must a clear, explicit policy to improve the quality of the organisation's DNA across the board.

The performance triangle explained and detailed in Chapter 5 can be used as a framework to help make this happen. To do this we will look at the four main levels in the organisation:

- junior
- middle
- senior
- leadership.

Bear in mind that the following are purely example frameworks. Each organisation will need to decide which of the performance elements are important and at what levels, in relation to its particular direction, goals and strategies. In addition the tables setting out desired criteria will also vary significantly not just from organisation to organisation but role by role as well. Just like strategies, leaders will have different views on the things that are important to them and their organisation in the pursuit of high performance. In the tables below it is possible to argue that some attributes might be considered attitudes, or some attitudes might be abilities. In many respects I hope you are engaging in these thoughts as you read this section. It will mean that a questioning process is underway that recognises that at least the headings are relevant and it just comes down to personal preference and detail. Like all models nothing is prescriptive. Models need to be adapted to suit the needs of each organisation.

Junior-level recruitment

It is interesting to start at the junior level because in most organisations this attracts the least attention from the leadership. When did you last hear of a senior manager or a leader even checking to make sure that a receptionist was the best receptionist they could hire? Or that an apprentice starting on the shop floor was the best apprentice they could bring in to the organisation? And whoever checked to see if the person recruited fitted not just the job specification but had the attributes, attitude or other facets that matched the aspirations of the leadership and the company? Quite simply, if you don't start making changes at the bottom they will never happen at the top.

When recruiting at the junior level there is clearly a need for someone, usually the line manager or department head, to draw up a job specification that includes all the requirements of the role. For an organisation seeking to recruit the highest calibre personnel to help achieve its high-performance aspirations it must have a much more robust assessment and filtering process than just a job specification. Introducing the requirement to also assess applicants against the elements addressed by the performance triangle provides this robustness.

When recruiting for a junior role perhaps the two most important criteria are attributes and attitude. The rationale being that for someone at a junior level skills and ability will probably be minimal and in any event these will be areas that the organisation will want to develop. It will be far more important that the individuals have the right attributes and attitude qualities that fits the organisation's aspirations for high performance. See Figure 25.

Having drawn up a job description and decided that attributes and attitude are the two key aspects that are essential to match with the organisation's drive towards high performance we need to integrate them into a framework for selection. Table 8 sets out a sample template for how this might be done. It can been seen that there is a ranking of elements in order of their importance at this level.

You may well be questioning what goes where and which elements are really necessary. This is far less important than the fact that there is real recognition that every job or role has to be assessed and drawn up using a far broader and deeper set of assumptions than purely job description and responsibilities. Even if the organisation is too large for a leader to see what is happening at the junior levels it can be seen that top-level drivers can be included to help guide the process. However, even in a large organisation this would not be enough. The people department must be much more than just a pay and benefits, terms and conditions entity. If they are a real people and organisational development group they will have all the skills and abilities required to help anyone who is recruiting, at any level, in ways that are strategically linked and meet the organisational development and high-performance aspects required. This group would also be involved in the selection

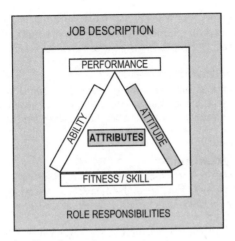

Figure 25: Junior-level requirements.

Table 8: Sample for junior-level recruitment characteristics

Job/role being assessed: Market Analyst			
Organisation requirements: • Organisation's vision: what it means at this level • Organisation's strategy/goal congruence statements and guidelines and impact on this role • Organisation's ethos/philosophy statements and guidelines and impact on this role			
1st: Attributes	2nd: Attitude	3rd: Skills (fitness)	4th: Ability
General/broad requirements			
High intrinsic motivation	Determined	People skills	To be developed
High self-esteem	Persistent	Organisational skills	
Above-average IQ	Enthusiastic	Communicates skills	
Above-average EQ			
Graduate-level education			
High energy			
Job/role specific requirements			
Interested in others	Drive to succeed	Statistical and analytical	Ability to cope with pressure
Self-starter	Desire to learn and improve	Presentational	Decision making
Self-disciplined	Ambitious	Time/deadline management	
Collaborative		Software/computing	

and interviewing process. As a result of their involvement the key attribute and attitude requirements could be formally tested (by internal staff) in addition to just relying on interviews.

In sporting terms, junior levels in organisations may be seen as being similar to the academy or development squads in most high-level team sports. If you fail to select the right starting talent and fail to give it the amount and quality of development attention it deserves you will fail to have the high quality 'feed stock' for the next levels of progression.

Middle-level recruitment

The middle-level roles in most organisations are the 'doing' roles. This is the level where most of the delivery activities of the organisation are achieved. It is perhaps the most critical area in which to get talent selection absolutely right.

When recruiting at the junior level there is clear recognition that with the right attributes and attitude there is time to develop the skills and abilities the organisation needs as well as enhancing the attributes and attitudes that made the candidates attractive in the first place. Thus it will be some time before junior levels are required to work at the coal face.

Conversely, in the senior roles there tends to be a movement away from the coal face. This is definitely the case for the top-level and leadership roles. It is the middle level that is firmly and squarely swinging the pick and getting the coal to the surface.

Consequently it can be argued that recruitment at the middle level of any organisation is the most important in terms of securing high performance in the day-to-day working of the company. It is the level where most business decision making takes place. These are not the large, strategic decisions but the high-volume, small decisions on which the organisation's lifeblood, its cash flow, usually depends. This middle level will usually also be the level of the organisation that has the most direct and most frequent contact with the external environment: customers, suppliers, regulators, etc. As a result, people recruited into this level must be able to hit the ground running. To do this those recruited will need to be assessed equally on all four aspects of the performance triangle. See Figure 26.

Table 9 below sets out how typical aspects of the performance triangle may be used with respect to recruitment at the middle management level. It can be seen that, in line with the arguments set out above, all aspects are equally important at this level.

Selecting and bringing in poor raw material will introduce a double weakness into the organisation. First it will dilute the existing talent pool. More importantly, the engagement of poor performers will be visible to those already in the organisation and if the situation is left unresolved the performance of those around the poor performer will degrade.

In sporting terms, the middle levels of an organisation can be seen as the backbone of high-performing teams: highly competent, high-ability athletes performing at the

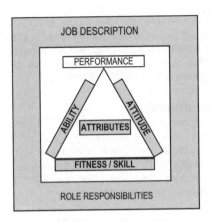

Figure 26: Middle-level requirements.

Table 9: Sample for middle-level recruitment characteristics

Job/role being assessed: Marketing Manager			
Organisation requirements: • Organisation's vision: what it means at this level • Organisation's strategy/goal congruence statements and guidelines and impact on this role • Organisation's ethos/philosophy statements and guidelines and impact on this role			
=1st: Attributes	=1st: Attitude	=1st: Skills (fitness)	=1st: Ability
General/broad requirements			
Task orientation	Persistence	Good organisational skills	Decision ability
Initiative taking	Enthusiastic	Good people skills	High functional ability
Leadership	Desire to succeed	High level of functional skills	Excellent planning ability
Collaborative	Passionate	High implementation skills	Ability to make things happen
Attention to detail			Ability to work under pressure
Job/role specific requirements			
Strong customer focus	Team player	Team building	Plan and organise tasks
Perfectionist traits	Completer/finisher	People/team motivation	Plan and organise people
Focused and driven	Accepts change	Good analytical skills	Source/synthesise information
Likes people		Good presentation skills	Ability to create 'intelligence'
Strong 'external' focus		Deadline management	Ability to manage change

top of their abilities and ensuring their team stays towards the top of the league. They may not be the star players in their team who are selected for international or Olympic competition but without them their team would be more likely to face relegation. Having a visibly poor performer in the team that the coach does nothing about is the fastest way to cause a team to disintegrate.

Senior-level recruitment

When selecting for senior roles, skills (fitness) and attributes should be a given and the focus will be on ability and attitude. How good and competent they are at executing in a senior role is critical but as important is their attitude. Anyone being considered for senior level roles must have the attitudes that are aligned with its high-performance culture and which create the drive and desire to continue delivering that performance. See Figure 27.

Too often in organisations the promotion to senior level is poorly managed, often by design. Quite often, promotion is a reward for long service. It is often the result of cronyism or an individual's skill at corporate politics. The reality is that the people at this level are in high-performance critical roles. They are the knowledgeable bridge between the leadership at the top and the 'delivering' middle. They have the high-functional experience that ensures the proper translation of top-level visions, missions and strategies into workable, functional strategies and plans that can be implemented in the reality of the workplace.

Those that are capable of moving from middle to senior levels must be able to demonstrate an ability to rapidly adapt their middle-level skills and how they are applied to a completely different requirement. They must also demonstrate a desire and ability to learn and add to their middle-level talents. It is not just the change from short-term, day-to-day functional thinking to longer-term tactical and strategic thinking; it is the requirement to develop the concrete from the abstract and to

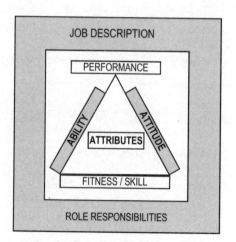

Figure 27: Senior-level requirements.

engage in elements of imagining futures and scenarios. It is the need to employ high levels of empathy, to understand where people's fears and concerns may derail otherwise brilliant plans and devise ways to allay and overcome those fears. Most importantly, senior levels must demonstrate high attention to detail (or use this ability in others) and have the energy, stamina and skill to ensure it is attended to.

It is at this senior level of organisations that the root causes of strategic failure lie. It is almost universally accepted that around two-thirds of all strategies fail and that they do so as a result of poor implementation. It is this senior level that is most closely associated with ensuring strategy implementation happens. This level is the one that bridges the gap between the top-level strategic thinking and the lower-level planning and doing. It is the level responsible for developing plans and implementation strategies that will align everyone in the organisation and for ensuring everyone works towards delivering the high performance the vision and top-level strategy seeks.

Table 10 sets out how the typical aspects of the performance triangle may be used with respect to recruitment at the senior management level. Again the ranking has changed to reflect the relative importance of the key elements of the performance triangle as it applies to this level.

In sporting terms senior-level people can be likened to the top-performing athletes and players in their teams. These are the ones who are able to use their experience to direct key elements of the team's performance and help less experienced team members to maintain performance especially under pressure. They are the star players in the team and are the ones selected for international duty.

Table 10: Sample for senior-level recruitment characteristics

Job/role being assessed: Head of Production			
Organisation requirements: • Organisation's vision: what it means at this level • Organisation's strategy/goal congruence statements and guidelines and impact on this role • Organisation's ethos/philosophy statements and guidelines and impact on this role			
=3rd: Attributes	2nd: Attitude	=3rd: Skills (fitness)	1st: Ability
General/broad requirements			
High order people skills	Energetic	High management skills	High order advocacy
Attention to detail	Persistent	High implementation skills	High ability to persuade
Attention to big picture	Resilient	High communication skills	Excellent storytelling ability
Good empathy			

Job/role specific requirements			
Decisive	Calm and considered	High functional knowledge	Turn strategy into plans
Innovative	Committed	Financial literacy	Ability to solve problems
Cool under pressure	Questioning	Strategic and tactical skills	Ability to simplify complexity
Inclusive/ collaborative	Embraces change	People skills	Ability to initiate change
		Relationship building	

Leadership-level recruitment

This is where things become both difficult and easy. When recruiting at the leadership level, e.g. at the board level or subsidiary company leader level, one should be able to assume that skills and ability are in place to a very high level (and are desirable ones for the organisation and the role being recruited for). This is the easy bit. For this level we are really back to what was important for the junior level roles and as we can see from Figure 28 these are attributes and attitudes. These are probably the most important aspects that someone in a leadership role can bring to the organisation. They must be able to set the tone for the organisation and set examples for everyone around them. It is the attributes and attitudes of leaders in everything they do, say or impart that will set the ethos and philosophy of the organisation and its followers. As has been well documented the most effective communication is via actions, symbols, behaviours and other forms of non-verbal

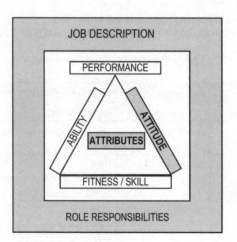

Figure 28: Leadership-level requirements.

communication. Leaders must exhibit the attributes and attitudes that will ensure all modes of communication signal high performance.

Table 11 sets out a ranking order for the aspects of the performance triangle required for leaders. It shows some of the high-order attributes, attitudes, skills and abilities leaders they will need to bring to the role.

Table 11: Sample for leadership-level recruitment characteristics

Job/role being assessed: **Chief Executive Officer**			
Organisation requirements: <ul><li>Organisation's vision: what it means at this level</li><li>Organisation's strategy/goal congruence statements and guidelines and impact on this role</li><li>Organisation's ethos/philosophy statements and guidelines and impact on this role</li></ul>			
1st: Attributes	2nd: Attitude	=3rd: Skills (fitness)	=3rd: Ability
General/broad requirements			
Confident and balanced	Perseverance	People skills	Ability to cope with ambiguity
Curious/questioning	Fearless	Relationship building	Ability grasp complexity
Embrace challenge/ adversity	Energetic	Financial literacy	Ability to synthesise solutions
Strong work ethic	Enthusiastic		Ability to create change
Reliability	Resilient		Balance detail and big picture
Disciplined			
Job/role specific requirements			
Gravitas/authority	Calculated risk-taker	Coach	Excellent storytelling
High stamina	Does not accept status quo	Mentor	Ability to solve problems
High order empathy	Opportunity seeking	Strategic and tactical skills	Ability to simplify complexity
External and internal focus	Committed	High advocacy skills	Ability to motivate
Visionary			Ability to lead
Positive outlook			

In sporting terms this role can only be compared to that of the coach except that in business the leadership role is significantly more complex. Nonetheless, as has been stated earlier, great leaders are generally also great coaches.

SUMMARY

When seeking to build a high-performance squad out of which to develop a top-performing team, coaches select exceedingly carefully. They are fully aware that they are about to embark on a significant and lengthy performance development programme. The amount of detail they go into, the amount of time they take and the amount of testing they do prior to any selection is immense. In all of my experiences with businesses I can categorically state that I have not seen a single one invest anything like the care, attention and time in recruiting across the organisation that coaches in sport take with their athletes.

Leaders can make the job of talent selection and development a great deal easier by putting in place a people department that has all the attributes, skills, abilities and attitude in itself that the leader desires for their people and organisation. This department must share the leader's vision and have the capability to make it happen. Even more than the operating departments, this people department must intimately understand, and be able to link, the organisation's visions, strategies, plans and programmes into effective frameworks that will guide talent selection and its development over the years. This department must be full of very bright, high-empathy, business-savvy individuals who like people. Without this support any leader will be unable to implement their vision and will fail to secure the performance he desires.

The ramifications in sport of success or failure is merely the addition or the loss of some silverware. In business, failure will certainly mean the loss of revenue and profits but it may lead to the loss of jobs and livelihoods or even the loss of the business. When the ramifications of failure are so important the casualness of the recruitment process and its lack of focus on securing high-performing talent that is in tune with the organisation's vision and direction should be of concern to any leader.

CHAPTER 10
TALENT DEVELOPMENT FOR
HIGH PERFORMANCE

There is a great desire in me on improving – getting better. That makes me happy! And every time I feel I am slowing down my learning process [or] my learning curve is getting flatter it doesn't make me feel very happy. And it applies not only as a professional, as a racing driver, but also as a man.
Ayrton Senna, triple World Champion, Formula 1

We have now arrived at probably the most interesting and most rewarding area for any great leader or coach. This is the development of the individuals, teams and groups for whom you are responsible. High performance can only be achieved by developing high-performance people. It is in the development and motivation of people that great leaders and great coaches lay the foundations for high-performance teams and organisations. What we are talking about is effectively the organisation's character. This character comprises all the people that make up that organisation and just like parents with children, leaders are fully responsible for the character of their organisation and its development. They are responsible for equipping it with the skills, abilities and attitudes that will see it become a highly successful entity. If it turns out to be delinquent it will be because of a failure in leadership.

This chapter assumes that the leader has created the right environment (Chapter 8), recruited the right type of people (Chapter 9) and has the leadership qualities (Chapter 13) to deliver their vision for the organisation. Given your own style, experiences and background you will probably already know how you want to shape the organisation to suit its particular character, its circumstances and the competitive pressures upon it. You will also recognise that this no easy endeavour. It is one that requires energy, persistence, stamina and drive. In addition, you must ensure that both the big picture and the minutiae of the details are fully covered. If you thought all these undertakings were tough they are as nothing when compared with the sustained effort and attention required to both setting the people and organisational development environment and ensuring it is constantly achieving all the things required of it.

LEADERS MAY SHAPE A BUSINESS BUT FOLLOWERS MAKE IT HAPPEN

I know leaders keep saying 'People are our greatest asset' but, when you examine the evidence, saying it is generally all they do. It may be obvious but it is worthwhile just looking at an example organisation in Figure 29 and reaffirming just why people are the greatest assets.

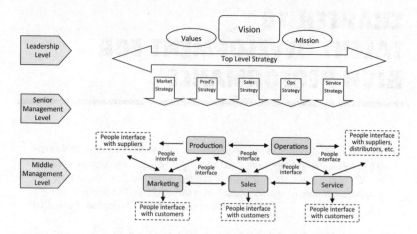

Figure 29: Leaders may shape a business, but followers make it happen.

Even in this highly simplified diagram it can be seen that it is the employees (the followers) that are dealing with the external world of customers, suppliers, distributors and partners; it is they who are doing the business and making the money. It is the employees who are dealing with each other internally and making things happen. And it is the employees who are solving the problems that four-year CEOs and other transitory leaders (with potentially limited domain knowledge) may not be equipped to solve. So even if leaders have accepted the ideas in previous chapters and selected the best talent to make up these people it will come to nothing if there is no people strategy to ensure they are developed in order to grow with the company's plans for achieving high performance.

There are two ways of developing and implementing a people strategy. The first is to hand down the top-level, vision-delivering, overarching strategy to the various functional executive directors and business leaders and leave them to translate the top-level strategy into individual functional strategies – including people strategies. The second is to use a top-level, cross-functional group to derive a coherent set of functional strategies – including a coherent, company-wide people strategy.

Many, arguably most, companies follow the first method with each functional head being allowed to interpret their own needs in their own way with perhaps only a check on headcount and budget from HR and finance. This means that all the problems of talent selection discussed in Chapter 9 are multiplied five or six times by each functional head (executive directors). They are then multiplied countless times by senior managers, department heads, etc. Sub-cultures and tribal proclivities can dilute the carefully selected gene pool even further. This dilution will accelerate over time as more and more people are poorly, or possibly idiosyncratically, developed by their line managers. It may also be that new people are recruited and developed under departmental processes that are less than rigorous in terms of cohesive and coherent ideas of exactly what is required across the organisation.

The second method requires much greater discipline to implement and it also needs good oversight by the leader. A top-level, cross-functional group is used to develop an organisation-wide people strategy. This same group is then used to develop the broad thrust of the people strategy for each functional area while ensuring it remains coherent with the overarching organisation-wide strategy. Leaders must be closely engaged if they want to ensure that the development of the talent in the organisation adheres to the precepts required by the high-performance vision. I hope it is obvious that there are two levels to this people development strategy:

- the organisational level
- the individual level.

While there is always some latitude in how development is achieved at the level of the individual, at the level of the organisation the plan must be highly structured and detailed. The core thrusts of how, where and when talent is developed must not only be planned over time but it must be monitored closely for both implementation success and for desired performance increases. This last element of monitoring is critical. Without monitoring and measuring outcomes it will be impossible to check for success or make adjustments to prevent failure.

WHY TALENT DEVELOPMENT IS A CORNERSTONE FOR HIGH PERFORMANCE

Designing and running an organisation-wide development programme is like painting the Forth Bridge: it is never-ending. Coaches in sport start out with a long-term development framework and then, from the results and feedback from continual testing, will constantly adjust the programmes to get the best out of the wide variety of athletes in their squads. In addition, the best coaches are continually monitoring the latest trends and ideas in sport and sport science to see what improvements can be made to their development programme. They do not just monitor their own sport but will see what is happening in other sports and indeed in the performance world outside of sport. Leaders who desire high performance in their organisations must be no less committed to excellence in their development programmes than top-level coaches in sport. There is, however, a major difference between a leader and a coach in this respect. A coach is normally responsible for a single team and the squad of athletes that feeds it. The coach is not responsible for the whole club or all the other athletes, teams and squads within it. The leader of an organisation is very definitely responsible for everything that makes up their 'club'. Consequently, the leader's world is vastly more complex than that of the coach.

In terms of people development the leader is absolutely responsible for making sure that the development process energises the people in the organisation and produces the broadly desired, not just the narrowly needed, skills and abilities. The leader must also be forward-thinking enough to be shaping the people development environment not just to meet the current requirements but to meet those future needs required by their vision. He is also responsible for inculcating the right attitudes – the ethos and philosophy – by which the company is to be guided.

This aspect of development guidance and governance is critically important when seeking to design a people and organisational development programme over many years in line with a vision and long-term direction. One of the useful aspects of the performance triangle is its ability to encapsulate what it is a leader is trying to do when developing the performance aspects of an organisation. The model relates just as well to groups, departments, divisions or regions within an organisation in addition to all of the individuals or teams and groups that make up these various entities. Figure 30 demonstrates how the triangle can be used to show this representation in simple, outline terms. Clearly organisations are much more complex than this simple diagrammatical representation but more detail can be included as and where useful.

Regardless of how the people and organisation development plan is articulated, all good leaders must have a clear understanding of the individual elements that make up their organisation and where problems and tensions are likely to arise.

The starting place for all people and organisational development is the creation of a top-level development requirement and its associated delivery programme. This must be inextricably linked with the direction the leader wants to take the company in. This vision and direction is what simultaneously both harnesses and drives the organisation's strategies and objectives. Until all of these vision and direction elements are clear and set out in some detail it will be impossible to design a people and organisational development programme that is cohesive and has coherence over the long term. Without a plan, without coherence and without clear linkage to the long-term aims of the entity it will not be possible to achieve development for high performance.

What often happens is that organisations are driven to produce financially focused plans: operating budgets, headcount requirements, capital expenditure plans, etc. What they often end up with is a year-by-year (even quarter-by-quarter) finance

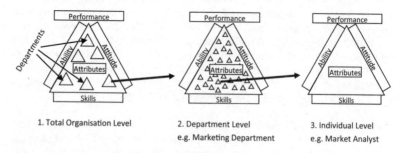

1. Total Organisation Level

2. Department Level
e.g. Marketing Department

3. Individual Level
e.g. Market Analyst

Figure 30: Organisational development path: organisation-, department- and individual-level performance triangles.

department driven plan providing financial targets that so many firms call 'perform-ance management'. There is nothing wrong with financial targets so long as they are not mistaken for performance targets, as they relate to the goal of seeking true high performance to meet the long-term aspirations and positioning of the organisation. Growth, product (or service) innovation, revenue, profit and customer delight all derive from the actions and competences of people with excellent domain knowl-edge doing things better, faster, cleverer, with fewer errors, etc. These are all people-centric activities and this is the real world for organisations. Spreadsheets, figures, financial manipulation, creative accounting, analyst briefings, etc. do not affect this real world of the organisation nor do they improve real-world perform-ance. This is done by great leaders committing to developing already good people into excellent ones, thereby turning average entities into high-performing organisations.

PUSHING THE BOUNDARIES: ACHIEVING STRETCH IN TALENT DEVELOPMENT

While the model in Figures 31, showing the organisational development path, can clearly be used to guide not just individual development but that of groups, depart-ments, divisions and indeed whole companies, it does not help in understanding what that development should be. In this respect, Figure 32: Development and per-formance thresholds, shows in simple graphical terms what it is that people and organisational development programmes are seeking to achieve. In terms of organi-sations it can be seen that even for an average-performing entity there are mini-mum organisational thresholds of attributes, skills, abilities and attitudes that are required to enable the organisation to survive in its market. If an average company

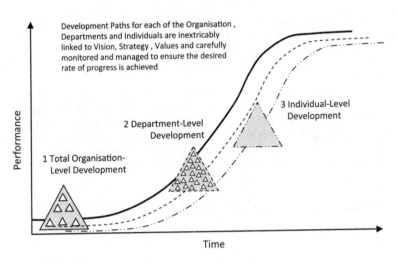

Figure 31: Organisational development path for organisations, departments and individuals.

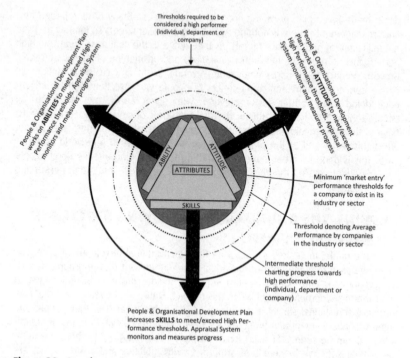

Thresholds required to be considered a high performer (individual, department or company)

People & Organisational Development Plan works on **ABILITIES** to meet/exceed High Performance thresholds. Appraisal System monitors and measures progress

People & Organisational Development Plan works on **ATTITUDES** to meet/exceed High Performance thresholds. Appraisal System monitors and measures progress

ABILITY

ATTITUDE

ATTRIBUTES

SKILLS

Minimum 'market entry' performance thresholds for a company to exist in its industry or sector

Threshold denoting Average Performance by companies in the industry or sector

Intermediate threshold charting progress towards high performance (individual, department or company)

People & Organisational Development Plan increases **SKILLS** to meet/exceed High Performance thresholds. Appraisal System monitors and measures progress

Figure 32: Development and performance thresholds: the organisation's character.

has an idea of what skills, abilities and attitudes are required just to meet the market survival thresholds then the enlightened leader, with their clear vision of the future, should have a clear view (albeit mainly top level) of what development is required in order to become a high-performance organisation.

Most firms in an industry or sector will operate at or slightly above that minimum threshold, which may be assumed to be the threshold of average performance that has been referred to many times in this book. Very few firms move beyond average, and of these even fewer move beyond good. This book and this chapter in particular are about how to move individuals and whole companies beyond good and into the high-performance thresholds. The next section effectively combines Figures 30 and 31 with Figure 32, as shown below in Figure 33.

A PROGRAMME FOR PEOPLE AND ORGANISATIONAL DEVELOPMENT

Where does developing for high performance start? The impetus to move from the current position to a new and hopefully better one is the leader's vision. Without a leader with a clear view about where they want the organisation to be in the future (and having the power to make it happen) any vision becomes little more than a

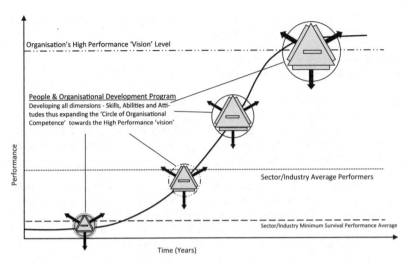

Performance

Organisation's High Performance 'Vision' Level

People & Organisational Development Program
Developing all dimensions - Skills, Abilities and Atti-
tudes thus expanding the 'Circle of Organisational
Competence' towards the High Performance 'vision'

Sector/Industry Average Performers

Sector/Industry Minimum Survival Performance Average

Time (Years)

Figure 33: People and organisational development: expanding the competence thresholds over time.

dream. I know that many people dislike the term 'vision' and frequently use words such as direction, long-term goals or objectives. The reality is that the terminology is far less important than the articulation and translation of the long-term vision or direction into concrete, definable and executable elements. It is these elements that can form the basis of measurable plans and programmes. With reference to people this means an organisational development programme (PODP).

It is also clear that the main components of the PODP are the attributes, skills, abilities and attitude that the organisation embodies and manifests, i.e. its organisational character and its competence in the industry in which it competes. We also know that this organisational character derives from the combination of the attributes, skills, abilities and attitudes of all the people who comprise that organisation. The aim of the PODP is to set out what the organisational character must look like (some defined number of years in the future) to deliver the leader's vision of the high-performance organisation. Top athletes develop strong mental powers and use powerful imagery to envision their futures. Leaders must be able to do the same. With this future vision held firmly in mind the hard graft of working backwards to the current position can start. This requires the detailing of every aspect of the organisation's character (skills, abilities and attitudes) in order to clearly set out what must be developed in each area and by when, to move the organisation in the direction of high performance. The PODP is much more than the skills gap analysis undertaken by most HR departments in average organisations. It must be inextricably linked to the long-term vision and strategy. It must be absolutely coherent with all the phases and timing of that strategy. It must be highly detailed and through that detailing, able to be closely monitored.

This is not easy. To be even more accurate, this is extremely difficult for almost all organisations. It is difficult for two reasons:

1. it is hard, grinding, detailed work
2. it is intellectually highly demanding.

This is good news because if it were easy all your competitors would be able to do it. It is important to note that while strategic thinking is fun and often excitingly intellectual, at some point in time it must devolve into the sheer hard work of developing a strategy, its associated plans and the implementation regimes required to make them happen.

Sadly, even in those cases where a leader does have a vision and a desire to develop their most important assets, what generally happens is that a broad and often poorly articulated requirement is communicated to the HR director or manager and the leader entrusts the detailed development of the people plan to HR. From both my personal experience and that related by many other senior people I speak to, the modern HR departments are primarily pay and rations organisations designed almost exclusively to 'keep the troops fed, watered and disciplined and the leaders out of trouble with employment legislation'. What is required for a true POPD is high-order strategic competence, intimate business knowledge and experience, detailed knowledge of organisations and outstanding people knowledge, skill and empathy. Last is the need for brilliant planning abilities with strong future orientations.

Developing the people and organisational development plan
The following steps are required to develop a PODP.

1. Translate the high-performance vision into a clear idea of what the organisation will look like when the vision is achieved
2. Identify what competences it will need to exhibit at that future time as a high-performance entity.
3. Break down the overall competence requirements, identify and detail what these mean in terms of the attributes, skills, abilities and attitudes (and numbers) to meet this future vision.
4. Analyse what attributes, skills, abilities and attitudes the organisation has currently, and identify and detail the shortfalls.
5. Develop a detailed plan that is time-phased and that details the competences required by the end of each phase and the resources required to deliver the plan.

While this list may on the surface look quite straightforward it is in fact extremely complex. When we use the words 'identify' and 'detail' we are disguising a vast amount of work. The people, their roles and the attributes, skills, abilities and attitudes required for each role in every part of the organisation need to be analysed, detailed and measured in terms of the existing requirements versus the requirements of the vision. Even the organisation's structure itself must be examined to see if it is fit for purpose in relation to the vision.

This may best be shown through the use of an example. Let us say that the vision requires an organisation that is currently a national one to expand its existing activities internationally and grow the business threefold in seven years. The first thing that is required for developing any element of the organisation's strategy is to break down the vision into more detail and thus more clarity. What does 'international' mean? Is it all countries around the world or is it more targeted, for example a few specific countries in north-west Europe or the BRIC nations (Brazil, Russia, India and China)? What does 'grow the business threefold in seven years mean'? Is it revenue, profit (and what type of profit?), market share and product volume? Is it perhaps new business growth? Until the vision is turned into concrete elements and clarity achieved as to what things mean, developing a high-performance strategy cannot begin. So, let's assume 'international' means north-west Europe focusing on France and Germany and that threefold growth means both revenue and operating profit at an agreed ratio. Even in this very simple scenario it may be seen that the attributes, skills, abilities and attitudes of the organisation are going to require significant attention at all levels and in all departments. It is also likely that staff numbers are going to increase dramatically.

At this stage a considerable degree of discussion, imagination, open-mindedness, scenario planning and any other form of envisioning the future organisation should occur. It is important at this juncture to obtain the best picture possible of what the organisation might look and feel like in the future when the 'trebling-size' vision is realised. It is also critically important to recognise that whatever scenario the group charged with this task comes up with it will be wrong. The future never works out as we envision! But this must not stop leaders who seek high performance from at least trying to get a best approximation of their destination before rushing into detailed strategies and plans to get them there. Just selecting the group of people charged with undertaking this exercise is a crucial responsibility for the leader. If this group is not open-minded, intellectually bright with broad interests and knowledge, honest and rigorous in its approach and subsequent analysis, it will fail to develop the richness from which good strategic options can be developed. Once this initial picture of the future organisation is developed its competence thresholds (attributes, skills, abilities, attitudes, even the number of people it requires) can be approximated.

Starting with the leadership team, questions can be asked about what is required at this level to become a high-performance organisation working in France and Germany and at three times the size of the current organisation. For example does the CEO have to be multilingual? Do marketing and sales directors need to be multilingual and/or local nationals? What level of knowledge of import and export issues must the operations director be aware of? What knowledge must the technical director have of differing and local regulations and standards? How commercially and financially aware does the leadership team need to be for a transnational organisation three times its current size? How will risks to the organisation change and how well equipped are the leadership team to deal with them? What will rapid growth do to quality? And so on. The questions and analysis can become and should become detailed. In addition, the questions and the analysis have to drill down level by level, department by department. It is from this detail that the difference between what the organisation can do now and what it must be able to do in seven years' time can be derived.

Once the future picture has been detailed (however fuzzy some might think that to be) and the current situation assessed against that future then constructing the PODP can begin in earnest.

SUMMARY

In many respects what this chapter discusses is not particularly new. You can hear in most organisations variations on the following theme 'Where are we now?', 'Where do we want to get to?', 'How do we get there?', 'Let's carry out a gap analysis and see what we need to do to make the journey'. The problem is that much of the thinking work that goes into deriving the answers is not translated into the hard, detailed work from which strategies and plans are drawn up. Even if it is brilliantly translated into great strategies and plans it often seems difficult, even impossible, for organisations to control the strategic process over the time spans required – even where the CEO remains for longer than the average four years. There are myriad statistics from learned institutions about the success rates of corporate strategies. The generally quoted figure is that approximately 70% of all strategies fail to achieve their objectives or desired outcomes. The reasons most frequently cited for this are: a failure to align the organisation to the strategy, a failure to have the mechanisms in place to monitor and measure implementation over time and a failure to make the necessary adjustments such feedback may require.

There is another reason and that is 'leadership fatigue' or, in its worst form, 'leadership boredom'. As I have said before, being a high-performance and successful organisation requires sustained effort, energy and stamina over the long term from its leaders. A year or two into a programme (sometimes even just a few months) the excitement and the novelty wear off. Keeping all the strands of a high-performance programme on the rails is sheer hard work. Many of today's leaders prefer the excitement and the buzz of strategic thinking rather than the effort of strategic doing.

I have worked with a number of organisations, some very large and global, with what, on the surface, have appeared to be very sophisticated people appraisal and development systems and processes. However, I have not seen a single appraisal and development system that is coherent over the long term or tied into a clearly articulated long-term vision and direction. Once a POPD is agreed the next problem becomes one of making it happen and monitoring its success. This is the province of measurement and appraisal – otherwise known as performance management – and is covered next.

CHAPTER 11
INTERNAL MEASUREMENT
FOR HIGH PERFORMANCE:
THE PERFORMANCE APPRAISAL
SYSTEM

A high wage will not elicit effective work from those who feel outcasts and slaves, nor a low one preclude it from those who feel themselves an integral part of a community of free men. Thus the improvement of this element of the supply of labour is an infinitely more complex and arduous task than if it depended on wage alone.
**Sir Dennis Holme Robertson, 1921, Economist,
Cambridge and London Universities**

Appraisal systems in organisations are rarely universally liked or applauded as being useful or fair. Leaders and leadership teams often see them as a tiresome but necessary process to show they care and (more honestly) as a mechanism to apportion rewards. Most line managers see them as a hugely demanding, time-wasting exercise that is often flawed. Employees also often see the process as flawed, open to abuse and bias, unfair and failing to address poor performers.

Despite this almost universal antipathy towards performance appraisal systems across organisations they remain the performance-driving tool most relied upon by substantial organisations.

While it is impossible (and even unhealthy) to be prescriptive when addressing performance appraisal systems, this chapter seeks to examine why and where modern day systems are weak. It also identifies those areas and elements that can make such systems more properly and effectively the drivers of high performance.

AN OVERVIEW OF REWARDS AND PERFORMANCE
Since the previous chapter has discussed the development of high-performance talent it would be quite natural to move directly into discussions about how to measure and appraise just how well that talent is improving and meeting the aspirations of the high-performance organisation. Certainly the measuring and appraising elements are very normal and usual activities in organisations, even though, as this chapter will explain, they are rarely undertaken rigorously or well. However, before moving on to such detail I would like to place a few questions in your minds.

- If your organisation has an appraisal system what is its primary function?
- If your organisation employs rewards (and by default punishes by withholding such rewards) as the primary means of talent motivation what evidence do you have that the rewards are achieving what was intended?
- Is your performance management system seeking to promote questioning, challenging, learning, initiative taking, innovating behaviour that constantly challenges the status quo; or is it merely seeking compliance and the meeting of objectives?
- If you were to list the long-term goals you would have for your people (what you would want them to be able to do, what you would want them to be like, how you would like them to behave, what values you would like them to have, etc.), how closely will that list match the aspects and elements included in your appraisal system?
- How closely would that same list match the vision, direction and aspirations of the organisation itself?
- When was the last time you read the latest thinking on the theory of measurement and reward systems?

None of these questions are flippant, especially the last one. Alfie Kohn in his 1999 book *Punished by Rewards* puts it thus:

> There is a time to admire the grace and persuasive power of an influential idea, and there's a time to fear its hold over us. The time to worry is when the idea is so widely shared that we no longer even notice it, when it is so deeply rooted that it feels to us like plain common sense.

I mention this because there is a large body of work that does not just question the theory of carrot and stick type rewards but believes them to be counterproductive.

Hopefully the following interesting experiment will spur your interest in the subject of rewards. In 1962, Sam Gluxberg, Professor of Psychology at Princeton University, worked with MBA students using the Candle Problem. Originally developed by psychologist Karl Duncker as a cognitive performance test to measure functional fixedness, the candle problem provides participants with a box of thumbtacks, a candle and a book of matches. Using only these three items the task is simply to fix the candle to a wall above a table so as to ensure no wax drops onto the table when the candle is lit. Gluxberg took this problem a stage further. He divided his test subjects into two groups. To each participant in one group he explained that he was trying to develop an experiment to apply to various problems and was seeking to establish norms for the time it took to solve the problem. He said that he was asking for their help to set these benchmark norms. To the individuals in the other group he said that depending on how fast you can solve the problem you will win money: if you come within the top 25% you will win $40, if you get the fastest time you will win $80. In a test where the fastest solution is only a matter of a few minutes the group working for money were on average three and half minutes slower than the group working to help provide norms.

Now this simple experiment clearly does not provide proof positive that extrinsic rewards always result in poor performance. What it certainly does show is that people's motivations are very complex and that there is a question mark over extrinsic rewards as triggers for both motivation and the achievement of high performance. There is a great deal of published work on the theory of rewards and what is clear is that simple extrinsic rewards (such as bonuses, exotic holidays or material goods) do not lead to the highest levels of performance. More worryingly, rewards, especially high ones, often lead to highly undesirable behaviours. What rewards tend to produce is compliance. In terms of objectives they will at best drive people to meet the objectives but little more. At worst they can create an adverse climate causing objectives not to be met. Even where the rewards are very high and structured to make people continue stretching to meet ever higher objectives, i.e. larger rewards for greater results, it predominantly results in performance behaviour that is good for the individual or the narrow interest group but detrimental to the long-term health (and sustained high performance) of the whole organisation. Think of mercenaries (i.e. those motivated by desire for material gain, even greed) in almost any form of endeavour. They perform primarily as individuals and any group cooperation has to be 'bought' by further rewards. Mercenary groups are notoriously difficult to manage, rarely achieve the highest possible performance and often fall apart under real competitive pressure.

With all the above thoughts in mind we can now look at performance management systems with what I hope is a more enlightened and healthy view.

A CRITICAL LOOK AT PERFORMANCE APPRAISAL SYSTEMS

This section takes a different look at the traditional performance management or appraisal system and shows how it can more effectively be designed and used to help obtain high performance. All the time we are discussing the design of performance management or appraisal systems I would ask you to bear in mind the questions asked at the beginning of this chapter. The best systems and certainly those that help develop high-performance individuals are not about carrot and stick and mere compliance. They genuinely seek to provide a solid platform for the development of the individual, albeit in ways that ensure such development is in line with the organisation's aspirations and direction of travel. An important aspect of the well-designed system is that it also highlights extremely quickly when the aspirations of the organisation and the individual are no longer aligned.

You will remember that in the previous chapter we discussed the ways in which the competence thresholds of the organisation need to be developed to meet the positioning requirements of the vision or future view of that organisation. You will also remember that this can only be achieved by developing the individuals, groups and teams that comprise that organisation over that same time span. The top-level people and organisational development plan (PODP) introduced in Chapter 10 guides the more detailed, functional-level, process and performance plans that will have been developed at the same time as the POPD. These business unit and department-level plans are critical in order to make strategy happen and ensure it does so in the right ways and in the right time scales. Making it happen is not some magical alchemy jealously guarded by a few arcane practitioners in the bowels of the organisation. Making it happen devolves to all the people – the very same people who have been so carefully selected to deliver this organisation's aspirations of high performance. The key performance device that ensures the successful development of this talent is in line with the vision and the strategy is the performance management system – more generally known as the appraisal system or performance appraisal.

There are probably as many performance management or appraisal systems around as there are organisations. They range from the ad hoc, unwritten and informal through to the very sophisticated and slick consultancy-provided frameworks. This book does not provide a prescriptive framework for developing such systems. In reality, developing people and assessing how they develop is a very human and personal activity. No matter how it is prescribed or managed by an organisation's system it is, at its most fundamental level, about people talking and listening to each other in intelligent ways and striving to create a learning environment. As a result any system, no matter how sophisticated it may look, will have all the strengths and weaknesses that human beings will bring to such a highly interpersonal activity if it is not constructed very carefully.

I have looked at many performance management systems and most try to address the usual elements you would expect, such as the following.

■ The formalisation and documented review of employee performance.
■ Employee performance measured against some previously derived objectives.
■ Monitoring/measuring the value or worth of employees.
■ Monitoring/measuring the potential of employees.
■ A system used to encourage and motivate the employees.
■ A system that may be used to determine employee rewards (and more rarely, employee termination).

An appraisal system is usually linked to some overall HR plan. What these narrow appraisal systems rarely do is include all the elements that will help ensure the development of individuals (and thus the organisation) into high-performance ones. In broad terms, the elements that need to be addressed can be described in the following three ways.

1. The organisation's culture: the effects and impacts of the organisation's past history projected into the present

We have already seen that organisations have a character or personality partly derived from their history and past experiences. This is otherwise known as its organisational culture. Failure to develop an appraisal system that takes account of key aspects of an organisation's character (and the impact on it of its future ambitions) will create tensions at odds with securing high performance. This is in no way suggesting the culture cannot be changed. Often a new direction and its associated strategies and plans absolutely require it to change. What is important is that the culture is understood and account taken of it, especially in the early period of introducing a new approach to achieving high performance.

As an example, take a highly bureaucratic, risk-averse, rule- and procedure-driven, state-owned monopoly. Suddenly, asking people to use their initiative, take big decisions and be measured on them is not only going to be counterproductive; it will stress people significantly and probably lead to lots of decisions that are dangerous to the health of the entity.

Performance management systems must harness the character of the organisation, at least initially.

2. Current organisational behaviour: how it looks and feels to the outside world

It is often stated that organisations reflect their leaders and this is true in many respects. However, as far as those coming into contact with the people carrying out the day-to-day activities of the organisation, i.e. customers and suppliers, it is the character and behaviour of the employees that dictates how the organisation looks and feels to the outside world. The influence of employees combines with that of the leader to create the personification of the organisation's character.

If you have selected the talent in your organisation for high performance they will expect to have clear and demanding personal development programmes. They will want (and expect) to be monitored and measured – how else will they know they are progressing? As importantly, they will want their leaders to know they are developing. Most importantly, they will want the external environment, e.g. customers and competitors, to know they are good at what they do. It is likely these will be predominantly highly intrinsically motivated individuals. Their desire to improve over time will come from them knowing they have done and are continuing to do well. In sport this is easy to measure. In business it is difficult but it must be achieved if you are not to lose these types of people.

3. The 'something else' that harness desires and aspirations: ethos and future ambition

The journey towards high performance is a tough one and it is first and foremost the power of the vision, and its transmission with utmost clarity to the followers, that will provide the harnessing power. However, without 'something else' this vision could be achieved in ways that are thoroughly unpleasant at best and criminal at worst. We have only to look at the banking sector, journalism or politics today for examples of this. All the corporate governance codes in the world have not prevented bad leaders doing bad things and contaminating their people with their disease.

Thus, the 'something else' is the core ethos or guiding philosophy by which the leader wishes to achieve their vision. Even though it may be the leader's core ethos and philosophy, if it is too far removed from the existing character of the organisation it will be doomed to failure. In such cases good and astute leaders will understand the situation and adapt. They may adjust the vision's strategy in the early years or adjust its timescales and thus take more time to alter the character (culture) to increase the chances of eventual success of the vision.

With these three elements in mind, what the best high-performance appraisal systems manage to achieve is the combining of the character of the organisation with the needs of the followers (the organisation's talent) and harmonising them with the requirements of the leader's vision, and the direction and the strategies that they generate. Elements critical to this type of high-performance development that should be included in an appraisal system in addition to the more usual ones cited above are:

- direct and integrated linkage with the top-level vision
- direct and integrated linkage with the top-level strategy
- direct and integrated linkage with the organisation's ethos, philosophy and values
- the explicit reference and inclusion of the element of development over time, i.e. linkage with the timescale of the vision
- the development of organisation-wide 'goal congruence' and 'one tribe ethos' – link objectives across functions, departments, etc. to encourage cooperation
- statements from each individual, agreed with superiors, of their personal aspirations, and how they intend to commit to them and over what period they expect to make them happen.

CONSTRUCTING A PERFORMANCE MANAGEMENT/ PERFORMANCE APPRAISAL SYSTEM

With all the above in mind the question is how does one construct a performance appraisal system that ensures all these hard and soft, immediate and future-oriented elements are captured in ways that invigorate the organisation and its people and helps drive high performance? It makes no sense to be prescriptive with respect to this question. Organisations are dynamic entities and any appraisal system must reflect the organisation it serves. However, I believe there are some very basic building block requirements that must always be taken into account – Figure 34 sets these out in diagrammatic form.

With the introduction of the concepts raised in this diagram it is worth making a few comments on where the main differences may be between the average and the high-performance appraisal system.

The first is that the vision, together with the strategy and ethos it drives, are all included in the appraisal system. On every individual's appraisal form there should be clear guiding statements as to what the vision is, the top-level strategies it is driving and the ethos that the company wishes to embody. The statements around these top-level elements should be crafted to provide the anchoring tenets of the more detailed elements of the appraisal system.

While the vision is often a bit of a 'motherhood and apple pie' view of the future, the strategy and ethos elements are very real and hard edged, even at the top level of the organisation. It is these elements that are translated into the lower-level strategies, plans, values and behaviours that all combine to deliver the long-term direction and goals embodied in the overarching vision. It is the skill, breadth, depth and detail with which these top-level elements are translated into lower-level strategies, plans and codes of conduct that will help provide the glue for the organisation – how it does business, how its people reflect its philosophy to the outside worlds (and to each other) and how they develop towards high performance.

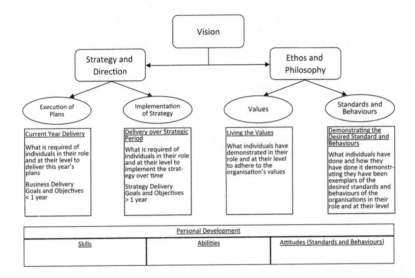

Figure 34: Performance appraisal system: building blocks.

Execution of plans (<one year)

Most average appraisal systems focus almost exclusively on the execution of plans. This element is by far the easiest from which to extract measurable objectives and thereby provide people with hard, succeed or fail types of goals that suit many managers. The reason it is easy is because plans tend to be those elements drawn from strategies for implementation in the current year. They form part of the finance/business plan for the year, which in most organisations is the only driver for top-level and organisation-wide performance. Focusing almost exclusively on such short-term elements will not only fail to achieve high performance – it will ultimately ensure average performance as followers come to recognise that:

■ there is only an interest in short-term results
■ there is little or no recognition for accepting short-term performance 'misses' for a much greater long-term gain
■ average performance secures some rewards and that above-average performance often does not secure commensurately greater rewards.

There is nothing intrinsically wrong with the use of short-term, well-defined targets and goals, provided they are combined with all the other elements that are critical for high performance sustained over the long term.

Implementation of strategy (>one year)

It is extremely rare to see included in the average appraisal system long-term objectives, complete with adequate measures that:

- let people know that implementation and execution of strategies and plans over the long term is crucial and of importance to the organisation
- derive meaningful implementation objectives from the longer-term strategies and plans
- put in place meaningful recognition factors that drive the desire to achieve the best implementation and execution of longer term strategic plans.

Having a system that successfully manages these elements can have a number of beneficial effects other than driving high performance. Demonstrating commitment to strategies and plans for the future and tying individual performance into them can generate those things that followers need, i.e. senses of purpose, belonging and excitement. Tying recognition (even rewards) into performance over time can help with employee retention, which is crucial if you have gone to all the trouble to select high-performing talent. And the most obvious of all: if your whole organisation is tied into longer-term performance objectives then your strategies have a better chance of succeeding and not being consigned to the 70% that generally fail. High performance would not be far behind if all of these were achieved.

Values

The value of values is covered in some detail in Chapter 8. A few average appraisal systems may include some references to values. In almost all cases an organisation's values are statements made up by the leader or their top team, primarily for external show. As such they are little more than a few marketing slogans handed down to the followers. If this is how an organisation's values have been created then they generally have little meaning for the followers and become elements to which only lip service is paid. In such cases making them part of the appraisal system will have no effect. However, where values are real and meaningful to all in the organisation then they must be explicitly and expressly included. Linking specific values with objectives (both short- and long-term) and standards and behaviours will have a significant impact in the following ways:

- have a harnessing effect on everyone's efforts, bringing cohesion and a one-tribe approach to all that is done
- bring a quality approach to everything that is done as people take pride in what they do and how they do it
- strengthen the requirements of the role for each individual and build people's levels of responsibility in their roles
- strengthen initiative taking, decision making and support at all levels and across all functions in the organisation.

This values list looks at values as they affect appraisal systems. Chapter 8 provides more detail on just how and why they can be such powerful mechanisms for high performance if constructed in conjunction with the involvement and support of followers.

Standards and behaviours

The ethos and philosophy elements of the leader and their vision are crucial for deriving the standards and behaviours that not only the leader desires but that the organisation should embody. In terms of the appraisal system these can be translated into very clear requirements and guidelines around roles at every level of the organisation. The standards can be included along the lines of the 'what' is required of each role and at each level. The behaviours can be translated as the 'how' or the manner in which the roles and their standards will be undertaken and delivered.

I have only ever seen one appraisal system that came even close to incorporating most of the elements shown in Figure 34. All elements were written down, articulated in appraisal discussions and, most importantly, they were able to be rated on a meaningful scale. Not unsurprisingly that company was a market leader in its field and had been for some decades.

APPRAISAL SYSTEMS: PROBLEMS WITH RATINGS AND SCORING

This is an area where there is a huge body of research which, among other things, indicates the following.

People giving appraisals unconsciously apply a range of psychological biases

Leniency errors, halo effects, affective reactions, attribution bias, stereotyping, recency bias, personal effect and many others have an impact that skews the rating or scoring of one individual over another that may have little to do with their actual performance.

Most people intrinsically dislike differentiating between people

Michael Beer, Professor of Business Administration, Emeritus at the Harvard Business School, argues:

> Managers do not want to differentiate and no system will be successful in making them do it. Managers understand that to make [distinctions between employees] will create several problems ... When managers are forced to make them, as they are when asked to award a merit increase, they rate everyone on the high side. That is because they do not want to damage an employee's self esteem, thereby demotivating the employee.

Scoring is problematic

Scoring a) marks lower than average people upwards, and b) shows a bias where the proportion of higher than average scores is always higher than the proportion of lower than average scores.

In a series of studies of 7,000 employees of pharmaceutical company Merck it was found that over 95% of the sample were marked as average or just above average and that 3.7% were scored as well above average but only 1.3% were marked as below average.

The inference is that a) people producing below-average performance are hidden by the biases, and b) that the overall performance of an organisation's people is inaccurately being portrayed as better than it is.

Culture affects scoring

In a number of multinational organisations I have worked with, the effect of cultural bias in appraisal system scoring is clearly evident. Real-life examples are that in Japan giving and/or receiving very high scores to individuals may be considered culturally difficult and embarrassing, whereas in the USA receiving average or below-average scores is deemed completely unacceptable by the person receiving them. In one particular multinational organisation the appraisal rating for every individual in the US divisions was above average. When these scores were attempted to be 'normalised' in line with the rest of the global organisation there was uproar from the US divisions.

The real problem is that the employees themselves know exactly what is happening. Real, daily performance is not hidden from them. Poor performers generally know that they are poor performers. More damagingly, high performers know who the low performers are and that they are not being properly identified and addressed.

Since performance management systems cannot get away from some form of rating in scoring it is critically important that these issues are addressed as far as is possible and their effects minimised. In large and very large organisations some form of rigorous analysis of appraisal ratings will be undertaken. In very large organisations this can be high order statistical analysis capable of identifying regional/national variations. In most organisations some form of levelling or adjustment mechanism can be employed post-analysis. Regardless of the size of the organisation, proper education and guidelines for all engaged in the appraisal system must be employed. This education must include clear instruction on the expectations of the leadership when applying the totality of the performance management system.

PERFORMANCE MANAGEMENT: AN EXAMPLE

To put this in perspective an example may help. In one squad at my rowing club there are 32 athletes. They train between 16 and 20 hours each week and this training takes place on six days of each week. In a normal week the training generates a minimum of eight performance measurements per athlete. In a testing week, usually once a month, a further 20 performance measurements are generated. These are all logged and posted on the training board. In addition each athlete has their own personal profile in which qualitative assessments are included along with the quantitative training data. Discussions with the athletes take place at training sessions where there is genuine two-way feedback. This whole process is managed by a single, voluntary coach in addition to full-time work outside of rowing. The motivation, the desire to train and the desire to compete are achieved without a single extrinsic reward. Whilst athletes are understandably a self-selecting performance group, the key is that they are predominantly intrinsically motivated to achieve high performance. The reason they do this is because they are predisposed towards trying to achieve the top two drivers in the hierarchy of needs outlined in Chapter 2, namely esteem and self-actualisation. There is no reason why a good leader, with good people and the right approach cannot elicit similar (albeit less intense) desires to achieve high performance.

While the above example is of a very intensive and very high-performance targeted system, it is worth comparing this amateur sports performance appraisal system (done for fun) with what the average organisation does when seeking to survive in a competitive, even hostile, environment. I would argue that the average organisation is intrinsically laissez faire when it comes to its performance management system and often sees it as an unproductive and costly way of apportioning rewards rather than a true high-performance tool.

In sport, in high-performance squads and teams, failure to provide good and personally stretching development for high-class athletes means only three things:

1. your athletes become demotivated, disgruntled and not as good as they could and should be
2. your team begins to lose increasingly frequently
3. your athletes leave and/or are easily poached.

It is no different in an organisation that has selected talent for high performance. If the organisation fails to provide its people with all that they need to meet the psychological drivers that feed their intrinsic motivations, they will fail to perform.

SUMMARY
This chapter has looked at the primary elements that need to be addressed when motivating and managing high-performance individuals but has done so by ensuring that development also works in conjunction with the character of the organisation. Similar to a person, if you try and force an organisation to work in a way that is alien to its core character, it will become stressed and ineffective. This chapter has therefore looked at how the character of the organisation can be assessed and then harnessed. It has provided a number of models that help guide how this can be achieved.

Perhaps most importantly this chapter has identified that the performance appraisal system plays a critical part in monitoring whether the desired high performance is being achieved. Having identified where almost all such systems fail, this chapter provides guidance on the crucial aspects that must be integrated into the appraisal system to drive all elements of high-performance achievement. In the modern era where so many organisations have failed, not just financially or commercially but more critically have failed morally, the notions of values, standards and behaviours take on even greater importance. This chapter shows how these aspects can be incorporated as measurable elements in a performance appraisal system.

Managing people is extremely hard work. Managing people to achieve high performance in a high-performance environment is hard work in the extreme. It also requires an attention to detail and the application and dedication to ensure that detail is addressed. This work and requirement for detail is no excuse for not putting in the effort and energy required to construct and manage a system that gets right to the heart of what it is to develop high-performance people.

CHAPTER 12
EXTERNAL MEASUREMENT
FOR HIGH PERFORMANCE:
COMPETITOR COMPARISON

Champions do not become champions when they win the event but in the hours, weeks, months and years they spend preparing for it. The victorious performance itself is merely the demonstration of their championship character.

T. Alan Armstrong

If you are an athlete or a team that is committing to an intensive training and development programme, spending tens of hours a week in the gym or on the road, getting ever fitter and ever better at what you do, there is a natural desire to want to see just how well that hard work is paying off. If you are in a competitive environment then you positively want to pit yourself against the best in your class. Otherwise what is the point of all that hard work?

Organisations have no choice. The imperative to compete is thrust upon them whether they like it or not. Most organisations choose, metaphorically, not to go to the gym. They choose not to engage in intensive training. Despite this 'disengagement' they have no choice. They are not only entered into the competition but are taking part in it every single day of the year, every year!

It is not possible in a single chapter to provide an exhaustive treatise on how organisations should measure themselves in their markets and sectors, nor even on what they should measure. These elements are organisation- and market-specific – sometimes even idiosyncratic to the leader. What this chapter does seek to provide is an outline of the benefits such external measuring brings to an organisation and some ideas for the approaches to take.

BUILDING ON SAND

The business-planning process
In looking at devising performance measurement most average organisations have a planning model that is driven predominantly from internally derived processes. Figure 35 shows how an average organisation might manage its business-planning and associated performance-management process. The diagram depicts a typical 1 Year Plan, 3 Year Projection derived from a typical organisation's business-planning process. The business may have a number of targets and this represents one of them, e.g. earnings before interest and tax (EBIT).

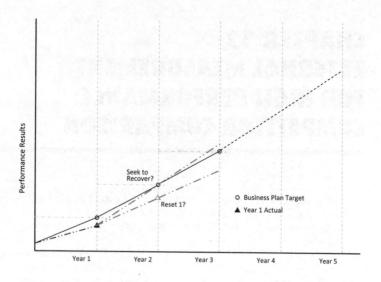

Figure 35: Business planning and performance management.

On the surface this looks perfectly reasonable. Numerous people within the organisation will probably have been involved in the business-planning process. It may even have some links towards what might be achievable for whatever is the current strategy. There are generally two problems with this type of approach. The first is that it is normally a process that is driven by the finance function and focuses on hard financial measures. This is understandable because they are relatively easy to derive and provide the comfort of being easily quantifiable, in theory. The second is that usually it is only the current year that is grounded in any sort of numerical reality. A one-year plan for most organisations is not generally considered to be strategic. It is just an annual operating plan. On this basis Year 2 and Year 3 are effectively only financial projections. Consequently, they are generally not strategically derived and directed imperatives. They are thus unlikely to be tied into meeting the performance levels aspired to in the vision.

I have been involved in the formulation of many annual planning exercises in my 30 years of running departments, business units and companies. Some of these have even been called strategic planning. I have often been involved in proper strategy formulation processes but only once in 30 years have I seen the finance department play second fiddle to the strategy process when it comes to drawing up and submitting the numbers. The numbers planning is often done with only a nod towards the strategy and almost always in glorious isolation from the vision. I have even been told on more than one occasion by a FCO to redo my numbers because my growth projections did not fit the plan. In one spectacular case I was told 'The sales figures are fine but your capital expenditure is too high' and the CFO's 'view' was submitted. In an asset-intensive business we could not achieve the figures in the sales plan without the assets in the capital expenditure plan. Predictably we failed to make the numbers.

Questioning the assumptions

The reality is that the golden rule of business plans – 'question the assumptions not the numbers' – is almost always ignored. I have seen forecasts and projections submitted that are close to nonsensical: sales volume forecast that a couple of simple questions would have exposed as wildly optimistic; an expansion plan that was not supported by costed and planned resources and took no account of maintaining quality (support and training) as the work force grew threefold; or project delivery results that ignore previous experience and outturns. Questioning the assumptions underpinning anything based on flimsy (even lazy) thinking quickly exposes weaknesses. For example:

■ what market share increase does this represent?
■ which competitors will you take it from?
■ how will they respond?
■ at what stage of the sector lifecycle are we in, and can we really achieve this sort of growth?
■ what risk factors have been identified for this project, how have they been assessed and ranked, what mitigation actions are there for each and what is our history of managing these in the past?

What happens if Year 1 targets are missed?

Even these things are not the main problem. The key issues arise if the organisation fails to meet its Year 1 targets. If the Year 1 numbers were based on what internal functional experts believed was achievable in the market in Year 1 and they failed to make the numbers, how do you work out how to deal with the Year 2 projection requirement? Do you accept the Year 1 missed target position and reset so that Year 2 starts from the lower base? Do you try and work out what the magical something is that you can do to double the projected growth rate to recover the original plan position? And if you can do this, why did you fail to meet Year 1 targets?

The other area of questioning arising from a failure to meet the plan is what caused it? If it was a shortfall in sales do you accept the sales director's explanation at face value? If it was a delivery or execution failure is the operations director's explanation at the board meeting a true reflection of its cause? If it was a productivity failure is it because the machine line is old as the production director states? Or is it because people just failed to meet their Year 1 objectives as HR and department heads might report? Whatever is said internally, unless there was a real and quantifiable market downturn, the reality is you did not perform as well as your competitors and they beat you. Unless you know why and where they beat you then whatever you do for Year 2 and beyond will be flawed. It will end up being just another financial estimation cloaked in the term business planning.

Coaches, athletes and teams know absolutely why and where they get beaten. This is because they have detailed internal performance metrics and they gather as much data and information on their competitors as possible at both team and individual level to ensure detailed comparison. Once they have as much competitor data and information as possible they analyse it intimately and turn it into intelligence that can inform and direct the next steps. These may be at the individual or team level. They may focus in some cases on people's fitness and generate specific fitness regimes to address particular areas. They may focus on people's technical abilities or the team's joint ability. It might mean getting into the area of mental toughness and resilience and developing even stronger mental skills and attitudes. Quite often being beaten results in significant changes as key weaknesses are removed and replaced with strengths.

When the success of organisations, even average ones, is so vital to so many parties, e.g. customers, suppliers, people in the organisation, shareholders and economies in general, it is bewildering to compare the casualness of competitive performance assessment in business with the obsessive thoroughness in sport. Some of the most valuable people in professional sports are those who gather and analyse competitive data, assess and organise it into useful information and finally synthesise it and present it as intelligence to be acted upon. Until this has been done all the sports scientists in the world may be considered to be 'undirected'. With real information and intelligence, fitness coaches can modify training regimes. Technical coaches can think of better ways to develop ability. Nutritionists, psychologists, physiologists – all can use the intelligence obtained to improve and develop their regimes.

This is all well and good. Sport you might say is a very well-defined, well-bounded and simple environment in which to run such competitor comparisons and upon which to act. I would agree that it is a simpler environment in which to gather competitor comparisons. I would certainly argue that how they are used is as complex and difficult as the business environment but that argument is not required here. What I hope is obvious is that, as complex and as difficult as it may be in business to gather such competitor information, that obstacle alone is no excuse as to why it should not be done. In the beginning it may be a messy and only partial process but as it is committed to and the techniques, methods and skill of the people involved improve, so will the knowledge of the competitive environment and all those competing in it.

BUILDING ON SOLID GROUND

As was mentioned at the beginning of this chapter it is not possible, nor does it make sense, to try to provide specific competitor information and intelligence gathering regimes. Every business is different. Every competitive environment is similarly unique. What is set out below is a broad-based example that seeks to show how an organisation might undertake an effective process to understand all the elements relevant to its unique position. In the same way that coaches and athletes know intimately what areas of development will make them both competitive and successful, organisations must have the same detail and clarity of their corporate bodies, their competitors and their competitive arena. Only with such detailed knowledge is it possible to know exactly why, where, what and how to train, to develop, to expend effort and allocate scarce resources.

In looking at any organisation it is possible to identify its critical activities and distil them into key distinctive areas. These may be considered as being not just the organisation's fundamental activities but the competences it requires to be success-ful in creating value for its customers and consequently for itself. Figure 36 shows a simple diagram for a typical specialist engineering organisation designing, manufac-turing and selling systems that are key components in their customers' operations.

While this can be seen as being a useful exercise in beginning to graphically visual-ise what is key to the organisation's success, it is only when it is broken down in two further ways that it becomes very powerful as a business tool. The first is to understand how these activities are viewed by the customers in order of importance to them. The second is to identify in more detail the critical activities and compe-tences that make up each main functional activity. This ranking and a sample of sub-activities are shown in Figure 37.

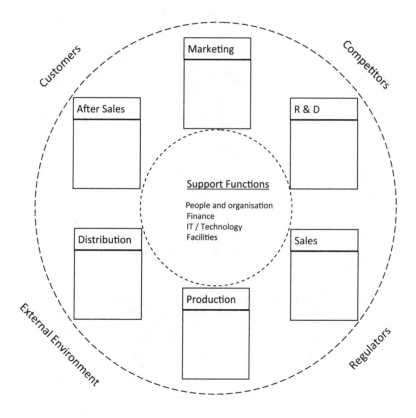

Figure 36: Distinctive activities and competences.

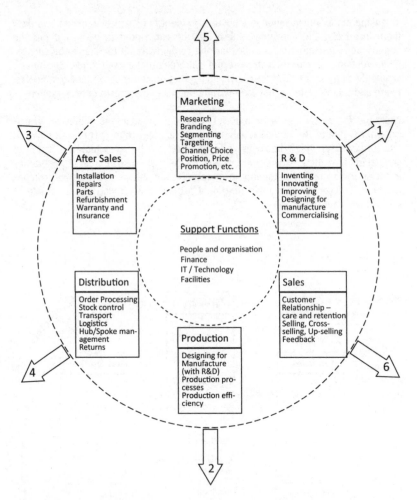

Figure 37: Ranking and detailing distinctive activities and competences.

If we assume that these represent the core competitive activities that the organisation needs to excel at in order to secure high performance, then we need to find ways in which to a) measure the competence in these activities and sub-activities and b) do the same for the competitors. This means that we have to examine all the activities that make up a functional area's core competitive competencies and see what, where, when and how these can be measured. Once we have worked out those things that would be useful and valuable to measure, we need to assess which of them can usefully be measured given real-world constraints. We need to examine how we would get such data and information on our competitors. This disaggregation of the function's activities and assessment of them must be

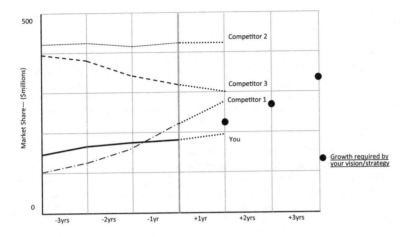

Figure 38: Market share: competitor comparison over time.

repeated in all of the core competitive functions and activities undertaken by the organisation.

In this respect let's focus on marketing for the sake of this example. Some of the competitive advantage elements might, among others, be:

- marketing budget
- scale and scope of the marketing department
- volume, prominence, media route, sophistication and frequency of advertising
- customer insights and knowledge
- market share
- brand value.

It is clear from this list that some items lend themselves relatively easily to data gathering and hard measurement and others do not. In some cases the information will be easily quantifiable and in others it may only lend itself to qualitative judgements. In some cases the raw data will need to be normalised in some way to allow an equal comparison between differently sized organisations, for example, brand value. As a single figure the brand value for Hewlett-Packard will not compare directly with Acer, however a ratio of brand value per dollar of marketing spend or per dollar of income may normalise the comparison. Eventually a number of valuable and measurable comparators can be developed. These should then be plotted over time. Figure 38 shows how this might look for a measure of market share.

It can be seen that the value of such work is not just a competitor comparison as a snapshot in time but as a tool capable of providing some indication of competitor trending. This trend analysis is not just useful from a competitor intelligence and response point of view. It can also indicate how realistic or difficult your visionary desires might be to achieve. If the solid black circles represent the market value growth requirement of your vision it is quite clear you have some significant challenges ahead given the current trend.

If this exercise is repeated for all of the other key and measurable marketing elements, a powerful comparative picture of you versus your competitors in the marketing arena can be developed. If this exercise is repeated for all the other functions a considerable amount of valuable comparative intelligence is available to inform not just visionary and strategic long-term decisions, but also short-term tactical responses to competitors and market environmental changes.

An example of another useful exercise that can be done from an overall organisational perspective is comparative mapping of the distinctive activities and competences. It should be possible to find ways to recombine for each function the separate elements of the competitive intelligence now obtained and to arrive at an overall view of just where your organisation sits in competence terms compared with the competition. It may need some clever statisticians or mathematicians (or just some creative flair) to achieve this aggregation but if it is done properly there is considerable value to be obtained because it provides a clear overview of your strengths and weaknesses in comparison to your competitors. Figure 39 shows how this might look.

It can be seen that the distinctive activities are ordered with respect to their importance to the customers. Once there is a degree of confidence in the data, information and intelligence that gives rise to all the above it is possible to relentlessly focus resources and effort on those elements and sub-elements that really add value to the customer and avoid wasting them on marginal, peripheral and low-value adding activities.

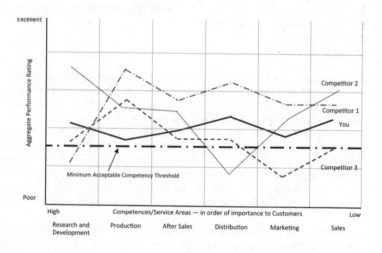

Figure 39: Distinctive competencies: comparative mapping.

SUMMARY

The purpose of this chapter has been to show the importance of undertaking external data and information gathering and turning it into useful competitor intelligence. There are, of course, as many models and datasets available to clever analysts as you could wish for. This chapter has sought only to demonstrate the weakness of average approaches to performance and the potential power of detailed competitor comparisons.

I hope it is evident that while financially focused business plans have an important role to play in shaping the future of any organisation, it is a very limited tool in the absence of intelligence that places it in context with its market environment – especially with respect to its competitive environment. To use a sporting analogy, financial planning on its own may deliver you the best five-meter pole ever constructed. However, this is of little use when you turn up at the pole vaulting tournament to find that the top athletes are using six-meter poles.

The high-performance organisation knows almost as much about its competitors as it does about itself. As importantly, its knowledge and understanding of the environment in which competition is taking place should be unrivalled. It is this application of knowledge about itself, its rivals and the arena in which the competition takes place that will set the high-performance organisation apart from the average one.

CHAPTER 13
WHAT IS REQUIRED OF THE
HIGH-PERFORMANCE LEADER?

Men will follow this officer anywhere – if only out of curiosity!
Army officer appraisal, anonymous

In setting the scene for Part 1 of this book, Chapter 2 touched on leadership and the similarities and differences between leading and coaching. It deliberately sought to switch the focus over to followers and in particular to the key elements that followers want and that, if met, will secure the highest levels of performance from them. The needs of followers are the most critical aspects to understand with respect to achieving a high-performance organisation. Any aspiring leader overlooks these at their peril.

You might ask then, what does this leave for a single chapter on leadership and leading for high performance? When one considers the thousands (possibly tens of thousands) of ancient manuscripts, sage writings, scratchings on broken pottery and innumerable books over the last 5,000 years that have sought to study and explain leadership, how can a single chapter add anything at all? And, of course, in the last 30 years we have had the advent of the business schools, the academics and the consultants who have probably trebled in three decades the volume of texts on leadership that the previous five millennia achieved.

So, in the face of such overwhelming treatises on leadership what can this one chapter in this one book possibly add? What it seeks to provide are two things. The first is some food for thought. Some of this thinking will be non-contentious but I hope you find some of it extremely so. When you read some of the more controversial theories I hope you will see that they resonate with the parlous state of the modern organisation (even the modern world). They certainly have validity when the quality and ethics of contemporary leaders and the state of modern leadership are considered. The second element I hope this chapter provides is some new insights into leadership and the role of leaders in the modern organisation.

This book has shown how leaders can select followers and develop them in ways that will provide the highest possible chance of achieving high performance. If, however, the leader of high-performance followers is only average then the performance of even above-average followers will trend back to average as well. In fact it may become worse, because followers who want to deliver high performance will become more frustrated than those who are quite happy bumbling along in their normal fashion. Think of a team of top athletes, all the very best in their sport and position individually, and then provide them with a poor coach. The result might look something like the 2011 England rugby team! Thus, the following sections in this chapter set out key elements leaders need to address if they wish to fully harness the potential of their followers and achieve the highest levels of performance their people and organisation are capable of.

THE PSYCHOLOGICAL CONTRACT

I will start by a making a point about leaders and organisations that I have not seen made before. The point is that the moment someone sets themselves up to be the leader of an organisation they enter into an unwritten, psychological contract with everyone in that organisation. Most leaders enter into this contract without ever knowing they have done so. All those in the organisation below the leader will almost certainly have entered it without knowing they have done so. Despite this lack of awareness of the psychological ties followers will have expectations of that leader from the outset and requirements they need fulfilling. They will expect their leader to deliver the four things they need (see Chapter 2 and below). They will expect their leader to be competent and deliver, among other things, wealth, security of income and the feeling they are doing something worthwhile and for which they are valued. In fact the very lives and livelihoods of the followers and their families are inextricably linked with the skill and competence of their leader.

Consequently, whether they are consciously aware of it or not, the followers will be looking for signs, signals and actions that tell them their new leader can deliver their security, wealth, sense of purpose, etc. If those signs, signals and actions are positive and consistently so, the leader will be creating a climate where followers will trust and commit to that leader. The converse is also obviously true but with a major warning. Human beings are genetically wired to give bad news greater attention and credence than good news. Therefore leaders have to work harder at sending positive signals and eradicating negative ones.

LEADERSHIP: EGO AND REWARD OR DUTY AND SERVICE?

Why do leaders want to become leaders?

I am always fascinated by the answers I hear in response to this question. Taking on any leadership role involves a person putting their hand up and taking responsibility. Not just responsibility for a task or activity but for that key difference that leadership means: taking responsibility for other people, for their performance and for all the situations in which this will take place. The minute you put your hand up to take responsibility for other people and their performance you have accepted a dramatic increase in personal risks. These risks are to your own performance, the outcome of the work itself, your reputation, your relationship with subordinates, peers and superiors – pretty much everything that makes up you, your role in the organisation and the outcomes others seek from you. It often also means subtle (even not-so-subtle) changes in relationships outside the organisation.

So why does anyone put their head above the parapet just to risk having it shot off? No matter at what leadership level this question is asked, the formal, interview-type answers nearly always tick all the right, politically correct boxes. What is interesting is that the higher people climb towards the top of an organisation the more the informal, underlying motives appear to change and the more even the formal responses change.

The lower down the organisation the leaders are (and the younger they are) the more closely answers appear to reflect their real underlying desires:

I enjoy my work, I seem good at it and my boss has encouraged me that this new role with some direct reports would be good for my development.

or

I solved a few problems last year and I enjoyed the feeling of satisfaction helping other people gave me. When this new role came along where I would be responsible for my own team I wanted the responsibility and sense of achievement I felt last year.

Answers mostly reflect the genuineness of people taking their first steps on the leadership path, the enthusiasm of youth, the excitement of the new.

As this question is asked of more senior leaders, on their pathway to the top, words such as ambition, lead, self-determination, control and to be the boss, start to creep in with ever-increasing frequency. However, the biggest change is that the more self-effacing reasons for taking on leadership roles espoused by lower-level leaders, and even the type of language used, is progressively replaced by more assertive (if not outright aggressive) rationales and language. In many cases, the closer leaders get to the top the more they seek leadership roles for non-leadership reasons. Money, status, power, position, control, ego, etc. seem to figure more highly than vocation, duty, obligation and service. In the current aggressive and materialistic societies these old-fashioned words receive scant attention in public. In private, I have heard them ridiculed.

Are leaders necessary?
If, in an averagely performing organisation, most of the day-to-day work is being done adequately by middle and senior management, is the leader providing any value? Elsewhere in this book, organisations, especially very large ones, have been shown to survive even inordinately incompetent leadership. If the average tenure of leaders in large organisations is only four years, can they really create a lasting high-performance impact? Unless an organisation is visibly out-performing competitors, what is the leadership doing? Given that this book is about achieving high performance in organisations, none of these arguments are advocating that leaders and leadership are unimportant. What they are saying is that average leaders leading average companies, especially where their tenure lasts only the average period of time, have very little impact on performance.

High reward does not equal high performance

US professor and business school dean Roger Martin's book *Fixing the Game* makes this point supremely well. His premise is that making stock and stock options a very large proportion of the compensation package of leaders and leadership teams, far from having had a beneficial effect on performance, has at best had none and at worst reduced it. The watershed year he uses is 1976 when a highly respected paper was produced by two American university professors (Meckling and Jensen). This paper introduced what we now know as Agency Theory. This postulated that to properly align the interests of the managers of the firm (the leadership) with the owners of it (the shareholders), the managers should have stock as a large proportion of their compensation. Martin's research elicited some interesting findings. Between 1933 and 1976 the average adjusted compensation for CEOs was $850,000 per annum. The average performance of the Fortune 500 stocks on adjusted annual basis was 7.5%. Between 1976 and 2006 the figure for CEO compensation had increased sixteenfold to $14m per year but the average stock performance for the Fortune 500 had fallen to 6.5%. Martin makes the point that the stock performance figures can be altered by changing the start and finish periods but what he is very clear about is that the sixteenfold increase in CEO compensation had not resulted in any increase in performance.

Can the leader really do the job?

There is one other aspect that is worth raising at this juncture. This is that, very often, leaders of modern organisations, unlike coaches and team leaders in sport, have not been truly tested. In sport, coaches and teams deliberately and frequently place themselves in the spotlight of intensive competition. In business and organisational life, it is rare for a leader or the leadership team to find themselves in an ultimate win-or-lose situation. Winning or losing is generally by small degrees: winning a tender here or losing a little market share there. Even in these situations the process of winning or losing is codified in procedures and processes, managed by departments and business units. Most leaders are so far removed from the reality of competing at the edge of the organisation that they see and feel little of what it is their people and organisation are experiencing. In general, for the leaders of large organisations the pain of losing and the joy of winning is far removed from the visceral feelings of competition in sport – and if the leaders are of the worst types already outlined above, they will care little for such things anyway.

The good news is that, in all of the above, I am talking about average leaders in average organisations. There are organisations that achieve significantly higher performance than their peers and do so through exemplary leadership. This means that for leaders and their organisations that embark on a high-performance path the scope to outperform the pack is very high.

THE CLIMATE OF LEADERSHIP IN THE MODERN WORLD

Over the last two decades we have seen spectacular failures in governments, corporations and institutions. The parlous times we are currently living in are the result of a systemic failure in leadership in many of our significant national and international institutions and organisations. This is not because of some sudden onset of a global epidemic that bizarrely targets anyone who appears to be a good leader. There appear to be four main reasons.

The fallacy that the desire to be a leader confers automatic competence to be one

This first point goes to the heart of what average means. Most people are by definition average and in many cases this means that many leaders are just averagely good, averagely competent people who find that, either through time or circumstance, they have arrived at a position of leadership. These types of leaders often do the least damage in that they are benign and actually want to do a good job; but ultimately they are average and therefore, ultimately, so is the performance of the organisations they lead.

Since we are talking about average organisations and average people you may be thinking 'surely anyone who seeks out leadership roles can no longer be considered average'? The reality is that just being ambitious does not suddenly confer above-average skills and abilities that equip someone to be a leader. I have come across incredibly ambitious, aggressive people who you would not leave in charge of a wheelbarrow, let alone people and organisations. I am almost certain all of you reading this book will have stories where a slick, fast-talking show pony has seemingly flown to the top of the corporate tree, despite having been awful to work with and having no discernible talent to those that have had to work closely with them. Again, in average organisations with average leadership, you don't have to do much to stand out, so even the ambitious but average performer can do well.

The philosophy and ethics of leaders

The second element that conditions the leadership climate is one already outlined above and which goes to the heart of the matter. That is the character of leaders. In other centuries, while many of today's current venal attitudes also existed, there is evidence of people having a greater sense of duty, calling and service to their country or organisation. Max Weber in his book *Protestant Ethic and the Spirit of Capitalism* highlights just how powerful the attributes of duty and obligation were and how they pervaded almost every thought and action. How far removed is Weber's capitalist from the ethics of today's leaders. Today, even high political office in the most powerful countries in the world is often used only as an opportunity to indulge the ego or even just to get rich – mostly after tenure but sometimes (and scandalously) during it.

Interconnectedness: the microscope of the wired world

A third factor affecting the climate for leadership is the blinding glare of the modern world's near instantaneous communication platforms, extremely pervasive media and a globally connected population on a multi-layered network that is almost impossible to censor or disrupt. These three elements combined are able to examine and expose human frailty to a degree never before imagined and then beam it to the world. These factors have had a major impact: from exposing fraudulent and criminal practices by the leaders of organisations and governments to the toppling of dictators responsible for repressive regimes. How these societal elements will continue to develop and combine in the future is uncertain. However, in the wake of the disastrous leadership and decision making that has created the current recession, it is highly likely that those who set themselves up as leaders in the future will be subject to considerably more scrutiny both from their followers internally and, if the organisation is big enough, from the media externally.

One major outcome of the exposure of appalling leadership over the last four or five years is that in the eyes of the typical follower, leaders (as a group) have become morally bankrupt and highly suspect. This will make the leader's role in the modern organisation a challenge but will also present a huge opportunity. If the leader exhibits the right characteristics in a sustained and coherent way such that trust and belief is established then the commitment to that leader by the followers may be greater than might normally be expected following the current global debacle. While looking hard for signs of failure in their leaders that will reinforce their preconceptions or prejudices, people will more likely become highly committed followers when they discover a true and constant leader.

Complexity, ambiguity and the impact of global pressures

The last factor affecting leadership in the modern world is the sheer complexity of the political, economic and societal structures. Throughout every generation, the young and ambitious rising stars have made the argument that the old leaders are out of touch, ill-equipped and unable to deal with the rapid pace of change. I believe that in this current world neither the young and thrusting tyros nor the conservative old guards have a clear idea about how to really get to grips with the issues and challenges the world currently poses. This is not a technology or pace of change argument. It is a social dynamic argument. Two primary factors would seem to drive what will increasingly become major and global societal challenges:

1. the inextricable interconnectedness of the modern world
2. increasing pressure on, even shortages of, primary basic resources, e.g. energy-producing resources, water and food.

What makes the modern, highly networked era different from previous ones is that knowledge of resource problems will become increasingly realised by mass populations. In addition, the extreme interconnectedness of the world's nations means that problems or actions in one country will very definitely and very rapidly impact on many others. National leaders can easily and quickly shape messages to the populace and mobilise them in ways that best suit them. We see examples of this manipulation of populations by leaders almost on a daily basis.

You may well be asking at this stage how does all this relate to leaders and high performance? The answer is that while the world is highly interconnected in terms of economy and resources it is still an extremely tribal place when it comes to politics, national interests and cooperation. Leading any organisation towards high performance in such an interconnected world will require knowledge of and sensitivity to these crucial issues. Leaders must understand the environment they are leading in. And this leads us to the next part of this chapter: how leaders lead for high performance.

THE TRUE AND CONSTANT LEADER

It's about character

All the things that this book has addressed in previous chapters relating to the people in the organisation – the followers – now come together at a single point, the pinnacle: the leader. The first thing that should be noted is that if you want a high-performance organisation and you recruit high-performance people and apply the ideas this books describes, you must ensure that you are a high-performance leader. In this respect, in the same way that we have applied the performance triangle to the followers we can now look at some key attributes and attitudes that high-performance leaders will need to bring to bear.

Attributes

- Strong, core-guiding philosophy: a core ethos than holds them true to their beliefs.
- A clear sense of purpose and direction: both internally as a life force and for the task in hand.
- High self-awareness: self-knowledge of strengths and weaknesses; ability to act on them.
- High self-confidence: ego without hubris; projection of confidence to followers.
- High mental resilience: mental toughness to absorb high pressure; ability to enjoy it and use it to advantage.
- Mental dexterity: ability to assimilate complexity and ambiguity and extract meaning/patterns.
- Ability to learn from failure as well as success: ability to use every situation for knowledge gain.
- Big picture *and* high detail: ability to sweat the small stuff and synthesise into attainable visions.
- Logical and creative: ability to be rational and assimilative and then apply a magical spark.
- Strategic and tactical: ability to turn visions into things that can be delivered and work out how.
- Competence: having real mastery of the things that matter to delivering high performance.
- Decisiveness: having the ability to act and the confidence to initiate action rather than react.
- Trust: the ability to secure the trust of others and the confidence to trust others.
- Authenticity and integrity: being a real person; leading in a way that is true to your character.

Attitude

- Absolute commitment: high self-motivation; prepared to sacrifice many personal things for end goals.
- Absolute focus: with goals set there must be an unwavering focus on achieving them.
- Determination and persistence: pre-requisite is stamina; ability to play the long game.

■ Desire to win: you cannot win unless you really want to win.
■ Driven: desire is only half the story, the drive to win is critical.

You may have read the above listed attributes and attitudes and feel a little daunted. In Chapter 2 I made it less daunting by focusing on the single most important question leaders must answer: what is it that followers want or need? Poor leaders interpret this as 'What is it **I think** my followers should have?'. This less-than-subtle difference ensures average and often below-average performance is secured from those followers. We know from Chapter 2 that followers want four main things:

1. the need to belong
2. the need to be stimulated
3. the need to feel valued and recognised
4. the need to believe in and trust the leader.

The leader who aspires to lead a high-performance organisation must address these aspects in ways that will ensure coherence with their own character and the variety of situations that the people and the organisation will find themselves in over time. The following sections outline the facets leaders need to address, manage or deliver for the followers if they are to elicit the very best performance from them. It is important to note at this stage that this chapter assumes that the leader is technically highly competent in their management abilities.

It's about being you
The word 'authenticity' gets used a lot in this context of leadership but it is important to understand what this really means, especially from the perspective of followers.

I have worked with many heads of organisations over the last 40 years, both from within the organisation as an employee or director (14 companies) and as a consultant to them (50 or more). The one common factor throughout them is that they have all been different. I have used the term 'heads of organisations' carefully and deliberately because in many cases they were not leaders in the true sense of what we understand leaders to be. What I have been able to draw from these experiences is that the best of them, those who were genuinely leaders, were real people. They were people whose characteristics and behaviour were constant and in whom you knew there was little or no artifice.

I will seek to expand on this by providing an example where the head of an organisation was little more than an actor, and a poor one at that. One company I was involved with was the subsidiary of a large, Fortune 100 US telecoms company that had a succession of CEOs. One particular CEO was almost a caricature of a corporate leader. This in itself was not the main issue but some of things he did will provide an indication of his personality.

There was an Asian dimension to the company and since the occasional karaoke session was de rigueur he took professional lessons to learn one song perfectly. He would sing this song and this song only and would not participate in the general

enjoyment of people singing badly, enjoying each other's company and building relationships. He also set up informal basketball sessions where he invited senior
managers to play and chat afterwards. However, he always had a core team around
him who were excellent players and it was common knowledge that you beat him
and his team at your peril. When embarking on a company visit he would surround
himself with an entourage not far short of those you see around people who believe
they are celebrities. His presentations were adjudged by almost all who received
them as being the worst kind of corporate speak, false and without conviction.

There were many anecdotes surrounding his behaviour and all of them pointed to a
man trying to present the facade of a Fortune 100 corporate leader who in reality
was nothing close to being a leader. What was obvious to all who came into contact
with him was that here was someone who was false and not to be trusted. That he
was later one of the dot.com bubble-collapse CEOs who sought immunity from pros-
ecution surprised no one who knew him.

It is impossible to maintain a charade over a long period of time. It is only by being
yourself that people will be able to make a true assessment of who you are and
whether you are someone they could and should follow. What they are looking for
is whether you are someone they can trust and place their faith in, and for whom
they will do something more than just turning up at nine o'clock in the morning. If
you are seeking to be a leader of a high-performance organisation you must be able
to display those characteristics that will elicit high-performance behaviour form your
followers.

Apart from being a 'real person', how else is this element of being a leader
achieved? One area that sets the best leaders apart is that they have a core ethos, a
guiding philosophy that shapes what they stand for and how they behave. It is this
(and making this visible) that provides the constancy and coherency that followers
seek from their leaders.

It's about knowing yourself

Self-knowledge also plays a very large part in what makes the best leaders. They
have a clear view of who they are, their strengths and weaknesses, their good and
bad points, their place in the grand scheme of things and what they bring to any
situation, positive or negative. What this self-knowledge means, in conjunction
with a core guiding philosophy, is that the best leaders seem very comfortable with
themselves – they are comfortable in their own skin. These attributes lend themselves naturally to reinforcing that aura of confidence and conviction that any leader
needs in order to secure the trust and belief of followers. It is from these fundamental attributes that the leader's visions will be shaped and communicated. If there is
any tension or falseness in these key areas then a coherent vision that holds its
shape over time will be impossible to achieve.

It's about being close . . . and distant

There have been many views about whether leaders should be close or distant with
their followers: whether they can be 'one of the gang' and still be a leader; or

whether they must remain apart and aloof and keep a sense of mystery about them. The simple answer is that so much depends on the character of the leader, the leadership situation at any particular time, the nature of the followers and a myriad of other elements. In this respect there have been many self-important views of leadership. These may be epitomised by Charles de Gaulle's description in his book *The Edge of the Sword*:

> *First and foremost, there can be no prestige without mystery, for familiarity breeds contempt. All religions have their tabernacles and no man is a hero to his valet. In the designs, the demeanour and the mental operations of a leader there must always be 'something' which others cannot altogether fathom, which puzzles them, which stirs them and rivets their attention . . . Aloofness, character and the personification of quietness, these qualities it is that surround with prestige those who are prepared to carry a burden that is too heavy for lesser mortals.*

This self-aggrandising view of leadership plays into the hands of the autocratic leader and those who can only lead by force-of-position power. In the modern world, and certainly in Western organisations, this style of leadership does not secure the best performance from followers. It is more likely with the current generation of followers and their expectations, social networking and associated cultural orientation that this style of leadership is likely to secure appalling performance.

This leads to the next point which is: how close do leaders let their followers get to them? What we find is that the best leaders are very good at allowing their followers a good view of them, including their weaknesses (although this is usually managed very carefully and often quite strategically). By this I mean that if followers believe they have been entrusted or included in a sensitive area, their commitment to that leader can increase. Where that leader's trust has been extended to revealing a weakness, especially if the follower can help, then the bond can become incredibly strong.

It's about constancy

Leaders must do what they say they will do. This is covered in more detail below, but in terms of being an authentic leader this means following through on words with actions. By far the most powerful manifestation of a leader's commitment to his followers is not what they say but what they do.

It is important to say that just being you does not automatically confer great leadership. I worked with a leader in one organisation who could not have been more true to himself. The problem was he came from a very insular, narrow and rigid cultural background, was parochial to the point of racism, was technically incompetent in the role and was incapable of seeing other people's points of view, let alone their value. Was he true to himself? Absolutely and unswervingly! Was he a good leader? I do not need to tell you answer to that question, I am sure.

It's about taking care of your people

Almost everything about leadership, especially achieving high performance, is about people. Since the four things followers want or need are deeply psychological, good leaders must understand that leadership is first and foremost about people and tapping into their basic drivers. In this respect, good leaders will do the following.

- Take a great interest in their people, throughout the organisation.
- Listen to their people: this also means sending signals (through action) that you have heard.
- Engage their people: by good and frequent communication, building common purpose, building stories they can relate to, taking the time to get the stories told and assimilated where necessary.
- Care for their people: taking time to display real empathy, doing the little things that send big signals.
- Motivate their people: by communicating a future (and a path towards it) that excites, enthuses and energises.
- Achieve all the above through the currency of getting the big decisions right, by picking the right strategies and executing them.

The above is not easy and requires real commitment to achieve success, which brings us to the next point.

It's about hard work

People can often be difficult, contrary, exasperating and demanding, among many other things. But they are also the engine and deliverers of high performance and can also be exciting, energising and exhilarating. In a global organisation they will be culturally very different. Organisations are highly complex organisms and leading the people that comprise them takes a massive amount of energy, stamina and sustained attention to minutiae. Leaders must have such attributes and attitudes and be seen by their followers to have them.

Add to the people challenge the requirement for the leader to deliver all the technical elements that make an organisation work – vision, direction, strategy, plans, effective management throughout the entity – and the characteristics of energy, endurance, stamina, persistence and attention to detail can be seen to be paramount.

Taking the elements of persistence and attention to detail a stage further, we have previously seen that around 70% of all strategies fail to achieve what they were supposed to do. The same studies almost always point to a failure in implementation as the cause. This failure to execute is always a failure of leadership. It is a failure to do the really hard, mind-numbing work of ensuring understanding, commitment and alignment of the people before rolling out the plans. It is a failure to design and establish robust monitoring and feedback measures. It is a failure to ensure constant follow-up on the variances from the monitoring and feedback system and then doing something about it. All of these things can slip through the net and destroy even the best strategies and plans if leaders do not care enough to expend the energy and attention over a prolonged period to ensure success.

From the very first company I worked in I saw intrinsically good strategies destroyed by poor leadership. In a UK subsidiary of a Netherlands company our strategy was posted to us as a document to be read and implemented – no involvement, no communication, no explanation and most importantly no follow-up, no measures and no monitoring of our results. In a UK telecoms company, after six months of a strategic process involving the top 30 senior managers, a strategic plan was derived. Subsequent to delivery this plan was not only ignored by the leadership but another quick-fix plan was imposed by them – again with no depth, no means of monitoring progress and worst of all no interest because the leader who imposed it left the company four months later. In another case, for the UK subsidiary of a very large US telecoms company three successive annual plans were accepted by the parent company's leaders but the things the parent was required to do under the plans were not done. The parent's leaders then fired people in the subsidiary for not achieving targets that the parent's incompetence had caused to fail.

This all means that as a leader you have to really want to lead. More importantly you have to be fully aware of just what that leadership will require of you. Yes, you can hand-pick the very best team to surround yourself with, but even they will be looking to you for leadership, especially at critical moments. Even with this top team around you, it will still be up to you as leader to set the tone, to ensure the right elements are in place to achieve high performance and that the things you expect to be done are done. It is worth reiterating that to ensure you are leading a high-performance entity you have to be a high-performance leader – and that is hard work if it is to be done with the levels of commitment it requires.

Finally, it is important to examine the motivation for wanting to be a leader. In the case of the best athletes, particularly those who remain at the top of their game for long periods of time, they are highly intrinsically motivated. Intrinsic motivation drives the inner desire for an athlete to be the best they can be. It provides the drive to always improve, the determination and persistence to train hard day after day, to be the best they can be for long periods of time. Results are their own rewards. Extrinsic motivation means that the athlete is predominantly motivated by more external rewards: wealth, recognition and status. While extrinsic motivation can work well for the right characters it tends to generate shorter-lived success and often at a lower level of achievement. Extrinsically motivated athletes also tend not to be the best in teams or squads. Without a burning inner desire to spur you on the years of tough and often lonely training can be hard to endure. Without the inner belief that your hard work is building steady development and improvement the losses and setbacks can be impossible to overcome. Many of today's leaders give every appearance of being primarily extrinsically motivated: money, position, status, power and ego are a poor substitute for intrinsic motivations of service, duty, fun, enjoyment and satisfaction.

If all this sounds impossible it may be helpful to look back at coaching in sport. There are many tens of thousands of volunteer coaches all over the world in sport, who, in addition to their day job, take club athletes from nowhere to the top of their sport by expending similar huge amounts of energy, enthusiasm, commitment, stamina and know-how over long periods. They apply themselves to the detail and make sure they good at what they do. They do this because they want to and because it fulfils some, if not all, of those four basic needs. The hard work becomes pleasurable and a natural part of their life. Leaders of organisations must have similar reasons for wanting to lead as the best coaches do for coaching. Without the right reasons the hard work is seen as just that and rarely gets done with the level of attention it should.

It's about adaptation

Chapter 2 presented a new model in Figure 2 that sought to show the situational aspects of leadership and the diverse skills and abilities leaders need to exhibit in different situations and contexts. Like all models it shows the extremes of the continuums in order to more clearly illustrate the differences. In the normal course of leading any organisation, while such extremes are unusual and unlikely, there will be always be different situations and contexts that leaders will have to tackle on a daily basis. Good leaders have an innate ability to sense situations, pick up on atmospheres, be aware of people's demeanour and detect tensions. Having done so they are able to shape communication, both the medium and the message, to suit the changed situation they have detected.

It is not just about communication or picking up on situations and reacting to them. Good leaders often want to change a situation or an organisational dynamic. Before they do so they will take 'soundings', often informally, by walking about, talking to a wide cross-section of people and sensing the environment they want to alter. Depending on their findings, good leaders will adapt their approach to ensure that the change initiative arrives into the organisation in a way that will ensure acceptance and success. In this way good leaders are able to shape situations and contexts over time.

This adaptation extends to the leader's own style. While core behaviours will and should remain consistent (see p.186 above) it is essential to adjust and adapt your style to suit a particular situation, subject, audience, etc.

This area of adapting to situations and contexts is one of the most difficult for leaders, especially new leaders, to get right. It often requires a subtle mix of facts and intuition.

In nearly all cases where the ability is not instinctive the fall-back position is to always be yourself. It may even be possible to tell people you sense something is wrong but you can't work it out and would like their help and guidance. This could be a situation where you manage to pull off a triple win. You show followers you are sensitive enough to notice an issue or concern, you show followers a small weakness and then elicit their help and support to overcome that weakness. Openness, two-way trust and lack of hubris go a very long way in building strong and enduring follower support. A by-product is that positive stories get told and the best ones become part of the organisation's folklore and culture.

It's about connecting

Perhaps the key role of leaders, assuming they are technically competent in the elements of organisational and competitive environment management, is to engage and mobilise the organisation's people. Not only must they be able to engage and mobilise people, they must do it in a way that ensures they want to work to the highest of their capabilities towards a common purpose and some future goal desired by all. Pretty lofty aspirations, especially if you lead an organisation of 50,000 souls scattered across the globe. Nonetheless, the very best leaders manage to do it. They manage somehow to connect in ways so that, even if they do not do it face-to-face with each individual, their message is known, clear and committed to. We now look at how this connection can be made by leaders today operating in the modern organisation.

In other parts of this book, reference is made to poor leaders using positional power and hierarchy to shield themselves against internal criticism of poor performance. The worst leaders inculcate a climate of fear and intimidation. Conversely, the very best leaders ignore hierarchy. They understand that their position and the hierarchy of the organisation do not automatically confer a) the right to lead or b) the ability to do so. Good leaders deliberately work hard at making themselves visible and, more than this, available. This visibility and availability is not limited to just their top team or one layer down; wherever possible good leaders will make themselves visible across the breadth and depth of the organisation. In one company in which I was a member of the board, part of our personal objectives was completely focused (with measures) on the efforts we had made to get out and about and into the depths of the organisation.

In creating a sense of purpose, which is one of the four things that followers seek, good leaders use a variety of methods and mediums for communicating. What they are aware of, either innately, or through personal development, is Albert Mehrabian's 7%, 38%, 55% rule, or indeed any of the studies on non-verbal communications undertaken since. While many of these studies are misinterpreted, the main thrust of them is that non-verbal cues are much stronger at conveying messages than verbal ones. From his studies, Mehrabian cites the elements through which messages are received and interpreted as 7% verbal, 38% tone and 55% facial. Good leaders therefore craft their key messages and how they deliver them very carefully. Extending this concept a little further, good leaders also know that different personality types like to receive information in different ways. Some like lots of data and detail, others like the big picture. Some like the written word while others work better with pictures or tables and diagrams. Consequently, the best leaders ensure that the methods of communication address the primary types of receiver preferences.

Followers also need a sense of excitement, and in addition to the methods and types of communication outlined above, good leaders also employ, either naturally or deliberately, other psychological devices. For example they can create and tell compelling stories. This is a key ability in situations where there is no immediate or visible emergency but where the leader's vision requires major change. Excitement is also generated by leaders creating an edgy, but positive, atmosphere or environment. This can be along the lines of top-level motivating stories for example 'us against the universe' or 'we are the trailblazers' through to devices as simple as maintaining a creative tension and uncertainty in relationships. This is the sort of thing that might elicit statements such as 'I never know what they are going to do next – life's never dull around them'. Another area where leaders can generate a sense of excitement is by being non-conformist. This also has to be managed very carefully since overdoing it or getting it wrong can move exciting into just plain weird. The culture of the organisation is another area where excitement can be generated, i.e. by seeking to change elements of it. This is a difficult area because the culture is embedded in the organisation psyche and generally any change requires careful thought, planning, engagement and alignment of people. Once you move into the planned process quite a lot of the excitement disappears.

Perhaps of all the things you need to have to be a great leader and achieve the connections outlined above, you must have a high degree of what today is called empathy. The ideas of empathy, emotional intelligence and its measure (EQ or emotional intelligence quotient) often get a bad press from those who see themselves as the hard-nosed, aggressive and no-nonsense thrusting types. Empathy is effectively no more than the now scientifically researched and written about ability, or more correctly capacity, to put yourself in someone else's shoes. The greatest leaders have this capacity in abundance – whether they know it or not! All science has done is to investigate, research, study and develop a broader understanding of it. Science has even devised methods of testing for it, although when we say 'it' we have to be careful because emotional intelligence has many strands. Just as IQ can be made up of numerical, spatial, verbal and numerous other abilities so does EQ comprise many facets, each of which equips individuals with varying levels of ability in different areas.

Empathy is often deemed another one of these soft capabilities like leadership, so there is as usual the esoteric debate about whether it is a nature or nurture concept. Personally, I believe it is both. I have met very few people who do not from time to time put themselves in someone else's shoes, even if it is for entirely selfish reasons. So the ability exists in all human beings but the capacity or degree to which it exists varies considerably.

It is quite possible, highly probable even, that any major change initiative by a leader will give rise to waves of angst and concern in the followers. That change will still need to go ahead despite such fears. What empathy does is allow the leader to understand there are fears, to more accurately pinpoint the extent and manner of those fears and then modify stories, methods and possibly even timescales to ensure as many of the psychological barriers fear generates can be removed. No bad thing if the change is, say, a major new strategic thrust – it might even go a long way to ensuring the strategy is not consigned to the scrapheap of failure where the 70% of other organisations strategies reside.

Carlos Goshn, CEO of Nissan, said:

> The leaders of tomorrow are going to have to be incredibly secure and sure of themselves. Leaders of the future will also need to have a lot more empathy and sensitivity – not just for people from their own countries but for people from completely different countries and cultures. They are going to need global empathy, which is a lot more difficult.

So we can see that empathy allows us to understand followers and use this understanding to deliver all those elements and aspects covered above. It is through the people based insights that high empathy provides an understanding of what followers are thinking and feeling. As a result, empathy enables good leaders to better inform their decisions. The type and manner of the decisions and/or the messages around them will demonstrate to followers (often at a subconscious level) that they have a leader who is at least sensitive to them even if it does not always mean they get what they want. This is the currency of trust and the building of strong bonds that will ensure that followers will want to deliver to the best of their ability.

It's about being competent

You may think it strange that the competence of the leader comes last on the list but in reality technical competence, i.e. that competence that can be ascribed to functional requirements based on a career in functional/managerial roles, must be a given. Another term used for this is domain knowledge; being an expert in your field. If a leader does not have technical competence or domain knowledge then the quality of decision making in the more functional requirements of the role – for example crafting a strategy, interrogating the translation of that strategy into operational plans, interpreting the feedback, challenging assumptions – will be suspect. The primary reason why a leader should be a leader is that they have all the attributes, skills, abilities and attitude that can engage and mobilise the organisation's people in such a way that they combine and work to the highest of their capabilities towards a common purpose and a future goal desired by all.

There are, however, areas of competence beyond the functional that are worth outlining here. In addition to displaying to a significant degree all of the elements described in this chapter the leader must be able to combine and use them to make assessments that are accurate and meaningful for the organisation and its people. In making these assessments the use of sagacious judgement is essential.

Finally, the leader must be able to make effective choices and select those that will achieve the leader's vision and organisation's goals. In making assessments, judgements, choices and decisions the leader must ensure coherence with the vision and goals, consistency of manner, behaviour, style and purpose and maintain a cohesiveness within the organisation and most importantly with all its people.

SUMMARY

This chapter has sought to describe the things that high-performance leaders need to do in order to create the atmosphere and ethos within which high, even great, performance can take place. Great performance is as much about the belief followers have than anything else and their belief is found in the following.

Belief in the vision
Belief in the ethos and values
Belief in the leader
Belief in the plans
Belief in themselves

And, most importantly:

Belief that they are trusted to make things happen.

If the above is what high-performance leaders need to do then what they need to have is an overwhelming desire to lead – and that desire must be for the right reasons. It is only through having this overwhelming desire that they will have the energy, enthusiasm, stamina and drive to undertake the unremitting pressure and sustained hard work required to turn an average organisation into a high-performing one.

BIBLIOGRAPHY AND FURTHER READING

Ackland, J., The Complete Guide to Endurance Training, **London: A & C Black, 2007.**

Aguirre, D., Burger, C., Krings, J., Tipping, A. Jul, Measuring and analyzing corporate values during major transformations, **www.booz.com, 2004.**

Bompa, T., Carrera, M., Periodization Training for Sports, **Champaign: Human Kinetics, 2005.**

Buchanan, D., Huczynski, A., Organizational Behaviour, **London: Prentice Hall, 1997.**

Bull, S., The Game Plan, **Chichester: Capstone Publishing Ltd, 2006.**

Bull, S., Albinson, J.G., Shambrook, C., The Mental Game Plan, **Cheltenham: Sports Dynamics, 2002.**

Burton, D., Raedeke, T.D., Sport Psychology for Coaches, **Champaign: Human Kinetics, 2008.**

Campbell, A., Sommers Luchs, K., Core Competence-Based Strategy, **Boston: International Thomson Business Press, 1997.**

Childress, J.R., Fastbreak: the CEO's Guide to Strategy Execution, **UK: John R Childress, 2012.**

Clausewitz, C.von, On War, **Transl. by Howard, M. and Paret, P. Princeton: Princeton University Press, 1976.**

Cole, G.A., Organisational Behaviour: Theory and Practise, **London: DP Publications, 1995.**

Csikszentmihalyi, M., Flow: The Psychology of Optimal Experience, **New York: Harper & Row, 1990.**

Csikszentmihalyi, M., Finding Flow, **New York: Basic Books, 1997.**

Deloitte LLP, What is business for?, The Millennial Survey, **January, 2011.**

Deloitte LLP, Societal purpose: a journey in its early stages, Economist Intelligence Unit, **2012.**

Dewhurst, M., Harris, J., Heywood, S. Jun, The global company's challenge, McKinsey Quarterly, **2012.**

Dobbs, R., Oppenheim, J., Thompson, F. Jan, 2012, Mobilizing for a resource revolution, McKinsey Quarterly.

Drucker, P., Managing for the Future, **New York: Truman Talley Books/Plume, 1992.**

Drucker, P.F., Innovation and Entrepreneurship, **London: Pan Books, 1986.**

Fahey, L., Randall, R. (Ed.), Learning from the Future: Competitive Foresight Scenarios, **New York: Wiley & Sons, Inc, 1998.**

Ferguson, N., The Ascent of Money: a Financial History of the World, **London: Penguin Books, 2008.**

Fukuyama, F., Trust: the Social Virtues and the Creation of Prosperity, **New York: Free Press Paperback, 1996.**

Furnham, A., *The Psychology of Behaviour at Work: the Individual in the Organization,* **Hove East: Psychology Press, 1997.**

Galbraith, J.R., *Designing the Customer-Centric Organization: a Guide to Strategy, Structure, and Process,* **San Francisco: Jossey-Bass, 2005.**

Gast, A., Zanini, M., *The Social Side of Strategy, McKinsey Quarterly,* **May, 2012**

Gibbs, T., Heywood, S., Pettigrew, M., *Encouraging your people to take the long view, McKinsey Quarterly,* **Sep, 2012.**

Gladwell, M., *The Tipping Point: How little Things Can Make a Big Difference,* **London: Abacus, 2000.**

Goldsmith, M., Reiter, M., *What Got You Here Won't Get You There,* **New York: Hyperion, 2007.**

Goodall, A., Pogrebna, G., *How to stay in pole position: hire a boss who has worked on the floor, Cass Knowledge,* **Cass Business School, City University London, Dec, 2012.**

Gratton, L., *Living Strategy: Putting People at the Heart of Corporate Purpose,* **London: Prentice Hall, 2000.**

Hamel, G., Prahalad, C., K., *Strategic Intent, Harvard Business Review,* **Jul–Aug, 2005.**

Handy, C., *Understanding Organization,* **Harmondsworth: Penguin Business Library, 1987.**

Harvard Business Review, *On Managing People,* **Boston: Harvard Business School Press, 1999.**

Harvard Business Review, *Teams that Click,* **Boston: Harvard Business School Press, 2004.**

Hawley, j., Burke, L., *Peak Performance,* **St.Leonards: Allen & Unwin, 1998.**

Hesselbein, F., Goldsmith, M., *The Leader of the Future 2: Visions, Strategies and Practices for the New Era,* **San Francisco: Jossey-Bass, 2006.**

Hofstede, G., *Culture's Consequences,* **London: Sage Publications, 2001.**

Hofstede, G.J., Pedersen, P.B., Hofstede, G., *Exploring Culture: Exercises, Stories and Synthetic Cultures* **Boston: Intercultural Press, 2002.**

Hopper, K., Hopper, W., *The Puritan Gift: Reclaiming the American Dream amidst Global Financial Chaos,* **London: I.B. Tauris, 2010.**

House, R.J., Hanges, P.J., Javidan, M., Dorfman, P.W., Gupta, V., *Culture, Leadership, and Organizations: the Globe Study of 62 Societies,* **London: Sage, 2004.**

Johnson, G., Scholes, K., Whittington, R., *Exploring Corporate Strategy,* **Harlow: Pearson Education Limited, 2005.**

Kohn, A., *Punished by Rewards,* **New York: Houghton Mifflin Company, 1993.**

Lombardi, V., *The Lombardi Rules,* **New York: McGraw-Hill, 2003.**

Martens, R., *Coaches Guide to Sport Psychology,* **Champaign: Human Kinetics, 2001.**

Martin, R., *Fixing the Game: How Runaway Expectations Broke the Economy, and How to Get Back to Reality,* **Boston: Harvard Business Review Press, 2011.**

Mayon-White, B., (Ed.), *Planning and Managing Change,* **London: Harper & Row Publishers, 1986.**

McArthur, J., *High Performance Rowing,* **Ramsbury: The Crowood Place, 2005.**

Melé, D., Guillén, M., *The intellectual revolution of strategic management and its relationship with ethics and social responsibility,* **IESE Business School, Oct, 2006.**

Montgomery, C., How strategists lead, McKinsey Quarterly, **Jul, 2012.**

Morris, T., Spittle, M., Watt, A., Imagery in Sport, **Champaign: Human Kinetics, 2005.**

Nickols, F., Four change management strategies, **www.nickols.us, 2003.**

Nolte, V., Rowing faster, **Champaign: Human Kinetics, 2005.**

Ohmae, K., The Mind of the Strategist, **New York: McGraw-Hill, 1982.**

Pugh, D. (Ed.), Organization Theory, **London: Penguin Books, 1997.**

Robins, N., The Corporation that Changed the World, **New York: Pluto Press, 2006.**

Rumelet, R., Good Strategy Bad Strategy: the Difference and Why it Matters, **London: Profile Books, 2012.**

Sheer, M., The Dynamics of Change, **London: Karnac, 2013.**

Smet, de A., Lavoie, J., Schwartz, Hioe E., Developing better change leaders, McKinsey Quarterly, **Apr, 2012.**

Smith, A. The Inquiry into the Nature and Causes of the Wealth of Nations, **Dunda Books Classic.**

Snook, S., Polzer, J., The Army Crew Team, Harvard Business School, **9-403-131, 2004.**

Tidd, J., Bessant, J., Managing Innovation. Integrating Technological, Market and Organizational Change, **Chichester: John Wiley & Sons, Ltd, 2009.**

White, J., An Interview with Willi Railo, The Guardian, **2001.**